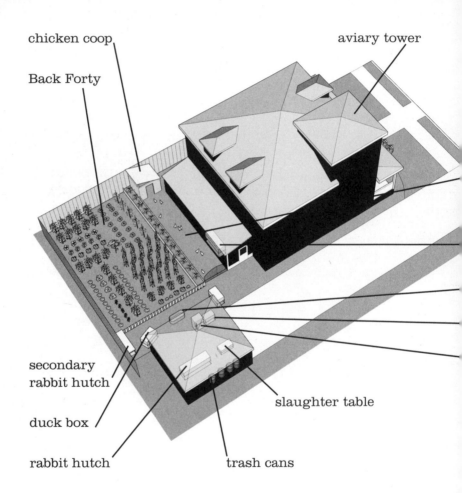

chicken coop

aviary tower

Back Forty

secondary
rabbit hutch

slaughter table

duck box

rabbit hutch

trash cans

chicken run

MY
EMPIRE
OF
DIRT

How One Man Turned His
Big-City Backyard into a Farm

FEMA trailer

duck pond

A Cautionary Tale

layer cage

refrigerator

Manny Howard

Scribner

New York   London   Toronto   Sydney

SCRIBNER
A Division of Simon & Schuster, Inc.
1230 Avenue of the Americas
New York, NY 10020

First Scribner hardcover edition March 2010

Excerpts from *The Art of the Commonplace: The Agrarian Essays of Wendell Berry* copyright © 2003 by Wendell Berry. Reprinted by permission of Counterpoint. Grateful acknowledgment for excerpts from *Conversations with Wendell Berry*, Morris Allen Grubs, Editor, University of Mississippi Press, Jackson, Mississippi, 2007.

For information about special discounts for bulk purchases,
please contact Simon & Schuster Special Sales at
1-866-506-1949 or business@simonandschuster.com.

The Simon & Schuster Speakers Bureau can bring authors
to your live event. For more information or to book an event contact
the Simon & Schuster Speakers Bureau at 1-866-248-3049
or visit our website at www.simonspeakers.com.

Designed by Carla Jayne Jones

Manufactured in the United States of America

1   3   5   7   9   10   8   6   4   2

Library of Congress Control Number: 2009033502

ISBN 978-1-4165-8516-9
ISBN 978-1-4391-7166-0 (ebook)

Frontispiece courtesy of Jason Lee
Photo on page 132 courtesy of Jos Howard
Insert photos courtesy of the author, except where indicated

For Lisa

If the land is to be used well, the people who use it must know it well, must be highly motivated to use it well, must have time to use it well and must be able to afford to use it well. Farmers must tend farms they know and love, farms small enough to know and love, using tools and methods they know and love, in the company of neighbors they know and love.

—*Wendell Berry*

CONTENTS

||||||||||||||||||||||||||||||||||||||||||||||||

Contents

PROLOGUE: THE RAFT

||||||||||||||||||||||||||||||||||||||||||||||||||||||||||||||||||||||||||||||||||||||||

Fifteen minutes gone that we can never get back and all
we are doing is staring through the wrought-iron rail-
ings of the Promenade fence out over the East River, two
eight-year-olds just stuck inside a day. There are no bullies
to run from in the park, no rats to stalk in the undergrowth
beyond the playground. Though, it's true, we have never,
either of us, ever seen a black party balloon before, still we
ran out of good stuff to throw at the one stuck in the tree
above us almost right away. Our bikes haven't turned into
police motorcycles yet. This is not an adventure at all.

A soot-smeared orange ferry on its way to Staten Island
drifts out of its decrepit, oxidizing dock at the Battery. A tugboat
with a gravel barge stuck to its nose pushes its way against the
current and, ever so slowly, upriver toward, and eventually
beyond, the Brooklyn Bridge. We lay limp against the fence,
both unable to imagine how we will survive this endlessly dull
day ahead, but both too polite to complain to each other.

1

Hey, wait. There it is right in front of us. We aren't pressing our faces up against the fence rails anymore; suddenly these are the twisted bars of a great, dark cage, and right there, staring back at us, is Adventure. "Let's build a raft," I breathe, too excited to speak the words.

Chris's eyes strain against the side of his skull, trying to see my face, gauge my intention without taking his head away from the sun-warmed metal bars. "A raft out of what?"

"Wood," I say, not certain that rafts can be built from anything else.

"Where would we go?" my friend asks.

"There." I point with my arm fully extended through the bars out across the river, north of the Fulton Fish Market, to the only visible sliver of beach on Manhattan Island.

"Where will we get the wood?" asks Chris, quickening to the plan.

"I'll show you," I reply, the plan coming together as I gallop the few yards to my bike. It is yellow, has a black banana seat, and best of all it has three speeds. The gear shifter looks just like one in a cool muscle car. Rather than being on the chrome handlebars, it's mounted on the crossbar. The selector has a pommel grip you pull toward you as you work through the gears. It shows the gear you're in with a red line next to each number, one, two, three. If I pedal hard enough, I have convinced myself, sparks will shoot out of the pipe at the back just behind my seat where the chrome plastic cap has fallen off and left an exhaust-pipe kind of hole. We mount our bikes and make our way north along the Promenade, fly down Suicide Hill to Old Fulton Street and the abandoned cobbled streets beyond, under the noisy roadway of the Brooklyn Bridge and down New Dock Street, which ends hard against the East River. Beyond the low guardrail that we are scrambling over, the river has long since swept the tar-flecked wooden mooring posts and concrete docking into a chaos of enormous, jutting, broken teeth. It functions as a maw, catching the flotsam of a river at its environmental nadir. Collected here among the filth is everything two eight-year-old boys in search of adventure could ever need to build a raft.

The rest of the day and—because Chris is sleeping over and then my mom says it is okay for us to spend the whole day—the next were filled scrambling across the collapsed pier, collecting odd lengths and diameters of rope and faded scraps of plastic—once umbrellas, municipal office-furniture upholstery, buckets, a red flip-flop. We pry planks and boards of waterlogged, tar-streaked wood from between the concrete slabs, slipping in up to our knees in the filthy, whirling eddies as the current first ebbs, then flows.

At the end of the second day when we return home near what we estimated to be dinnertime, Chris's dad, Mr. Dupassage, is waiting for us outside my apartment building. He leans impatiently against his orange BMW 2002, arms folded until we come to a tire-screeching skid a few feet from him. I'm sure that the orange BMW is the first European car I've ever seen. Chris says his dad can go a hundred miles an hour in it. Mr. Dupassage wants to know what is all over our clothes. Chris does not tell him that the tar on our hands and faces and shoes and jeans and our nearly identical terry-cloth polo shirts is from the wood we salvaged for the raft we are going to build.

Chris says he does not remember what it is. I straddle the

crossbar of my yellow banana-seat bike, studiously watching the derailleur move when I shift gears. I think that Chris might be ashamed of our raft adventure.

Opening the trunk of his orange European car, Mr. Dupassage tries another tack, asks Chris where the stuff all over his clothes came from. Chris says he does not remember that either.

Mr. Dupassage takes a lime green towel from the trunk and shakes white paint flecks off it onto the faded gray asphalt of the street and, draping it over the supple, beige leather passenger seat, warns Chris that he is going to have to sit right on the towel and not move a muscle the whole way home or he might get that stuff on his clothes all over the upholstery of the orange European car.

I wonder if sparks come out of the back of Mr. Dupassage's orange car when he goes one hundred miles an hour in it. Mr. Dupassage smiles when he says good-bye to me. He tells me to be careful not to touch the walls in the halls or in the elevator on my way upstairs, then he gets into his orange car. I think the car must be going almost one hundred miles an hour when it reaches the corner, but from where I am standing, still straddling my yellow banana-seat bike, I can't see any sparks flying out behind it.

Chris is French, or his parents are, or his father is. I wonder how long it takes to get to France from Pierrepont Street. My mom calls from the window on the second floor where we live. She wants to know if I know what time it is. I look at the red LED readout on my Texas Instruments watch and I tell her it is eight fifty-six.

In the elevator, when I lean against the wall, some of the tar from the raft wood wipes off my shirt onto the brown-

and-white-flecked enamel wall. I suppose that French people must not like rafts very much. French people like river barges better than rafts.

When my mom tells me to explain how I got myself covered in tar, I tell her that Chris and I are building a raft to sail across the East River.

The East River is not, in truth, a river. It is a tidal strait that joins with the Harlem River, also a part of the same tidal strait that was painstakingly, over twenty years during the nineteenth century, hollowed out to accommodate ship traffic. This strait connects the Long Island Sound up north to New York's Upper Bay and the Atlantic Ocean beyond to the south. Because the narrow waterway joins two such whopping great bodies of water, the tide roars up during the flow tide, then twelve hours later, down during the ebb tide. In its narrower stretches the tide moves at speeds approaching six knots. Manhattan turned the riverbank to stone on its western bank, as did Brooklyn and eventually Queens on the opposite shore, so now, call it a tidal strait or a river, it is more a sluice than a naturally occurring body of water. People who fall or dare to jump in it have few places where they can pick their way out. The East River hosts a handful of accidental drownings every year.

For this and many other reasons, the East River is no place for an eight-year-old to play. Another person's mother might have made this point immediately after her son announced his intentions to cross it on a raft that he and his buddy Chris Dupassage planned to build from found material piling up on the tide line along its rocky banks and fetid beaches. Not my mother. She supported every insane notion or scheme I ever presented to her. It was a conscious—determined, really—effort to shield what she considered my creative gift, to protect my imagination, my notion of the possible, from the crush of practical reality.

The lower reaches of the East River have teemed with traffic since the earliest Dutch settlements in the 1670s, and I spent most of my childhood living up on the bluffs above Old Fulton Street, the site where, in 1814, Robert Fulton inaugurated regular steamboat-ferry service between Brooklyn and Manhattan and made Brooklyn boom. The ferry kept Brooklyn's economy running, fueled its growth from Dutch farming village to throbbing Anglocentric factory town and international port until 1924, forty-one years after the Brooklyn Bridge was completed. The cobblestone streets bustled and the town became a city. The horse-drawn construction of the Eagle Warehouse and all the other warehouses and towering factories put an end to any doubt that Brooklyn was rising just as confidently as its neighbor across the river. By the 1970s, though, those factories and warehouses were slipping into decrepitude, creating a vacant canyon land where packs of dogs and kids on bikes from the various bordering neighborhoods competed for territory among the low-slung, Civil War–era brick warehouses with rusting, arched iron doors that still smelled of the pepper they once housed. Here on the flats stood a dozen monolithic, white cement factories built at the turn of the nineteenth century by the Scottish-born king of the cardboard box, the industrialist Robert Gair. In 1926, Gair moved his light-industrial empire upstate to Piermont. By the 1970s, "Gairville" had become a collection of empty

or emptying monuments to the slow death of urban manu-
facturing.

A week passes and Chris still hasn't returned to fix our raft.
During that gap I check on our pile of salvaged raft material
at least twice a day. If, when I get down to the river's edge,
any other kids happen to be hanging around on the north side
of New Dock Street, in the paved lot long since gone to seed,
forsaken by its owner, or the city or whoever abandons the
vast spoiled tracts in the landscape of my childhood, I wait
for them to leave, to leave without molesting our raft pile. I
position myself a calculated distance from our pile. Not so
close that I will draw attention to the salvage, but near enough
so that if some nosy kid does notice the pile, he'll know it is
mine and that I am watching him. I worry a lot about what
I'll do if the nosy kid who does notice our raft-makings also
wants to build a raft and sail it across the East River. I worry
especially about what I will do if that nosy kid who shares my
nautical ambitions is much bigger or more aggressive than
me. But I stay at my post by the pile all the same. I lie on
my back on the sun-baked pavement, my shoulders propped
against a discarded tire—hundreds and hundreds of tires are
heaped behind the concrete wall of the Sanitation Department depot on the south side of New Dock Street. I lie on
the hot sidewalk, my chin resting on my chest just like James
Coburn in *The Magnificent Seven*. His shoulders on his saddle,
his chin on his chest, his back in the dust of that West Texas
cattle station, he reclines, unconcerned and unmoving, while
dangerous men fuss needlessly around him.

Time passes slowly out here on the river. I catalog the hours. I count the days. Try to calculate the minutes until Chris returns to the raft. While I am not picking over the ingredients of our unmade raft, I am filling a composition notebook. It is a diary of the project, an account of the project and a fable of the adventures to come, with meticulously drafted plans for The Raft's construction. Chris never does return.

I am grown now. I am still restless. Often uncomfortable in my husk, feeling it tighten around me when the world falls quiet. Those who know me well have grown used to both grand gestures and grim antics. I come through in a pinch if a spasm of physical strength (and, on the rare occasion, bravery) is required. I fall down on the job if the most rudimentary clerical precision is called for. My mind is a whirl; concocting stories, nursing regret, scheming, and—more often than I like—suspecting the worst. I talk too much and I listen intently.

This past February, suffering through a three-month hangover, the result of a failed effort at a career change, I am untethered, undone really.

Years of magazine writing had taught me to trust that after a requisite period of inward-aimed anger, doubt, and pity, inspiration always returns. The plan had been to bide my time, await the rebound strategy, the plan for renewal or reinvigoration that has always been just one good night's sleep away.

If only I could sleep.

WHAT ARE PEOPLE FOR?

||||||||||||||||||||||||||||||||||||||||||||||||||||||||||||||||||||||||||||||||||||||||||||||||||||||

During the crisis of these last months I have satisfied my ambition by delivering the children to school—consistently twenty minutes late—retiring to a diner where I read three newspapers over a breakfast of sausage and bacon, two eggs any style, and buttered rye toast, all the while discovering new avenues of self-torture. An accomplished self-loather, I am rarely as fulfilled as when I cannot stand the thought, never mind the sight, of myself.

But after forty years, for the first time, now that I'm a father of two children—perfect, to my mind, in every way—my system, diligently honed over years of practice for self-destruction, suddenly fails me. Sitting bolt upright in bed on a predawn winter morning, I blurt, "I need to get a job!"

My wife, Lisa, does not stir. Never mind that the notion would not have produced the same horror in her that it has in me. Lisa can hold a job. I have never met a person who succeeds at one job all the while gracefully fielding ever-better offers of bogglingly well-paid alternatives as they stack up like airliners into La Guardia Airport after a summer storm.

Lisa is a successful and talented businesswoman who works hard for a privately held publishing empire producing the glossy magazines whose titles are shorthand in the vernacular of Western popular culture. For the most part, they are the very magazines I have spent nearly two decades scraping out a living writing for. Her day is spent constructing and negotiating deals that make millions of dollars for the publishing company. I don't believe that she will ever be paid what she is worth. That said, she is compensated exceedingly well.

Because of the money that these talents earn, we live in this three-story mansion with our two small children in a garden district behind Prospect Park in Brooklyn. If the home, dubbed Howard Hall by visiting friends from Montana, were not showing some of its 106 years, it could fairly be described as immodest. Standing at the window of our second-floor bedroom, an icy breeze drifting over my bare and mildly distended torso from between the original windowpanes, I watch nothing happen on the dead February street. The hoarfrost on the cars and the asphalt street, the century-old, dormant trees, are all as still as the night.

A job? What a thought. I have not had an honest job in a decade. As an editor near the top of the masthead at *Gourmet* magazine, the moment my first marriage failed, I got on my boss's calendar and quit. I sat, knees together in the narrow, yellow chair in the outer office of the editor in chief, juggling the attendant emotions of the circumstances of the past few years. The boss called my name twice from the threshold before I heard her. She ushered me in, offered me the seat across from her at her desk, and before she had a chance to sit down, I informed her that I didn't think that I was working out. Discourteous in my haste, before she had the opportunity to react, I gave two weeks' notice. "That seems about right?" I asked rhetorically, then crossed and recrossed my legs.

I was wearing one of the three new, expensive suits I'd specifically purchased for this profoundly civilized job, gazing out over Times Square while the boss processed my presentation. She asked me not if I would reconsider, but whether I was certain that this was the right time, right time in my life, she clarified, for me to be without a job, a place to go every day. A humane offer, motivated more by compassion than practicality; in truth I had been hopelessly ineffective at work for months. Then, as now, I lived my life out loud, and in the office, as was true most every other place I frequented at the time, the collapse of my marriage was common knowledge. "Yes," I answered, bright suddenly, animated even, "I am certain this is the right time."

"Maybe we can work out an arrangement?" she offered generously. "Maybe we can . . . we can put together a contributing-editor slot for you? You could write for the magazine, rather than edit?"

"Thank you. Let's . . . Can we sleep on it?" was my halting, distracted response.

"Fine, then," said the boss, grown weary of her compassion and generosity going unacknowledged. She began sifting through a pile of pink phone-message slips.

"Thank you," I announced, suddenly focused, strangely resolute, standing up and smoothing my still new suit.

"I do hope this works out, Manny," she offered, looking up from the notes without pausing their shuffle.

A yearlong contract was negotiated with the magazine; I wrote about food and travel, but always for the competition, never once for *Gourmet*. My contract was not renewed. This might not have been the case if I had once shown an ounce of interest, never mind gratitude, but I was so busy rebuilding myself I'm sure I never gave my behavior a thought. I had as much hostility for the image of myself as a senior editor at *Gourmet* magazine as I did for myself as a cuckolded husband, the job as much a symptom of my whingeing collapse of courage and my deluded determination to hold tight to the husk of a hobbled marriage.

For the years that followed, my travel assignments were diverse—random, more like: one week hunting for bear with petty mobsters in the new Russia and the next week at a four-star resort on Kauai, attending cooking classes taught by Roger Vergé.

I wrangled an assignment in Ukraine. My friend Evan was simultaneously directing a movie he had written in Russian and being held captive by the studio (in reality, an Eastern European gang who could not shoot straight, petty mafiosi who, he would come to believe, were using him as their "American filmmaker" in order to defraud investors in their business). At my request, Evan organized a bear hunt in the foothills of eastern Ukraine. It was hosted by his associates in the budding world of Russian film. The hunting party included the "don," recently released from captivity in a windowless basement by a rival "studio" with his head shaved and twenty pounds lighter than when I had last seen him at a restaurant in New York (where I'd arranged a dinner for him and Evan and their associates from Brighton Beach). Also in the hunting party was an Afghan war vet we nicknamed

Ajax. A muscular blond, he appeared to be a killing machine and developed a reasonably intense, if boyish, crush on me. Ajax continually challenged me to wrestling matches and various daredevilry. Most all of the challenges involved us both being naked.

In Haiti, after Jean-Bertrand Aristide's election, I reported on a United Nations mission to coax a legitimate police force from the Tonton Macoutes, a band of soulless, blood-soaked thugs who stepped on the public neck while despotic lunatic Baby Doc Duvalier raped his country.

Rather than become known, as I had fantasized, as the go-to for global political mayhem, I followed that assignment with a dreary snigger about a doomed son of Upper East Side privilege with a deadly monkey on his back. I continued to drift from my early ambitions. Staring at glass office buildings bobbing above a dense canopy of trees from the window of my room at the Four Seasons Hotel in Houston, Texas, I imagined I knew what the jungle of the city of Freetown must look like. But, try though I might, I wasn't covering fratricide in Sierra Leone; rather, I was holed-up with a plastic surgeon named Gerald Johnson, the self-described "originator and inventor of the belly-button breast augmentation procedure." Grown weary of sitting-in while Johnson fitted a torrent of unconscious, spring-breaking nubiles with a new set each, I was waiting at the hotel for the adult star Traci Topps to fly in for her downsizing—the bottom had just dropped out of the big-bust erotic entertainment market and I was Johnny-on-the-spot, breaking the news. I wrote inexcusably giddy profiles about supermodels (remember them?) and movie stars, and countless ditties about the good works of socialites (this before the advent of celebutantes). A dubious honor, I wrote the first of what would be a brief but intense avalanche of profiles about Colin Farrell. During the interview, held over breakfast at an ersatz Irish pub near the location of his second feature, *American Outlaws*, the indiscriminately affectionate enfant-terrible-in-the-making and I got so loaded on Guinness that I missed the day's last flight back home. There was some spiritual food, for sure: I proudly covered the cataclysmic flood in Grand Forks, North Dakota, staying on to volunteer for the Red Cross long after I'd gotten the assigned story. I scoured the south of France for truffles and learned the art of the perfect omelet with bold-name chefs at the dawn of that phylum of celebrity.

After years of searching, I tracked down a Chinese-American who agreed to make a traditional dog casserole and exposed David Bouley's profiting during the chaotic days that followed the September 11 attacks. One story at a time, my professional profile became that of the Grim Reaper of celebrity chefs, one of the few food writers who bothered to gather court records and call angry creditors, and who reported his stories even if it meant fewer gratis three-star dinners on the town. One day in 2005 I abruptly threw over magazine writing to work on a documentary about the war in Afghanistan. Finally a real adventure, I thought back then. A framed photograph of myself standing on the grand marble stairs at the Gandamak Lodge (once the Kabul home of one of Osama bin Laden's six wives), gripping a German-made StG 44 assault rifle, still hangs on the wall of my office.

My sudden desire for a proper job haunts me. I examine it warily, treat it like a symptom of something much more complicated, possibly an early warning of some terminal ailment. I ferry the children the five miles across Brooklyn to school without speaking or hearing a word. After returning to Howard Hall, I take up my station at my computer, relocated from the documentary production company's office suite on Park Avenue South to a temporary desk made of sawhorses next to the dining-room table, unambitiously downloading mediocre pornography—force of habit, more than the result of any specific animal urges. The home phone rings. I don't pick it up. Then, moments after the final ring dumps the call into voice mail, the same number registers on the caller ID of my mobile phone.

I answer it. Faye introduces herself, says she has, just this moment, come out of an editorial meeting at *New York* magazine and has a story assignment she wants me to consider. Faye explains that as soon as she presented the idea, the instant consensus in the conference room was that I was the very first choice as the writer for the piece. No runner-up was discussed, she assures me. "This one," Faye declares, without describing the assignment, "is the ultimate Manny Howard story."

Few compliments are greater—given you like the assignment—than being told that a roomful of editors agree that you are the best writer for their story. It suggests that your past writing has made a generally positive impression on some people in your field, and that the work is memorable, and, maybe most important, that you have a style that is identifiable, at least recognizable. Though feeling complimented and therefore beholden, I am practicing restraint, still trying to hold on to the notion that magazine writing is something I used to do.

Faye begins an excited description of the assignment. I

understand little of what she first says. I catch familiar words and phrases: locavore, food miles, greenmarkets, and the global food industry.

Faye asks if Lisa and I have a backyard. Faye asks because she wants me to write about the backyard. Faye asks because she wants me to write about using my backyard to grow food and then, eventually, eat only that food to sustain myself for at least one month.

Faye wants me to live off my backyard. She wants me, she announces, suddenly breathless again, to engage the groundswell of enthusiasm for urban agriculture. She wants me to confront the self-satisfied, well-to-do locavores cruising the city's greenmarkets. It is one thing to live in New York City and know the farmer who sells you milk or meat or whatever, she says. It is quite another to live in the city and be the farmer.

There is no stunned silence. Not at all certain why, in my heart I have already accepted this strange, mammoth assignment. Rather than say so, my reflex—honed after years of negotiating equally harebrained assignments from editors with unrealistic expectations—is to parlay for exceptions, specifically salt, pepper, and coffee beans.

I stop after three because, for reasons I do not yet fully understand, I agree with Faye's assertion that if I want milk, it will have to be produced behind the house. This meeting of the minds permits me to introduce the topic of livestock. During our first phone conversation we discuss the risks and rewards associated with keeping a milking goat.

Faye never uses the word *farm*, but before I hang up the phone, the editor's proposed arch, maybe cynical, critique of urban agriculture and the fetish of sustainability has become a fully operational farm in my mind.

What Are People For?

Berserk assignments negotiated during twenty-minute phone calls are nothing new. More of the same, I have been flown out to Trancoso, Brazil, to follow a celebrity chef and tease out a story—any story—finally settling on the earthy (if poisonous) joys of cooking with trans fat–laden palm oil. I have been paid to ghostwrite for an editor's own magazine a tale about his infidelities. I've been pulled off an assignment after arriving at a four-star resort halfway around the world because the editor did not realize that the publication's parent company underwrote the subject of the story. This assignment is refreshing by comparison: *New York* magazine has offered me a job that, contrary to most every other magazine assignment I've landed over twenty years, is a straightforward tale of intense physical labor yet to be completed. The most appealing aspect of this assignment is the promise of the backbreaking work it will require. Better still, taking this gig will certainly preclude hustling any other magazine work, which, though it has been the core activity of my career for ten years, is, of late, beyond imagining. Equally appealing is the advance understanding that the job will take eight months at a minimum to complete.

Faye and I negotiate the schedule, and eventually I secure unlimited reimbursement for expenses and what I consider fair compensation for the work and the writing—never mind that it is not nearly half a year's salary. All that is left before I officially accept the assignment is to check in with Lisa. After last year's trip to Afghanistan, I am anticipating little resistance. I might even be expecting a bit of grateful relief that I'll be staying so close to home.

* * *

Just two years after we first met, Lisa returned to her suite at the Fairmont, New Orleans, during a break from a working session at the appropriately luxe annual retreat her division made. I was holed up in the suite, working on a profile about chef Gabriel Kreuther, then the executive chef at the city's newly reopened Ritz-Carlton. Lisa opted not to return to the working session, and instead we broke the furniture until sometime after the dinner she was mandated to attend had begun.

I held her hand as we dashed across Canal Street, then hailed a cab to Commander's Palace in the Garden District, where her engagement was well under way. Opening the cab door for her, I gripped her firmly in my arms and kissed her quickly, before she stepped into the cab. I watched her cab pull into traffic, crossed the street to the Ritz, and visited briefly with Chef Kreuther in his kitchen as the dinner rush waned. Then I ducked back into the Quarter and took a stool at the counter of an oyster bar I favor just around the corner from police headquarters.

Not exactly how I'd imagined I would spend the evening that my future wife and I conceived our first child.

I arrived home before Lisa and was reading when she tumbled in the door, then undressed before me. Since we'd boarded the plane in New York, Lisa had been regaling me with stories of unsanctioned lost weekends and road trips to New Orleans that she'd taken with her teammates on the swim team. Half-dressed and entirely animated, now she proposed that, first thing in the morning, we visit Jackson, Mississippi. I protested mildly, pointing out that we would never make the four-hundred-mile round-trip in time for our afternoon flight. Lisa, smiling at the man, silly goose, in bed below her, was so eager to show me her childhood haunts, she insisted that as a teen on a booze safari, she and her friends could make the journey in less than two hours. "Really?" I asked sleepily, unable to convincingly calculate the necessary ninety-eight-mile-an-hour average land speed that such a trip would require while watching as she peeled herself out of her business rig and primped for bed.

The next morning, a Sunday, we woke just after sunrise because that's when, as Lisa had passed the front desk on the way upstairs a few hours before, she had arranged to have breakfast delivered.

Between sips of coffee and pieces of fruit Lisa again made her case for the road trip. The moment I nodded agreement, she picked up the house phone and confirmed the reservation for the car she had made with the concierge before ordering breakfast. "I got us the most loaded Cadillac available," she trumpeted. The only kind of car Charlie and Mama, her beloved paternal grandparents, had ever owned, she explained, excited. Then, catching herself when she clocked my furtive glance at my wallet on the dresser, she announced she was putting the car on her frequent-flier miles and wouldn't hear of me contributing. "This is my treat, my adventure," she said, bounding out of bed.

Once our ride was secured, Lisa announced that, rather than taking the most direct route, west out of town, then due north on I-55, running between lakes Maurepas and Pontchartrain, we should—"while we are down here"—visit Pass Christian, where she summered on the Gulf with her family as a child. "It's so beautiful there. You are going to love it," she all but sang. "It is so Manny Howard—very rustic, not Biloxi, the opposite. You'll love it. I swear you will." She smiled broadly while, all at once, fussing with the bodice of a bright yellow sundress and stepping into high sandals.

Choosing the route to Pass Christian was also important, she explained. There is a right way and a wrong way. If we were going to visit one of the most magical places of her childhood, we couldn't possibly take the state road northeast out of town toward Slidell. The causeway over the lake—Lake Pontchartrain—to Mandeville was the only proper route. "It's so pretty," she said. "You really will love it. I just know you will." I was so completely content watching while she made her third full wardrobe change that it didn't occur to me to say that I was, in fact, familiar with the drive, and the route she described constituted, even by the most optimistic, if feeble, math, a round-trip of over 450 miles, so that even if the traffic gods smiled and we did not get out of the car once in Jackson, the trip would take at least nine hours.

"Should we ask the hotel to pack us a box lunch, do you think?" Lisa asked, forgetting the question the moment she picked up her PDA to make sure she had no unfinished business from the retreat. "I can't believe I was late to *dinner!*" she exclaimed suddenly. "I got so much shit." She tossed her head, delighted, hair cascading down her back, arms straightening to the floor, PDA still gripped in both hands and disappearing between her strong thighs into the folds of her white skirt. I remarked that we should skip ordering lunch, probably just get a move on, if we were going to make our flight out.

* * *

Lisa was right, Pass Christian was "so Manny Howard." We visited in Jackson for all of twenty minutes, getting out of the car to gallop through the quiet country club where she and her brother and sister had learned to swim. I purchased some commemorative merch, a baseball cap, COUNTRY CLUB OF JACKSON, EST. 1914, a perverse disguise which I still enjoy wearing on crowded subways. We slowed the Cadillac in front of her grandparents' home and Lisa misted up, lamenting that we could not stop one more time. I got an enormous speeding ticket for tear-assing south down I-55 from Jackson.

I was only recently divorced (the legal nicety being completed three years after that first marriage had, in fact, died). Sure, I fell in love with Lisa on our first date. There was no question that I wanted to be with her. I did not want to have a baby and get married at all, though.

At least, I definitely didn't want to be a father. I probably was not as inelastic about getting married, but since my first marriage had begun to wobble on the wedding night, I did require that marriage be "fun" for a while before the unknowable preconditions of parenthood fastened themselves to us.

Lisa would not entertain the notion of terminating the pregnancy. Told me matter-of-factly that she was prepared to have the baby by herself, if I was not interested. I was aware of her formidable negotiating skills (then probably more acutely than now) and, because I was so impressed with Lisa's business acumen, truly considered this an opening offer, of sorts. But we had a difficult time "moving the conversation forward." Neither of us really had the words that could get us to what Lisa frequently described as the best outcome of any negotiation: a win/win.

I did not want the baby, only her—or so I said. My involvement as a father was her preference, but it was not necessary, she was having the baby with or without me—or so she said. Still ambitious for a win/win, I suggested we give up on conversation for a moment and proceed by employing a numerical system I devised to describe our feelings about our future: 1 = terminate the pregnancy and proceed together the best we could; 10 = have the baby and proceed together the best we could. Marriage, it was assumed by both of us, would follow the arrival of the baby, if there was to be one.

This worked inasmuch as it got us "throwing numbers at each other." For two weeks we met and exchanged numbers, usually 2 and 9 (both of us pretending to possess some flexibility), then would take a day off and spend it apart, me in a motionless daze behind the steering wheel of my late-model (full-size) Chevy Blazer parked outside a Laundromat on Atlantic Avenue. Lisa, likely a blur of corporate activity, rounded off by hopelessly sobbing into the pillows on her enormous white couch in the living room of her apartment on Central Park West.

One week on Lisa provided a new number: 3. I was shocked. I asked if she was sure. She said she was. I could not comprehend how she had moved so far, so fast, and I said so. She said she had been thinking about what I had said, saw some merit in the idea that we needed to be together, eventually even as husband and wife (maybe), before we could be a good father and mother to a baby. Faced with what I believed was Lisa's enormous sacrifice to keep me in her life, flattered, impressed—proud even—I could not stand the idea of being the one who convinced her that terminating the pregnancy was the right thing to do. I began a precipitous about-face. Two days later I announced that I was an unreserved 8.25.

Lisa was furious. She could not believe I could be so cavalier about this decision. She thought it best that she have the baby by herself. Offered to allow me reasonable visitation rights if I wanted them, but insisted on sole custody.

I was confused. "You were a 3 two days ago?"

"That's right. I am a 1 now. I am having this baby. I can do this without you. I make enough money to take care of this baby all by myself!"

"Wait? You're a 1?"

"Yes. And you're an asshole."

"A 1 is 'terminate.'"

"It is not."

"Yes. A 10 is 'have baby.'"

"It is not."

"Yes. That's what we agreed on."

"Fine, I am a 10 and you're an asshole."

"I'm an 8.25!"

"You are?"

What I ended up saying as a terrified 10 was "I love you. I want to be with you. That's all I know. I don't know if I want to be a dad. But I know that I can't be with you and not be a dad, so I'm going to be a dad with you. I don't know if it'll work, but I want it to. So let's have a baby and then see if we should be married, too."

When we called Lisa's mom and dad, whom I had met once on a family vacation on the Florida Panhandle, to tell them the happy news about the baby and the likely possibility that we would get married after the birth, they were happy for us, but not all that pleased about the order of things as we presented it. The pregnancy was not the problem. The problem was not being married and being pregnant.

We told them we'd call them back.

A few days later I called Lisa's dad, John, and asked him for his daughter's hand. He said, "Lisa's a wonderful girl."

I said I agreed. He said, "You take care of my little girl, now."

I said that I would. "No, Manny," said John, with deep concern verging on outright menace. "You take care of my little girl."

When I had caught my breath, I said that I understood and repeated that I would take care of Lisa. "Well, that's fine," said John. "I'm going to hand the phone to Elise so she can talk to Lisa."

Though an objective assessment of the details of each of our biographies did not hold out much hope for success, our friends received the news of our hurry-up marriage and impending parenthood with less dread than Lisa's family. Well known by my intimates for being precocious and impulsive, it didn't help matters that I fell in love with Lisa while closing on her from twenty yards, watching her stride purposefully from cab to restaurant. It was a blind date. We arrived at the front door at the same moment. "Manny," she not so much asked as affirmed.

"I was hoping that was you," was all I could manage. Game over.

We have proved unimaginable, yet obvious, partners.

It struck me early in the third trimester that we weren't going to escape the phobias that all the other new parents we knew had fallen prey to. Why, then, fritter away maternity leave, the biggest chunk of paid leave anybody in the honest workforce ever gets, sitting around our apartment worrying that we were being terrible parents? If we were going to worry about being bad parents, we should probably just go be bad parents. Over dinner I announced that when the baby was three weeks old, we were going to drive across the country and back. Lisa was not immediately convinced. I reminded her that I was the one she had put in charge of adventure.

Once we had decided to have the baby together, Lisa insisted we replace my beloved late-model, full-size Blazer with a car recognized as "safe" by *Consumer Reports,* a brand-new Volvo Cross Country wagon—the Castratimobile, by my reckoning.

Since we now had a brand-new car that could make the trip, I needled, do you really want to waste maternity leave sitting at home? I continued to badger and Lisa finally agreed. Unlike me, she had never driven across the country. She was excited at the prospect. I spent the balance of the final weeks planning a route that would take us eight thousand miles in twenty-eight days, buying gear and calling the friends we would barge in on. Heath Ryan Howard (almost immediately dubbed HRH) was born at the end of October 2002. I tucked Lisa, Heath, and our pointer-Lab mutt, Fergus, into their compartment in the crowded wagon, and we left for our victory lap in plenty of time to spend Thanksgiving with Lisa's sister, Marian, and my stepbrother, Justin, in Northern California.

In September 2003, expecting our second child, Lisa and I begin looking for a larger home and are drawn to the broad, tree-lined streets of Prospect Park South, a well-manicured, landmarked neighborhood, part of greater Flatbush. A garden district with grand, columned houses, and a carefully land-scaped esplanade, it reminds Lisa of Jackson. I never gave much serious thought to moving out of the neighborhood that I grew up in, but I had taken Lisa on a tour of the neigh-borhood when we were courting, figuring it would warm her to the idea of Brooklyn, draw her away from Central Park West. It often takes a little bit of convincing to sell the bor-ough to outlanders who arrive in New York and spend years in Manhattan, chasing ambition without paying much atten-tion to the rest of the city. Not Lisa. The idea inspires her, and before the end of the week she has lined up a number of houses for us to view in Prospect Park South.

We meet the Realtor, Mary Kaye Gallagher, midmorning on a pleasant fall day outside what is to become Howard Hall. Gallagher is waiting for us on the broad front porch. "She's *porch-sitting!*" breathed Lisa with delight. "Just like home."

We are ushered into the dark green Italianate manor house that I immediately judge to be beyond our price range. Almost every building in this neighborhood beggars the established metric for reasonable square footage in New York City. Gallagher, the dominatrix of real estate in Prospect Park South and bordering neighborhoods in western Flat-bush, announces that the house sits on a lot one hundred feet deep and sixty feet wide. She says the interior dimensions work out to be six thousand usable square feet—give or take. Gallagher has toiled tirelessly for generations to return this garden community to its former greatness. One of her most consistent challenges to closing deals seems to have been the maintenance and housekeeping standards that the long-term residents consider reasonable.

The interior of this home, one of the first completed on

the block, suggests that nothing that has entered it has been discarded since it was sold to one Josephine Halback directly from Dean Alvord, the developer, in 1903. Gallagher begins apologizing to Lisa for the clutter—some of which is stacked in long, low rows and covered by bedsheets, to morbid effect, in the middle of the apparently long-vacant bedrooms on the second and third floors. One bedroom on the third floor has an alarming brown stain—that is *not* blood—in the middle of the dirty pea-green, wall-to-wall carpet. When I turn to Gallagher for explanation, she simply rolls her eyes in a way I will learn to love and suggests we continue the tour. Here, look, the home's most significant architectural feature, the nearly two-story-high tower room with pitched roof and two walls of windows in the southeast corner of the building.

A second couple, older than us by at least ten years, show up to view the property, but Gallagher runs them off. "Come back later," she commands. It appears she likes the details of our biography: one kid and one on the way, Lisa's fancy job title at an even fancier fashion media company, even my credentials as a writer (she's already recruiting me for the neighborhood newsletter). We do the real estate dance, and eventually Lisa offers a polite "We will be in touch."

Lisa and I turn from the house, walking close enough to each other to feel her dress brush my hand. On the way across the street to our car, having absolutely no idea whether we can afford to buy the house, I whisper advice to Lisa, who is transparently in love with the property. If she feels this strongly, she should go ahead and make an offer. The place is a wreck, but it looks like most of the work is cosmetic; nothing a floor sander, a skim coat of plaster, and some white paint can't fix.

In the contract, finalized in September, we insist that a provision be added requiring the removal of every single item inside the house. The odd-jobber who does the work reports that he removes eighty contractor bags before the job is complete.

On the same day in December that we move into Howard Hall, the return pipe for the furnace bursts, so moving men and plumbers jockey for position in the basement. At least once a month during the first three years some facet central to the operation of our home collapses in a heap requiring (after failed attempts at repair on my part) the skills of a professional of some description. Lisa and I try to stay philosophical about the costs of getting Howard Hall up on its knees and functioning adequately, often joking when the doorbell rings that answering it will cost us $2,000, as that is almost without exception what any guy in coveralls who steps over the threshold will bill us for fixing the plumbing, chimneys, electrical, windows, whatever. Two months after we move in, with the paint still drying on the walls and the solder still setting between the new copper pipes, our son, Bevan Jake Howard, is born.

Six months later, dinner is over. The kids long since in bed, we are sitting out back on the screen porch indulging ourselves, flirting while fantasizing about home improvement. What if we put in a hot tub before replacing all the failing storm windows? A long pause as the reality of how many responsible home-repair items trump installation of a hot tub washes over us both. Thoughts of dishes left unwashed and waiting laundry piles eclipse lottery-winning-based fantasies for a luxurious domestic future.

As we are about to return to our chores, a shambling presence reveals itself beyond the far corner of the garage. In the dim glow of a sporadically operating floodlight a raccoon crosses slowly in front of the garage doors. "A raccoon in Flatbush?" whispers Lisa.

I gesture *I guess?* and slip out of my chair and, in a knee-destroying crouch, make my way to the screen door.

The raccoon is followed by four offspring. When they reach the parent (I can't sex a raccoon), it stands up and begins using its nose in our direction. "It can smell our dinner," Lisa stage-whispers.

"Get a broom," I command. In the moments it takes Lisa to fetch a broom, the critters vanish across the yard and through a hole in the shambolic fence. The following day, I'm talking to my childhood friend Josh, who lives around the corner, and he says he's seen the raccoons around and heard talk that an entire colony, known as a gaze, live out of the Dumpsters behind Kentucky Fried Chicken on Coney Island Avenue. That makes perfect sense to me. Where else in Brooklyn would a raccoon find anything to eat? We don't see them again for many years and only occasionally hear stories about sightings.

For dinner the day of my phone call with Faye, I grill a Newport steak for the family. Lisa really enjoys a good Newport, salty black on the outside and blue, barely warm on the inside. I also steam some artichokes, not my favorite but certainly hers. As dinner winds down, Lisa is scooping the fur from the heart of the artichoke for the kids. It is time to introduce The Farm. "So, I got a call today about a magazine piece that I want to talk with you about," I say.

"I thought you weren't going to write magazine stories anymore? Where does the Afghanistan film stand?" she replies, distracted, smiling at our son, Bevan Jake, who's devouring the now bald artichoke heart.

"You know where it stands. I'm out," I growl, thinking darkly about disappearing the last two years of my work life: no more dumbed-down script rewrites, no more endless meetings spent biting my tongue, navigating fragile egos and dishonest careerism for the cause of producing half-smart journalism. "I'm not talking about that anymore. I am interested in this piece for *New York*, though—could be a nice size."

Determined to stick to broad strokes, I outline the project for Lisa, who is exhorting Heath Ryan, busy pantomiming a vomiting attack, to try the various artichoke parts on her plate. Lisa looks up at me occasionally, not entirely interested in the specifics of the assignment, but clearly curious about my newfound enthusiasm. Finally, she stands, clears the kids' plates, and announces that it's time to march upstairs for books and snuggles.

In the kitchen now, dishes clattering, she calls, "How much will this 'growing your own garden' story pay?"

"Don't know exactly, but if it's assigned at ten thousand words, then it could be enough to help get the garage redone once it's all over." This is what, during Lisa's wheeler-dealer day, is called my close, and it requires that I stifle my desire to correct her, to make sure she understands there will be no garden, that I am planning to build The Farm.

After reflecting for precisely the time it takes her to load the last two plates and close the dishwasher, she concludes the negotiation: "Okay, sounds good. You're excited. That's nice, hon."

I endure the verbal pat on the head. Then footsteps upstairs.

NEXT ACTIONS

||||||||||||||||||||||||||||||||||||||||||||||||||||||||||||||||||

I accept the story assignment. The kids are in school. Lisa is working. Now I'm working again, too. All is well.

There are two kinds of people, those who feel fine doing the bare minimum, and those who can't do anything without throwing themselves entirely into any project. I am both of these people. This duality leaves the door open for the question that dogs me through every endeavor, however: are you going to fail at this, too?

The phrase *food miles,* used to describe the distance food travels between producer and consumer, and more pointedly to quantify the modern consumer's alienation from the source of his nourishment, was coined by Tim Lang, a professor at City University in London, in 1991. It is the foundation of an enormously popular food movement in the developed

31

world known as locavorism, the core premise that food grown and produced locally is superior to food produced thousands of miles away. It is as personally affirming and proactive as it is politically subversive. In the United States a growing number of people have identified agribusiness as their current bogeyman and engaged in what is called urban agriculture in order to ward him off. Since a sustainability convention held in San Francisco during 2005, a vanguard interested in whole foods started describing themselves as locavores.

In November 2007, the *Oxford American Dictionary* added *locavore* to its pages and thus, some would say, to the language. Being a locavore in 2010 must be a very different experience from what it was in 1991. For one, the historically disinterested news media is suddenly providing affirming details about the crisis in food production, constantly squawking about the global food crisis. In 1991, as far as the population was concerned, food described as organic was still the manna of the lunatic left. Alas, the poor, doomed organic-food movement; just as it moved out of the yurts and freak caves toward the light of general acceptance, Big Food swept in, co-opting the term, undermining accepted standards for what constituted organic food, and plastering snack bags with shamelessly misleading claims: "Contents 70 Percent Organic."

The decimation of the organic movement by industrial food producers is still a painful memory for food-conscious folk. People who think about these things have come to believe the reliance on processed food—some of which, even when it was organic, journeyed an average of 1,494 miles to the dinner plate—doomed consumers of healthy food. This belief inspired locavores. Their solution was to buy food directly from the people who produce it, often accompanied by the promise that the food is grown and harvested in accordance with best organic practices, but always grown within one hundred miles of the market. This is not simply an individual purchasing decision aimed at improving the health of loved ones and one's self. Not for the locavore. The locavore believes that pursuing this personal philosophy is the responsible thing to do, as it might also have an ancillary beneficial effect for local farmers and, possibly, the larger environment. Chances are if you describe yourself as a locavore, you attach some political or moral importance to your consumer patterns. You shop better than other folks. Your shopping has more significance. It is important. Your grocery list is a declaration of principles. As a result, you likely identify yourself as a member of a virtuous, forward-thinking group. You are part of a movement possibly; and so, unavoidably, you define yourself in opposition to others. You can now more easily identify a foe—likely malevolent, probably dangerous, and possibly deadly.

My farm is not a pious exercise in sustainability. It is a calorie machine. I am a six-foot-four-inch-tall, forty-year-old man who, once upon a time, weighed 234 pounds. I am a big and enthusiastic eater. I am not hostile to the luxurious, if boggling, choice that the global food-delivery machine provides us. Based on condiments alone, my refrigerator would offer a four-star global culinary tour. So why turn my back on it?

Because I know I am not the first guy to be plagued by a vague but persistent sense that the universe has been coming unstitched for some time, and that the destructive, if unquantifiable, process is continually accelerating. I am no innovator when it comes to providing a solution, a straightforward way to sew it all right back together. But I do believe that we have lost a fundamental connection to the food we eat—a confident understanding of not only where our food is from, but also what is in it.

I am as casually creeped out by the clinical mechanization of the global food industry as any other middle-class dad who is grateful to be able to pay 120 percent more for grass-fed, hormone-free milk if it means keeping tits off my daughter until she reaches puberty. I am confident that one day pretty soon some sun-starved genius working in the bowels of Monsanto, or a similar food Death Star, will develop a Twinkie that shares most of its genome with broccoli, and I don't like the idea one bit.

Still, I don't know if I side with the locavore, or his critic, who claims that the titans of agriculture have it right, that massive quantities of food packed inside cargo containers hauled aboard enormous trains (which advocates say carry unimaginably heavy loads 435 miles on one gallon of gasoline) and in the holds of oceangoing ships are much less wasteful in the long run than weekly—nay, daily—parades of local artisanal producers trundling off to greenmarkets in beater cargo vans or late-model Subaru station wagons to sell their certifiably wholesome foodstuffs to eager urbanites, holed up, isolated, and ignorant, without the means or practical skills necessary to raise or grow their own food.

The news coverage, even the strikingly articulate, near-literary evaluations of what the locavore would like to call a movement, is arm's-length. The analysis is often laced with antiurban sentiment and occasionally mythologizes rural America as the dime novels did the Wild West.

Not that locavores and their scribes don't achieve their goal. They do. Locavores successfully reject the presumptions that most of us make about the food we eat; they most certainly make themselves aware of its source and the conditions under which it is produced. This brings them closer to real food, food that is healthy, supports the hard work done on small farms, and supports quickly vanishing artisanal food crafts. Still, is that urban locavore with his string bag and his burning mission an activist or is he just shopping? I say he is not as engaged in politics as he believes. I say he's making well-considered purchasing decisions.

But I have less and less time for such pedantry now. The Farm will remove me from the consumer loop. The locavore's dilemma is that, for all his thoughtful action, he's still a consumer. The Farm will put me one step deeper, make me the producer. Once food is tied to work and not money, even—worst case—its scarcity will teach the family something. Anyway, how hard is it going to be to sustain myself?

The Farm of my imagining is a closed system. That's the project's primary appeal. The available arable land may only be 800 square feet, but a 250-square-foot garage will make a fine barn, and its second bay will double as an outbuilding. In addition, I'll put four planters on the front lawn. That's it: the extent of my resources. If I don't grow it here, I don't eat it. If nothing grows, the theory is I starve—well, fail at the project at any rate. There is no room for extenuating, mitigating, or complicating circumstances. If entropy is the enemy—and, as always, entropy is most definitely the enemy—The Farm serves both as my weapon and my battlefield. On The

Farm I will have clarity of purpose and an objective under-standing of my progress. This might be true for the first time in my life. This prospect is exhilarating. On The Farm all the vagaries of my life will be stripped away. Finally, relief from all the unanswered, even the unanswerable, questions.

Typically aggressive and devoutly unrealistic, I begin the planning phase of my farm immediately after winning approval from Lisa. No sooner has the planning officially commenced than my ambitions begin to carom from inspired practicality to absurd grandiosity.

Most of the solutions to the problems presented by the limitation of space spring fully formed from my imagination. The plant nursery will be on the counter of the wet bar in the basement rumpus room.

Beyond the basement laundry room, nondescript if it weren't so dilapidated, behind an ancient door glazed with fissured white paint, is the rumpus room. It appears that late in Richard Nixon's first term, Howard Hall's previous own-ers turned their attention to the basement. They obviously had grand plans, wanted to be known as the kind of people who knew how to have and share a good time. The narrow, rectangular hinged basement windows are painted black. The stone foundation walls and brick retaining wall are pan-eled over with oak-stained fir paneling. The plumbing and heating systems for the house are hidden above a dropped ceiling of one-foot-square cellulose tiles into which recessed lighting is installed. To improve the ambience, eight impos-sibly ornate, floral, bronze double sconces are attached to the paneling and hooded with lampshades that were, once upon a time, spray-painted gold. Black-leatherette-upholstered banquettes are built against the walls. Because of all the built-in seating in the room, Lisa and I presume that deuces and four-top café tables must also have been part of the decor.

But the beating heart of the adult rumpus room is the wet bar. It stands, crouches really, in the corner closest to the room's only doorway. It is equipped with two Formica bar tops and its own independently switched, recessed lighting. After we scrub the place for a few hours and install a combination of low-wattage red lightbulbs in the fixtures, the room has the same appeal that the best Eastern European dive bars on Manhattan's Lower East Side had during the early 1980s.

To complete the effect, for Valentine's Day the first year in our new home, Lisa has a mirror for the bar back etched:

MANNYLAND est. 2003

Sinister in so many intriguing ways, this rumpus room could be the very place Calvin Klein first imagined when he dispatched one of his art directors to concoct a vaguely seedy, possibly sexually apocalyptic, retro-suburban, subterranean lair to set the advertising launch for his denim line. How disappointed he must have been when his man presented him with the comparatively tame set for that controversial 1970s teenage house party. And how relieved he must have been that his vision was not fulfilled when the public scandal broke. Rather than having a gold-hued orange shag carpet, our floor has marbleized black asbestos tile. After being washed with boric acid and treated to a polish specifically designed to return dazzle to such tile, this floor achieves a look that, if it had been used for the denim line, would not have resulted in a simple scolding and censure by the iconic fashion designer's culturally right-leaning critics. Our basement rumpus room, Mannyland, would have resulted in his exile.

The bar is stocked, the wood paneling washed. All that we need to throw our first basement house party is a few café tables and some bentwood chairs. We also need to install a brass pole. I had this clever idea about providing live entertainment in our den of iniquity. Lisa loved the idea.

But my attention wanders. Our daughter, Heath Ryan, is about to celebrate her second birthday. She needs a special present. I decide that no daughter of mine is going to enter her third year of life without a flock of one dozen songbirds in a cage large enough for her to walk around inside. A birdcage as big as the one of my imagining has to be fabricated in a shop. So, before Mannyland is ever inaugurated, it is retasked as a woodshop, a function it has served ever since.

Before we continue, careful reader, a set piece—a harbinger of things to come on The Farm. I marched into the store specializing in songbirds and other exotics on Thirty-second Street just west of Park Avenue South. No point buying Heath one bird or even a pair of birds. She was going to be two in the morning, and a two-year-old deserves a flock, I reasoned. When the saleswoman intuited the depth of my mania, she was more than happy to oblige. She nodded while I described the cage I had yet to build or even buy the material for. "When is your daughter's birthday?" she inquired pleasantly, and flinched visibly when I replied, just as cheerfully,

"Tomorrow." Reassuring her soberly, I explained that I had been planning the birdcage for a week already, just needed to hurry home and get to the Do-It-Yourself-Big-Box-Store for the necessary aviary building materials.

We packed the small cardboard box with a pair of society finches, a dazzling gouldian, a chipper spice finch, a brilliant zebra with an orange beak. Truthfully, by the time the saleswoman asked if I might want an electric-yellow canary, I had lost count of the birds, and nodded, dazed, gripping a five-pound bag of flaxseed.

On the subway, the thin cardboard box containing $1,100 worth of songbirds vibrated on my lap. At home, after stowing the box safely out of the way, in a closet, I announced that I had bought Heath some songbirds for her birthday. Lisa said that she thought that was lovely and asked how many. "Enough," I replied. "I need to run out to the building-supply store and buy some stuff to make a cage."

"I'm wrapping her present now," Lisa called after me as I closed the door and sprinted to the truck. By eleven o'clock I had barricaded myself in the playroom in the tower on top of Howard Hall. The aviary was built there because the ceiling is eleven feet high. I placed the foundation of the cage right in the middle of the room and began stapling half-inch plastic fencing to eight-foot-long strips of one-inch-by-two-inch poplar. Three hours later I tiptoed into our bedroom and woke Lisa. She grunted fearfully, jumping at my touch. "I need your help attaching the top of the cage," I explained in a whisper.

"Now?" she asked, crushed by the disturbance. "What time is it?"

"I'm almost finished," I said quietly, as though the whine

of the power drill going all night had not been enough to wake both kids.

"What time is it?"

"I just need another pair of hands. Just for the last steps."

Lisa stood blinking in the harsh light of the bare clip lights I'd ringed my work area with. She stared mutely at the cage, standing, its flimsy lumber torqued—twisted really—from the base. The cage stood nine feet tall. Three of the four sides were plastic mesh. The back, made of thin plywood, already had a perching branch bolted to it. "How many birds did you buy?" she asked, looking at the scraps of construction material and power tools strewn across the playroom floor.

"I wanted to make sure they had enough room and Heath could stand in there with them. See the door, here?" I said, gesturing. "During the party all the kids can take turns visiting with the birds inside the cage, through the door right here. See?"

"How many parakeets did you get?"

"Finches," I corrected. "They're songbirds—and one canary."

"How many? Where are they?"

"Ten. Ten, I think. They're in the closet, there."

"Ten?"

"Ten finches and one canary."

"Eleven birds?"

The final stage, attaching the roof, took longer than planned. The fragile poplar did not hold the weight of the plywood cap, so I had to design a mesh top and further secure the base of the cage. Lisa returned to bed after I barked at her for not knowing which clamp I was asking for.

I introduced the addled songbirds to their vast new home a few minutes before five.

Heath never did bond with the birds; the few times I coerced her into the cage, she looked around, laughed, and slipped back through the door as quickly as possible. I was disappointed, but once they started killing one another, I stopped encouraging Heath to play and bond with her birds.

The first bird to die was the zebra, easily the most expensive. I found the male society in a heap at the bottom of the cage a few days later. The female looked a bit hammered-on too, so I put her in protective custody in a small, portable cage attached to the outside of the mother ship. When she recovered, I reintroduced her to the flock, but by then another finch had been killed and it felt like releasing her into the general population was tantamount to feeding her to the sharks. The children were banned from the playroom, and before long I dreaded checking on the songbirds. Soon the cage began to stink.

All the while I suspected the canary. Twice as big as the finches, he seemed the obvious aggressor. Finally three male birds and the female society were all that remained of Heath's flock. Not that Heath noticed these murderous goings-on, or the waning population.

Well into a rum-soaked cocktail hour, Lisa traveling for business and the children long since asleep, I made a cursory check of the gladiator ring—the first in days. There in a corner of the bottom of the cage, the female society lay dead, strangely wet—ignoble. The canary flipped away off the common watering dish, the locus of so many skirmishes. "You killed the little girl!" I barked, tearing open the plastic netting with both hands. "You rotten fucking birds!" I howled, lurching inside the wobbling cage, the birds screeching, panic-stricken.

The three remaining brutes flew out of the precariously listing aviary and around the room. When I exited the cage in hot pursuit, it collapsed in a heap. One made a beeline for a closed window and died with a sharp pop on impact; the second flew straight out the door of the playroom and into the hall. I nimbly snatched the canary out of the air as it flew in circles, orbiting the overhead light above my head, palmed it delicately, and pitched it underhand into the wall, crushing it. I stomped out of the playroom in search of the last escaped savage raptor; he was nowhere in the hall. Striding into the bathroom, a rum-drunk ogre intent on mayhem, I found the bird dead in the constantly running toilet (have to fix that gasket), spinning slowly in the languid whirl of the current as the water leaked incessantly into the porcelain bowl, wings spread as though it had perished on Golgotha.

Crime scene mitigation: I gathered the carcasses, disposed of them in the garbage curbside, and dismantled the cage with my hands, vacuuming up whatever minced-corncob bedding the mice had not eaten and I had not managed to get earlier with the dustpan and broom.

"What happened to the songbirds, hon?" Lisa asked, a week or so after returning from her trip.

"They died," I replied.

"That's a shame," she said, truly saddened. "They were a lot of work, though, and they stank."

I nodded agreement, flipping a pork chop in the roasting pan.

*   *   *

On The Farm, Mannyland will double as both woodshop and plant nursery. I shall replace the forty-watt bulbs that shine from inside recessed sockets in the ceiling with full-spectrum UV lamps, and on the bar top I shall place the tidy plastic trays of peat-moss pellets, acquired from a Do-It-Yourself-Superstore in the Shadow of the Gowanus Expressway, from which my seeds will sprout.

Animal protein, the primary challenge as far as the editors at *New York* magazine are concerned, won't be a problem. I have plenty of room in my driveway for a ten-foot, bright blue, plastic fish tank. That tank is my tilapia farm, my primary source of protein. For years, I've been reading about how tilapia is favored for its resilience by aqua farmers. If tilapia is half as sturdy as fish folk say, I'll have no trouble raising them. I'll need to diversify my protein sources, but I'll address that once the tilapia pond is installed. I set aside exactly two days for fish-tank construction in my build-out schedule. The vegetables, once raised from seeds in the basement, will grow in the backyard until harvesttime.

Planned a little more than one hundred years ago as a fastidious knitting of the best that urban and rural lives have to offer, our neighborhood remains an arboretum. At the back of the houses, the trees are old and the canopy high and thick. Still, I spend the first few days charting the movement of the sun across the yard, staking out and precisely marking the sunniest patches, most only a few square feet across. At best the available sunlight is what farming journals and seed packets describe as "partial."

The yard is hard-packed clay, and since we moved in four years ago, it has successfully resisted our every effort to domesticate it. Every application of grass seed is repelled. In fact, any seeds we introduce take to the yard as they would a trampoline. Days pass before even the most cursory rain is absorbed (during which time the yard becomes a Baffin Island for mosquitoes). The backyard has yet to provide a single member of the family any prolonged joy or recreation. Forays to the outdoor space at the back of the house are undertaken, like a moon landing, with steely deliberation after exhaustive planning and liberal, some would argue dangerous, application of bug spray. Even the most optimistic visits undertaken in perfect weather typically devolve into a demoralizing retreat to the safety of the screen porch.

The Farm will offer a first best opportunity to actually use the space behind our home. I don't realize, of course, that within a month I will be shackled to it, as it transforms from our backyard to The Farm—from yard to patch, my patch—patrolling it at all hours to make sure it has not washed away, is not being invaded by predators, consumed by blight, or destroyed by foul weather.

Our tumbledown mansion has a front porch with broad square columns, and in the kitchen there's a 1943 Chambers gas range; morning light streams through stained-glass windows in the living room, and afternoon lights explode through the leaded glass window on the landing between the parlor and second floors. But the Japanese cherry tree in the yard had a special place in our hearts and played a pivotal role in our decision to buy the house. Because the cherry can apparently withstand the lead-poisoned clay that passes for soil, it was the only thing that ever grew back there. Each year since we'd moved in, the bloom had been increasingly feeble. Now, with the exception of one tertiary limb, the entire tree is free of foliage, very sick indeed. So Joe Gallo, the owner of the neighborhood landscape service G&D Landscape, pronounces the tree terminally ill. "Dead" is his term, delivered without inflection. "She is dead," he repeats, casting his professional, if merciless, gaze upon the neighbors' trees beyond our stockade fence for good measure.

"All of her?" I ask.

"Yes. Dead," Joe says, not looking back at our cherry, but studying a sickly Norway maple in a neighbor's yard, its hefty but bare branches hanging over our property line.

"Even that part?" I ask, pointing out the limb with the leaves and a few sparse blossoms.

"No. Everything else is dead, that part's alive," says Joe, without looking in the direction I'm gesturing. "You want I should take it away?"

"Dead?"

"Dead."

"How much?"

"Three hundred."

"I guess so." I shrug, looking at the blossoms on the one limb, trying to fix them in my mind. At least Joe doesn't charge two grand like every other guy in coveralls who passes through here. The tree was rumored, by the previous owner, to be from the same batch planted along the promenade on the neighborhood's main thoroughfare when Prospect Park South was first planned and developed in 1898. According to the brass plaque by the front door, reading only 1901, ours was one of the first houses built on this street. This assertion was bolstered purely by accident when, one Sunday afternoon, I was inspecting a soil map of western Long Island that I had bought years before we moved into the house and is now hanging framed in the library. Published in 1901, the map is a color-coded rendition of the numerous soil types that lay buried under the concrete that is now Brooklyn. Their variety and their location are an episodic source of fascination for me: Miami stony loam, Norfolk gravel, Hempstead loam, meadow, Galveston clay, and sassafras gravelly loam. In the right mood, the list reads like verse, and I imagine the first Dutch settlers of the area searching their homesteads for the perfect growing or building conditions. The map also provides a sense of the state of urban development at the time, offering proof that, by 1901, the city was well on the way to overtaking all seventy-two miles of western Long Island and had made inroads, via railway, in the direction of Long Island's east end. The development is incomplete, nonexistent in some places. Farm plots can be clearly identified. Not until we moved to Prospect Park South did I notice that, at the time the map was made, the grid of streets in the neighborhood had only just been laid. To my delight, our house is clearly visible, the first, the only home on our side of the street. Our cherry may well have been one from the original plantings.

"My wife is going to be very sad," I lament.

"The tree is dead," replies Joe, as though I am about to ask him to resuscitate it.

"Still."

Lisa returns home from a business trip to California just twenty-five minutes after Joe and his crew have driven away with our cherry tree in the payload of the forest green G&D Landscape truck. I salvage four of the largest trunk sections to use as outside stools and half a cord of firewood for the fireplace in the library. The G&D crew has been thorough, raking over the entire yard and even boring out the stump. It is as though our cherry had never existed.

The stockade fence that marks the perimeter of our property is almost exactly the same gray/brown shade as the earth it surrounds. Boards are broken. Some are missing altogether. It has seen better days. Just how tired our fence has become was not nearly so obvious when the tree, even in its own tragic decline, stood in the northwest corner of the lot.

Ah, well. At least now with the tree gone I can begin the serious work of creating a well-conditioned soil bed for my garden. Lisa is sorting through the bills and, purse still under her arm, office rig still uncreased, perched on tall, peep-toe slingbacks, is a vision. She is exquisite in her fashionable urbanity. I drag her to the yard, mail now tucked under her arm, to show her evidence of the first bold step toward building The Farm. Lisa does not see it this way. She insists that she is shocked to discover the tree missing; that we never came to a final agreement about its removal. "Joe said it was dead," I insist.

"It had blossoms on it," she retorts, incredulous.

"I pointed that out, too, but Joe said the entire tree was dead except for that limb," I explain, more defensively than I feel.

"So it wasn't completely dead," Lisa proclaims, victorious.

"Well, it's not like it's going to bounce back."

"Not now it's not." Lisa changes the focus of her attention, indicating that she has grown weary of winning this point. "So, just how much did you pay the guy who diagnosed and then removed our sick tree?"

"'The guy'? You mean Joe? And, yes, according to Joe it isn't sick, it's dead. But just what are you suggesting?" I feign outrage while doubt creeps in.

"Nothing."

"Three hundred and fifty: three hundred, plus tip."

"Hunh," she grunts. It's difficult to tell whom she is more skeptical of, Joe or me.

Judging from her infinitesimally more relaxed posture, more weight on her left foot, and a slight supine arch in her back, I believe Joe might be off the hook, but just for good measure, I offer a defense. "Joe's job is plants; he doesn't go around chopping trees down for an extra three hundred and fifty dollars." I spit, wondering if what I was insisting was, in fact, true, before being saved by my own cynicism. "You don't think he would have made more money by unsuccessfully nursing the tree back to health?"

"Practicality? Is that how you choose your vet, too?" asks Lisa, obviously ready to rejoin the fray and looking at our dog, Fergus, as if somehow my decision to remove the tree impugned my fitness as a dog owner.

"Please?"

"Please," she mimics, then something at the back of the yard catches her eye, and her expression grows stormy. "That fence is going to have to be replaced," she says in a tone I imagine she reserves for employees for whom a Human Resources Department file is already being assembled. "And that has to happen before anything gets planted in this yard."

"Farm," I correct her. "It's a field."

"What?"

"This is a field now, not a yard," I snap.

"The field needs a new fence," says Lisa, and turns back to the house.

"No problem," I shout as she turns the corner for the stairs. After all, how hard could it be to build a new fence?

THE STRANGER

||||||||||||||||||||||||||||||||||||||||||||||||||||||||||||||||||||||||

O ur neighbor Jen has recently sent a sample of the dirt from
her yard out to the Rutgers University Agricultural Extension in New Jersey to be tested for toxins. She doesn't have topsoil either, just this clay, this substrate. Jen is expecting the results
back any day now. The news is not going to be good, but just
how defiled the dirt behind our homes has become will beggar
our imagination. After reading the report, neither of us can ever
look at a child playing in the garden or on the lawn the same
way again; the idea of eating something grown in it, absurd.

Later that day, discouraged and confused, as I am standing
in front of the garage surveying the barren earth, my musings
about the potential of soil boxes as a means of avoiding the clay's
toxicity are interrupted. *The country we're living in here now is lit-
erally not the country that our ancestors inhabited. We're living on
a surface that wasn't the surface then.* The voice—that of an older
gentleman from the mid-South, a teacher maybe?—seems to be
coming from just over my right shoulder, just up the driveway.
Startled, I turn to address my visitor, but nobody is there.

49

If you see that a lot of topsoil is gone, then the thing you have got to do is think a long time about plows and how they are used. Then you ask yourself, what's in the mind of the man that ran the plow? continues the voice, unhurried and confident. I'm looking in the garage for a radio. Did I leave a radio out here overnight? This old fella definitely sounds like some hard-charger with a book to sell, doing his time on National Public Radio.

You can propose that a certain kind of person caused a gully, and you had better think pretty carefully about what went into the making of that gully, the assumptions, the cultural means and derivations, that went into it. The radio is nowhere. Our kitchen windows aren't open; neither are those of our neighbors the Feders. Yet it feels as if this guy is talking directly to me. *And then you can propose a person who would come along and stop that gully, and then you're asking what does he have in mind in order to stop it?*

I'm standing next door in the Feders' yard now, craning my neck to see if Skip, another neighbor, is holding forth in the back of his house. The voice doesn't sound like Skip's, but *. . . Because the physical, the practical action of stopping a gully is not all there is to it. It begins far back in the culture. There are two cultural themes here. There's a cultural theme of destruction and there's a cultural theme of preserving and cherishing. And they've existed side by side.*

"What's a fucking gully?" I call into Skip's yard. There is no answer; just the clanking and grinding of the hydraulic crushing arm on a city garbage truck.

With the cherry tree gone, the backyard cleared, it stands ready for its useful incarnation as a field. I am momentarily free to consider beginning work on other farm projects. So I begin to worry.

I worry because, rather than working, I have been thinking. I am building my urban farm to describe the effort required to disengage from industrialized food, but it dawns on me now the implications of stepping away from the food that everyone else eats bear examining. Despite these musings and the countless fantasies—heroic and catastrophic—about my immediate future, I never come close to imagining what I am in for.

An outside observer might regard The Farm as a way of making life unnecessarily complicated. Why grow food, she might ask, and for heaven's sake, why kill food, when you can buy it on the corner? If asked, I might answer that I don't see simplicity where she does. Rather, I understand the availability of food on the corner to be the result of unyielding complexity. The product of an authorless tangle of relationships—human, commercial, political, industrial, biological, and chemical—that will never be fully sorted. What does having food available at almost a moment's notice, twenty-four hours a day, really require of us? I'd explain that I wonder how many compromises, negotiations, promises, shortcuts, evasions, explanations, demands, declarations, and obfuscations I am required to make in the twelve hours between the time I wake up and the moment I pick up the telephone to call for takeout from Yen Yen, the local Chinese restaurant on Church Avenue, and exchange my bank-card number for an order of chicken and broccoli with white sauce.

Life on The Farm is going to be a series of spare declarations. I plant potatoes. I water potatoes. I harvest potatoes. I boil potatoes. I eat potatoes. I feed tilapia. I breed tilapia. I kill tilapia. I gut tilapia. I roast tilapia. I eat tilapia. At least that is my theory.

FOUNDING FISH

||||||||||||||||||||||||||||||||||||||||||||||||||||||||||||||||||

On The Farm I will wake up. I will pull on my Carhartts and my work shirt and begin the day, a day full of work. I will fix what is broken. I'll heal what is dying. Then I will feed what is hungry and water what is thirsty. If I think at all, it will only be to determine if there is a more efficient way to complete these four tasks. I will also, I learn quickly once the project is fully realized, dispose of an astounding quantity of shit.

This flood of feces is still in the offing, but when it begins it provides the first hint that my plans have not been transferred into action nearly as efficiently as I had imagined. Minimizing the amount of feces produced by my protein source and then disposing of what is generated is an integral operating principle of my first scheme for producing animal protein on The Farm. I am going to raise tilapia.

Tilapia is a tropical fish. To raise tilapia, little more than a pool twelve feet in diameter and three feet deep is required.

It's important to rig the pool with a dome designed to contain the energy from sunlight to heat the water to eighty degrees. For the most part the fish will survive eating the algae that grow in their tank. The algae is fertilized simply by suspending a burlap sack of dry horse manure over the tank and shaking it over the warm pool once a day until the bloom has matured so that the water is tinted green. If horse manure is not available, I have been assured that desiccated chicken or rabbit manure is a satisfactory stand-in. Since algae are the tilapia's primary food, no filtration system is needed.

Unlike most all other fish species favored by fish farmers, tilapia require only low levels of oxygen dissolved in their water, so they don't need a constant source of new water and can be grown in containers without so much as an aerating pump. This hardy fish thrives in nitrogen-rich environments, and—it can't get better than this—nitrogen is a principal component of their own excrement. But it does get better. The only recommended dietary supplement to their poo-generated algae diet might be easier to produce than the algae itself. A few small plastic garbage cans is the only gear required. Place fetid meat in each can. After a few hours or so, cover the cans. The thousands of housefly larvae and rat-tailed maggots that result will be more than enough animal matter for the tilapia population. Describing tilapia as robust is as inadequate an observation as calling Mike Tyson tough.

A single breeding pair of fish is said to be enough to start a population of a thousand or so offspring. For the offspring to reach the edible weight of one-half pound, the temperature in the pool must never drop below seventy degrees.

The original plans for the dome used in backyard tilapia farming were published in *Popular Science* magazine in 1968.

The dome, a geodesic design, is none other than the Sun-Dome designed by no less a personage than our first futurist, Buckminster Fuller. Fuller still holds the patent for the dome, but his estate only requires $5 for a copy of the plans. Back in the 1970s, advocates of backyard tilapia farming estimated that it could take as little time as five to seven days to erect a fully operational tilapia farm at a cost of no more than $25 ($122.63 today). As soon as the water hits eighty degrees, the breeding pair begin their work. As long as the temperature never drops below eighty, the spawning never ends. I become giddy as I read an account of backyard fish-farming in the January 1972 issue of the journal *Organic Gardening and Farming.*

Tilapia is an umbrella moniker for hundreds and hundreds of closely related fish, a majority of which originates in the Nile, and now dominates the southern Zambezi and the Limpopo rivers in southeast Africa. But where can my breeding pair of tilapia be had?

I know exactly where to go.

On Butler Street, just east of the Gowanus Houses public-housing project, there's a nondescript one-story warehouse. Usually a pair of tractor-trailer trucks are parked outside this warehouse. Loaded on the flatbeds sit four or more five-foot, blue plastic cubes that are continually leaking water onto the street. As part of my regular commute to school with the kids, I drive down this stretch of Butler Street at least twice a week, depending on traffic patterns. While planning The Farm I must have driven past these trucks four times before it dawned on me that the outfit was growing fish. Right here, tanks arranged on trucks parked at the curb on Butler Street, full to bursting with what must be thousands of the admirably indestructible tilapia.

Identifying the man in charge is easy. A commanding presence with a clipboard and a meticulously pressed navy blue polo shirt, the boss is Vietnamese and has the totemic, oaken face of a lifetime of real work. He regards me suspiciously as I explain my interest in his business. I am not asking for the world. I am working on a project. I am building a farm. The Farm is in Brooklyn, not far from here. I invite him to visit, to bring the kids. I want his fish, one of each sex. I need brood stock. I am willing to pay for as many as ten to insure that I get at least one female. I am willing to pay very well for his fish.

This urban tilapia farmer regards me. Stony, he tightens his deeply creased lips and his mouth disappears entirely. He shakes his head and looks for an employee to yell at. "No fish," he barks instead, at me.

He's right. I can't see a single fish anywhere; blue tanks filled with tilapia too numerous to count, but not one visible fish. I persist. I'll be willing to pay him considerably more than the $9.99 per pound that the nearby, upmarket fishmonger charges for his tilapia. "I am working on a project," I repeat, my tone intended to soothe, my words pregnant with portent. "Building a farm behind my home."

"No fish. No tilapia," the urban tilapia farmer insists. For an instant, I wonder. Maybe I got it wrong? Maybe the tanks are filled with . . . with . . . "Ten dollars per fish?" I insist, sensing my glorious, ingenious fish farm slipping away.

"No tilapia," persists the urban tilapia farmer, turning to walk away, checking something on his clipboard. "Thank you. Good-bye, mister."

"Twelve dollars per fish," I importune, following him into his warehouse. Even at that price, if I manage to spawn just a few hundred fish, my protein costs will be pennies.

Founding Fish

The urban tilapia farmer marches into the trailer, parked in the near corner of the warehouse, that serves as his office. I hear him turn the dead bolt as the vinyl-sheathed steel door closes firmly behind him. I peer through the small window next to the door—fluorescent light, ramshackle secondhand desk and chair, three mobile phones, and a plastic ashtray. Next to a Makita power-tools pinup calendar is a dry-erase board covered with smudged and faded numbers and what I take to be Vietnamese glyphs. Under the board is a maroon couch with bedding folded neatly on the arm farthest from the door. There is a coffee table and a thirteen-inch color television set. The urban tilapia farmer drops the venetian blind over the window. "Mister, no fish!"

It seems the first two will be the hardest tilapia to produce.

The next morning I awake in The Zero. A black mood—yes, I know, leave aside clinical diagnostics—that, most often, leaves me defenseless against even untethered fits of hopelessness and self-doubt, never mind specific, identifiable failure. This morning, though, my confidence about laying hands on tilapia brood stock torpedoed, rather than succumb to The Zero, I am moved by an uncharacteristic fit of prudence. Before my second cup of coffee, sitting in front of the computer, I reach out to members of the meat-rabbit community. As a group they are enormously accommodating and many patiently answer all my questions. By lunchtime, rabbits have joined tilapia among my best hopes for animal protein. These are early days. No decisions have been made. No reason to get Lisa involved just yet.

WHEN THE GOING
WAS GOOD

||||||||||||||||||||||||||||||||||||||||||||||||||||

This will never do. I'm going to need a second shopping cart. I haven't even hit the hydroponics store yet and I am dragging one hundred feet of four-inch PVC pipe; five pounds of drywall screws; a few hundred pounds of gravel (not nearly half of what I will need); a flat of full-spectrum lightbulbs; I don't know exactly how many aluminum clip lamps; and a bramble of extension cords. Where am I going to stow the weed cloth and ten of those just-add-water, peat-moss seed-starter trays?

If I am ever going to kick my home-improvement retail habit, it is not going to be today. This is the second big-box trip in five hours, and from the looks of things, on the first trip I forgot more stuff than I purchased. These surveyor's flags will come in handy; I should probably buy two packs just to be safe. Hinges, I need more hinges.

First step, extant clay must be manipulated so that water will drain from on top of it, otherwise the topsoil I plan to import will surely wash away during the first aggressive rain. Flipping through the latest issue of some home improvement porn mag on the subway a few days ago, I saw an item about something called a French drain. A graded trench filled with gravel, it is used to eliminate swampy spots on lawns. I extrapolate.

The notion of digging a dry well springs fully formed from my enthusiastic desire to tame the yard. All that is required to drain my clay swamp is some plumbing. I need to dig a drain and some graded trenches. The trenches will border the field and originate at all the outflows from the various roof gutters that border the perimeter. The French drain is a straightforward application of hydrodynamic theory. To understand the mechanics of this device, really just a channel, it is only necessary to know that topsoil contains a lot of air and is therefore exceedingly porous. Like everything else, water is pulled toward the center of the earth by gravity and always takes the path of least resistance. The French drain simply gives the water somewhere to go as it percolates through topsoil and flows down a drainpipe, a hill, or, in this case, the grade of the trench.

A traditional French drain functions best when it is installed on a naturally occurring slope of some kind. Because our yard is as flat as a pool table, it will only work if I use the French drain in combination with a dry well. I begin the project by determining how many drains are necessary and staking out the paths they will take to the well almost in the center of the yard at its lowest point. The first trench runs from the outflow of the garage-roof drainpipe, the second begins at the outflow of the gutter on the patio roof. The third runs along the border of the back fence on a grade of one inch every one hundred, where it meets at a T-junction with the garage trench. From there the two channels join, making a ninety-degree turn down a steeper grade to the point where I will dig the dry well.

The trenches will be a foot across. The longest run is eighteen feet. The plan is to line them with gravel. On top of the gravel I'll lay four-inch pipe made of the plastic polyvinyl chloride (or PVC) that I have cut lengthways. These half-pipes are the trenches' main channel. I will bury the lengths in gravel until they are four inches below the level of the yard and tack on landscaping cloth, a fine-weave nylon fabric. The cloth allows rainwater but not topsoil to drop off the clay substrate and into the drainage system.

If the trenches are graded correctly, rainwater that the soil cannot hold will seep through the topsoil and make its way along the surface of the almost impermeable clay into the trenches. Once in the system, the excess water roils through the gravel and into the half-pipe, following the grade toward the dry well.

My first efforts at digging the dry well reflect the self-congratulatory mood I'm in. I'm impressed that I have dreamed up the scheme. I fetch the brand-new posthole digger and ask the kids if they want to play in the dirt with me. I bought kid-size shovels for them, and when they enthusiastically throw their support behind my proposal to play in the dirt, I present them each with their own scaled-down shovel. "There's a tool for every job," I explain, overly serious, as if this might be the only chance I get to impart this pearl. "You always gotta have the right tool for the job."

Bevan Jake and Heath nod knowingly and begin digging up the flower bed we are standing next to. "Hang on!"

When I redirect them to the site of our dry-well excavation, they work hard for ten minutes, then Lisa presents them each with a juice box. "Don't work them too hard, honey," she scolds, hugging them both tight. "It's sunny out here."

All the same, the kids are excited by all my talk of building a farm and eager to help. We dig about two feet into the clay and call it a day. Enthusiastic high fives all around. I hide my grim concern: this is much more difficult than I anticipated; digging through this clay is just like digging through meat.

The real work begins the next day after the kids are in school. While walking Fergus, I pass Josh's house. The cement contractor working on his driveway is overseeing his crew and collecting a check from Josh. The three of us get to discussing my dry well. The cement guy comments that for the dry well to function properly I must puncture the layer of clay and reach the sand below. That is the missing piece in my plan. Until that moment I was not certain how a hole—even one three feet deep—would drain all the collected water. "Is there definitely sand down there?" I ask guilelessly.

"Yes," insists the cement contractor. Like so many basic agricultural facts, the geological truth that sand always lies beneath clay comes as a complete surprise.

On the farm of the blind, the one-eyed neighbor is king. I heed the words, immediately return home, and begin to dig. The next day, standing in a five-foot-deep hole not much wider than a trash can, I ask Carlos, the foreman on G&D Landscape's local crew, if there is any hope of finding sand beyond the clay. "In my country," says the El Salvadoran immigrant, "sand always follows clay. I'm sure it is true here also." I flash to the two-hundred-or-so-feet-high clay cliffs of Gay Head, now Aquinnah, on Martha's Vineyard, smile weakly, and continue digging.

Lisa seems increasingly distant during the excavation. I am so concerned with the planting schedule I never take the time to explain why I spend two entire days in a cylindrical hole and eventually disappear into the bottom of it. She knows nothing of my search for sand and has little interest in my energetic explanations of the powerful forces at work that will suck water from the surface of the earth. She clearly considers my behavior manic. She begins to complain regularly about the ring of filth that I leave around the bathtub.

At seven and a half feet I strike sand, but do not believe it and continue to dig for an additional four inches. Two full weekend days have come and gone. Lisa feels my absence more acutely on the weekends. During the week she can just about manage getting the kids to bed before she collapses.

Once convinced that the posthole digger is finally picking up sand, I sit cross-legged at the bottom of my spider hole. I have nothing to do down here anymore, and because nobody knows I am here, no one will ask me to do anything else. This is a good place. Dazzling sunlight rims the top of the hole, but it is cool and damp down here. Fergus stands tentatively at the mouth of the spider hole, staring down at me. His whole life I have ferociously discouraged him from digging holes in people's gardens.

Not until I scramble out of my spider hole does our neighbor Jane Feder, who has been watching the work intently from her kitchen window for two weeks, call out to me. "You don't have to tell me if you don't want to," says Jane, standing somewhat tentatively on our driveway, "but what are you doing back here?"

When I tell her that I am building a farm and plan to live off it alone for a month come harvesttime, she says, "I knew it. I told Al"—her husband—"that you were gonna build a farm." Jane is instantly excited, and she stays excited. Jane isn't put off by the growing mountain of refuse, nor is she concerned when I tell her about the necessity of earthmovers in the driveway. The introduction of farm animals doesn't bother her one bit. She is thrilled to learn that squirrel traps will probably be required. She occasionally brings friends and neighbors to the back of the house to show them the progress I am making on The Farm. On a few occasions I am inside for these visits, and I overhear her explaining the project, repeating verbatim all the grand plans I have shared with her. She is proud of me. She is a witness to my hard work and is impressed by it. I am grateful for her confidence.

The Feders' generosity and patience overwhelm me. Their casual response to my encroachment across their property line is a constant source of worry for Lisa, however. I store lumber and building equipment of every description by leaning it against our garage in their yard. I also use their yard to abandon a vintage bicycle rickshaw from China that I purchased months before in which to convey the children to school every morning. I rejected this plan before I even arrived home with the three-wheeled bike. I'm still not clear why I continued to pedal the gearless, poorly balanced heap up the moraine to Howard Hall from Cobble Hill, where I purchased it.

The Feders, like a number of my neighbors a generation or more older than Lisa and me, inherited their home from a parent, Jane's mother. "The one good thing about moving back into your mother's house as an adult," quipped Jane during one of our first conversations years ago, "is that you don't have to change all the toilet seats." I develop an immediate, and enduring, crush on Jane and, at the same moment, try to recall if I have ever changed a single toilet seat in any of the homes I had moved into.

As a lifelong city dweller, I bring the right perspective to my new project. Eight hundred square feet is a spacious one-bedroom apartment in Manhattan. I employ this organic metric as I proceed and rarely feel oppressed by the limits. Rather, like any good New Yorker, I start looking around for unoccupied or underutilized square footage and equipment to commandeer. The Feders' garage, I know, is empty except for a rusting exercise bike, an American flag, and a rotting armchair. I can double the usable space in my own garage if the Feders will let me use it to store the seventeen-foot sea kayak I started building six years earlier for the duration of this project. They will. In an instant their garage is full. When Lisa hears about this arrangement, she struggles to conceal her annoyance. The kayak was a Valentine's Day gift from Lisa. She gave it to me hoping that it would transport me across the East River, thereby accomplishing my boyhood ambition. The kit, the instructions for which estimated that construction could reasonably be expected to be complete in sixty hours, seemed like a manageable project when I excitedly opened the eight-foot-long cardboard box and began work. Six years later, watching while I tuck the half-built hull safely away in someone else's garage, Lisa shakes her head slowly and turns back toward the house without saying a word.

When the Feders leave for their annual retreat from summer in the city to the ocean breezes of Long Beach, Long Island, I miss Jane terribly. She has been the only witness to my tireless work to bend my naive plans to reality, and as such my only comrade.

While digging my spider hole, my hands became increasingly numb. I complained to Lisa. She did not seem particularly concerned—strange for a woman who passed out cold upon seeing me anesthetized in the recovery room after a simple hernia operation. All the same, fearing the unidentified worst, I consult my primary-care physician; he refers me to a respected neurologist. The neurologist says my hands are numb—and shaking slightly—because I drink too much. I protest, "Can we consider other contributing factors here, Doc? I mean, have you ever dug a seven-foot-deep hole straight down into the earth—*the clay!*—using just a posthole digger?"

"No," he replies, and writes me a prescription for electromyography. Electromyography, or EMG, vindicates me. I may drink too much, but I also have a pinched nerve in my cervical vertebrae, and that's causing the numbness in my hands. My hands get better after a few months, but the day will come when I shall beg for the return of numbness to my hands. I buy a second bottle of wine on the way home.

The One That Got Away

||||||||||||||||||||||||||||||||||||||||||||||||||||||||||||||||||||||||||||||||||||||||

After two weeks of delay a delivery truck with the material for the new fence arrives. There are a dozen panels and corresponding crosshatched caps, and fourteen cedar fence posts. I demolished the existing fence weeks ago and it lies in chunks on the refuse pile under the living-room window.

Joining the two incarnations of our back fence are nearly one thousand linear feet of PVC pipe and a dozen elbows and T-sections, a few dozen fifty-pound sacks of gravel, a short stack of plywood, and countless boxes and bags brimming with all the various fasteners, adhesives, and doodads that the projects ahead of me require. I draw great satisfaction from the refuse pile. The bigger the pile of garbage, the more incoherent its contents, the more like a proper farmer I feel. I'm delighted to find the enamel coat on the fridge in the garage/barn showing the first signs of rusting out—like acne spreading across the ivory skin of a preteen. Things rust on farms, garbage piles up. But on a farm nothing is garbage, everything might have a secondary use.

This is what makes installation of the new cedar fence so problematic. The new fence is a beautification project. Every other job on The Farm is about increased utility—or, at least, is planned that way. The arrival of the new fencing provides what Lisa describes as the one bright spot of her entire week. She considers the completion of the fence the only remaining measure of my commitment to her and our marriage. Ever since I agreed to build the new fence, it is the only aspect that she has demonstrated any curiosity about—even offering, after delivery of the material is delayed a second time, to call up the fence supplier to "light a fire under his butt." Like an increasing number of inanimate objects out back here on The Farm, the fence is now the symbol of Lisa's and my competing interests and concerns, and that, predictably, makes the work pretty slow going because, now, while erecting the new fence, I am working for the boss; everything else is, well, mine.

During a break navigating the fence-construction project and finishing the French-drain and dry-well project, I visit the urban tilapia farmer. This will be my fourth and, I have determined, final visit.

When the urban tilapia farmer sees me pulling up, he turns on his heel and double-times it to his trailer. I follow and pull the door open before he dead-bolts it. "Good morning," I announce cheerfully as though I have not been stalking him for two weeks.

"No fish!" he insists, tugging on the doorknob.

"C'mon. You have thousands of fish. I don't even want twenty."

"We are closed today. Sorry."

"You're not closed," I say, trying to empathize. "Ten fish at retail and you'll never see me again."

"I'll call the police," the urban tilapia farmer threatens.

"I am the police," I respond reflexively. It's an unusual response, I know, but it's one my friends and I have overused with little success ever since we were old enough to convince anybody that it might be true. Why I might think it appropriate to, even casually, impersonate a lawman at this moment has less to do with getting fish than recovering a measure of respect. A cop of some kind—Fish & Wildlife, FDA, Sanitation, who knows how many different regulations his curbside fish farm violates?—is what the urban tilapia farmer had suspected from the moment he first saw me. Since then his estimation of me has plummeted. I release my grip on the brass-plated doorknob. The door slams shut. I turn and walk out of the warehouse. Standing alone on Butler Street, with no tilapia and no respect, I am two weeks behind on my meat-production schedule.

What was the name of that rabbit breeder across the river in New Jersey?

Back at The Farm, with hands still numb, I dig a series of graded channels all leading to that seven-foot-deep hole. I cut the bottoms out of a pair of thirty-eight-gallon Rubbermaid garbage cans, place them bottom-to-bottom in the hole, and fill them with rocks and stones unearthed during the excavation. The graded channels are lined with gravel. The PVC pipes are sawed in half lengthwise and perforated using a drill; they are then filled with gravel. The channels, now filled with pipe and gravel, are covered with weed cloth. This will allow water to drain into the system but keep silt and dirt from clogging it. An additional five hundred pounds of gravel is purchased to cover all the trenches.

The underpinning for my field is complete. All that remains is to take delivery of five tons of the most fecund topsoil that eastern Long Island has to give, which I ordered from Joe and his son, Angello, at G&D Landscape, and dump it right on top of all my work. Angello says it should not be too long now. Spring is a busy season—his busiest—and he's got too much work to let one of his two trucks go all day to get my soil. "It's too much, Manny," he explains.

"It's gotta be worth the three grand you're getting from me, Angello," I reply, stepping through the back door and into my barren yard.

"Manny, please, I am working on it. Three days, a week most."

"A week's too long, Angello." I scrape at the mud with the toe of my shoe. It's as hard as a tennis court.

"I'm moving mountains, Manny."

"If you say so."

I'm only aggravated by the principle of the delay, the effect that it has on the schedule I am keeping in my head. I don't know anything about plants, nothing useful at least. I don't really care all that much about them, certainly not in the abstract. I'm pretty certain that I have added little to my knowledge about plants since my first biology class in junior high school, and knowing that makes me a little twitchy about the next step. My friend Tex, a beloved mentor who lives outside Bozeman, Montana, and the one person responsible for inspiring in me an appreciation of the real rural world outside the Five Boroughs, has bored me near to tears on numerous occasions, railing against the dangers of "alien invasive species" of wildflowers to his beloved high Western desert.

I know that photosynthesis has two stages: the first exchanges carbon dioxide for oxygen, and the second, the Calvin cycle, generates the energy for plant growth by producing glucose. I know that xylem and phloem operate as the plant's circulatory system and skeleton, and that water and nutrients flow up from the roots, and that water and sugar (the result of the Calvin cycle) flow down from the leaves.

It would not take all that much reminding to get me conversant on the topic of osmosis. That's about it for book learning, though.

In my heart I know that most plants need more sun than my garden gets to generate enough energy to produce edible fruit, stems, or roots. I am nothing if not adaptable, however, and I am convinced that by force of will and continuous hard work I will make the plants in this tiny field produce food for me.

There's no point starting a vegetable garden in New York City that is designed to feed me without starting all the plants from seeds. I return to the Do-It-Yourself-Superstore in the Shadow of the Gowanus Expressway and buy still more ready-made disks of peat moss, load them with seeds of every description—cantaloupes, acorn squash, Green Zebra tomatoes—and place them on the dusty wet bar in my ramshackle basement.

Finally, a constructive use for the still-to-be-completed rumpus room once known as Mannyland. Dormant for months, this space is all but ready to function as a plant nursery. I replace all the red lightbulbs with full-spectrum UV bulbs and set up a battery of clip lights with the same bulbs: endless ersatz sunlight from every angle. In only days I have evidence of growth. I am just as thunderstruck as my son, Bevan Jake, had been when he was two years old and, at playschool, his dry, red kidney bean had exploded from the dirt in a Dixie cup into a tender two-leaf shoot. This early success encourages me to redouble my efforts. I insert multiple seeds in single peat disks and plug in still more artificial sunlight.

As though racing one another from the bar top to touch the sunlight plugged into the ceiling, my seedlings soar, nimble—okay, wiry—ever upward. This, my cousin Gabe informs me when I invite him to witness my success, is exactly what they are doing. "Your lights are a little high, Cuz," he says clinically, if a little apologetically, as though delivering the news of a terminal diagnosis. "These seedlings are a little too spidery to survive outdoors."

"Balls," I reply. "They'll do fine. They're standing stock straight down here, aren't they?"

"There's no wind down here, is there?"

Within a few days, still in the basement and without the presence of any wind at all, the seedlings begin to collapse under the weight of their own ambition. I try to transition them to the outdoors by moving them to the sunporch, but the collapse is pandemic, and within a day hundreds of seedlings lie dead and dying across the vast expanse of water-swollen peat pellets. I am not an organic greenmarket farmer dedicated to sustainable practices. I am a Mesolith, not yet a subsistence agrarian. Both in style and substance, for all my grand schemes, my mighty works wrought, I have made surprisingly insignificant gains on a hunter-gatherer.

Successful gardeners call the process hardening off. After

the seedlings have grown strong and gained a leafy appendage or two in a controlled indoor environment—and mine
never did because, for starters, I failed to cull the weakest
plants, which stole vital nutrients from their stronger siblings,
thus compromising the entire crop—the successful gardener
chooses an overcast day after the weather has grown mild to
introduce his young plants to God's creation. In this pains-
taking, maddeningly gradual process, the plants first spend
a few hours in partial shade. Time outdoors for the young
sprouts is gradually increased until seedlings spend a half
day, then a full twenty-four hours outside. Only then, careful to protect them from wind, does the successful gardener
usher them into direct sunlight. This process is also episodic:
a few hours become a few days, and finally the plants are
transplanted to their place in the world.

THE CONTROL OF NATURE

IIIIIIIIIIIIIIIIIIIIIIIIIIIIIIIIIIIIIIIIIIIIIIIIIIIIIIIIIIIIIIIIIIIIIIIIIIIIIIIIIIIIIIIIIIIIIIIIIIII

I pull into a parking space around the corner from a hydroponics superstore in Queens. Staring out the windshield,
momentarily mesmerized by the eight lanes of careening traffic on the Long Island Expressway just twenty yards away, I
half recall a conversation with my cousin Gabe, who insisted
that all serious hydroponics stores in the city are under con-
tinual surveillance by the police and/or agents of the Drug
Enforcement Agency.

Emerging from the truck onto the treeless, sun-bleached
block of Flushing, I am dressed in a yellow floral-print shirt
of Italian origin, white jeans, and flip-flops. If for no other
reason than I am dressed like an extra from *Miami Vice* (the
movie), I momentarily inhabit Gabe's fantasy, scanning the
street for indiscreet unmarked vans and open windows on
the second stories of the brick-faced row houses that face
the hydroponics store across the yawning trench of the
expressway. In this drama I suppose that I am the rogue

vegetable farmer, grown weary of toiling over cabbages and green beans, ready to take on Johnny Law and try my hand at a real cash crop. It did occur to me as I began my work on The Farm that any small family farmer in America who does not allocate some of his land or energy to growing high-quality marijuana is either a dullard or a coward, plain and simple.

The hydroponic supermarket is a squat, one-story stucco structure, a muttered obscenity of a building with nine-foot-square windows on which the weekly, monthly, and daily specials are written in soap.

Once I'm inside, the distraction of my ganja-grower fantasy is swept away by the striking potential of applying some scientific method to The Farm, which is expanding before me. If only I knew the first thing about the science of hydroponics. I am transfixed by the enormous variety of gear in the showroom. Rows of plastic containers—jugs and pots and barrels of every description, spools of clear and opaque tubing in countless diameters, waiting to be applied to the project of plant growth without soil or sunlight. Stocked on beige painted aluminum shelves and stacked on the mottled white linoleum floor are pumps and filters calibrated for every need. Reflective plastic foil hangs in rolls from brackets near the ceiling, undulating like Christmas tinsel in the breeze from the industrial air conditioner. I walk the aisles gawking at the hardware, confounded that a gear freak such as myself has only just now encountered this pastime. Imagine applying such equipment-intensive science to vegetables? Forget survival, I will win prizes for growing zucchini as big as forearms. I will need construction cranes to remove pumpkins. Consumed by the effects that these tools will have on my vegetables, it never occurs to me that based on the price tags alone, this specialized precision equipment is not designed for growing mere vegetables.

How many times have I told Heath and Bevan Jake? There's a tool for every job, I say in sober tones. It's important to use the right one every time, even if it's not the one nearest. Even as I look around the showroom, a broad smile splitting my face in two, between visions of beets the size of softballs and cantaloupes like beach balls, I catch the eye of the taller of two salesmen—clean-cut guys in their early twenties. I arrange my visage, attempting to communicate the boy-could-I-use-some-help-buying-a-whole-lot-of-shit-that-I-know-nothing-about message. Eliciting no reaction whatsoever from the tall salesman, I abandon all subtlety and opt, instead, for the direct approach. "Excuse me?" I bellow cheerfully to another clerk two aisles away. He looks at his watch, then arranges his face in a heavens-is-that-the-time? expression, spins on the heel of one of his skateboard sneakers, and heads for the stockroom like the White Rabbit down the hole. I approach a third clerk, ask for assistance, and I am instructed in a mildly irritated tone to wait a minute.

"Hey, friend," I spit, "I'm trying to spend a little money in here."

The young man dedicates way too much time working his triceps. His head swiveling on the first vertebra, he turns to face me. He works to make the muscles of his arm twitch. "I wanna grow vegetables in my basement," I bark at this, the third clerk, who seems more eager to fight than sell. He stops. Takes a deep breath.

"What kind?" he asks petulantly.

"I don't know. What grows fast?"

"All kinds of things," he replies, not the least bit curious or engaged.

"I'm working on a project," I begin to explain slowly, clocking the first salesclerk circling us, apparently trying to listen in on the conversation. "I don't know anything about hydroponics, but I am trying to grow enough food to sustain myself for a month, and I only have eight hundred square feet of outdoor space to work with. I need to grow plants in my basement. My cousin shops here. He says he put a garden in his closet. He purchased it here."

"In your basement? What kind of plants?"

"I don't really care."

"You don't care?" the clerk asks, incredulous.

"No," I press on. "What I need is a flexible system. See, if the first crop dies, I need a system that can grow more than one variety of plant, of vegetable," I add for clarity.

Suddenly it strikes me: why stop at vegetables? "Hey, can I grow fruit using this equipment?"

"Some people grow strawberries," he says, looking around the showroom.

"That'd be a good start," I say, rubbing my hands together enthusiastically. "What do I need for them?"

"Look, I don't really know how to help you," says Triceps. "Maybe Chris can help you? Chris!" Triceps shakes his companion, the first guy to ditch me, out of his eavesdropping rapture. Triceps strides away from me without gesturing in my direction. "Can you help this gentleman?" he asks rhetorically, making his way quickly toward the front of the store to begin organizing what looks like a collection of bathroom wall vents.

"Chris," I exclaim, trying to sound cheerful. "Help me, would you? My name is Manny. I want to buy an entire growing system: soup to nuts."

"What do you plan on growing?" Chris asks, deadpan.

"Fruit, like strawberries, and vegetables."

"There are lots of vegetables," Chris says, sounding suddenly bored.

"Okay, Chris," I say, flashing on the only vegetable my kids will consistently eat. "I want to grow broccoli. Broccoli. Yes. I want to grow that."

"Broccoli's complicated. You're going to have to watch the temperature with broccoli, cauliflower, too. It is tricky keeping the temperature below sixty degrees, trickier than it sounds, but it's vital or you will stunt the plant." He regards me, clearly profiling me, trying to make sense of the white jeans, the flip-flops, and especially the floral-print, yellow dress shirt. After a considerable pause he speaks again. "Hey, you know who's smart about low-temp growing? David," Chris answers his own question. "David! This guy wants to grow broccoli," he calls to the White Rabbit just reentering the sales floor from the stockroom.

"It doesn't have to be broccoli," I try to correct. "I don't really care . . . just easy," I sputter.

"Help him, would you?" says Chris, walking away toward what appears to be bottles of shampoo—actually humic acid. Pulling a cloth from his pants pocket, he begins to dust and rearrange the opaque brown bottles with their colorful labels. Chris is still looking over his shoulder at me while his associate begins the conversation anew. "You want to grow broccoli?" asks David amiably.

"Not necessarily. I am working on a project. I need a

hydroponic system that is flexible. I am not sure what plants I want to grow yet."

"Plants? What kind of . . ."

"Vegetables," I correct myself.

"What kind?"

"I don't really care," I sigh.

"You don't care, huh?" asks David, looking around the showroom.

"I just want to grow what's easiest."

"None of this is easy," David says steadily, looking over my shoulder to Chris, trying to disguise his expression, one both angry and confused.

"I'm sure," I say, growing weary of being addressed as a child. "How about this?" I ask, grabbing at a reflective zipper bag that looks as if it should line the inside of a good-size closet in a prewar apartment. "If I get this, what can I grow and what else will I need to get started? Let's put a list together."

"You are going to grow broccoli in a closet?"

"No. I'm going to use my basement. It's about four hundred square feet of usable space."

"Then you won't need that," David says, walking toward a display of paddling-pool-size, black plastic tubs. "What you might want is a reservoir. You're going to need, like, thirty square feet."

"No problem," I say, feeling the first signs of traction in this frustrating retail experience. "A reservoir and what else?"

"We can start you out with this five-gallon reservoir," says David, holding up a black plastic container about the size and dimensions of a busing tray from a Greek diner. "You'll also need tubing, nutrients, grow nets, some grow medium. Do you have a pH kit?"

"I don't have anything, David. How many plants will that hold?" I gesture forlornly at the entirely inadequate plastic reservoir that he is filling with gear.

"Six, about six," he says without looking up, reaching for a package of six blondish, oversize steel-wool-looking pads.

"No good, David. I need to grow closer to sixty plants."

"Sixty? Sir, you gotta walk before you can fly," he says, then that pause, and that scrutinizing once-over. I flex my toes in my flip-flops while enduring his examination and wish that I had not. "Sixty of what kind of plants?"

"Vegetables."

"What kind of vegetables?"

"I don't care, remember? Whatever works."

"You better talk to Paul," says David, suddenly very clipped, looking around the room nervously. "He's the manager."

"I don't want to talk to anybody else, David. I want you to sell me a rig so I can grow good stuff to eat in my basement. I have a huge basement and I have got to grow enough food to live off of for a month. Will you sell me enough gear to do that, or not?"

"Talk to Paul," David says, pointing to a man with a tight-clipped beard wearing a retro Houston Colt .45s baseball cap.

David begins to unpack the plastic tray and calls, almost yelling, "Talk to this guy, wouldya? He wants to grow sixty plants in his basement."

"Vegetables," I clarify, though more out of habit than anything else.

I walk the length of the store toward Paul before he lifts his eyes from a wholesale catalog he's marking for order. When I arrive at the counter, I stand in silence waiting for him to put his pencil down and close the catalog. "You want to grow sixty plants in your basement?"

"That's right."

"You don't care what kind of plants?"

"Vegetables. I would like to grow vegetables."

"Broccoli?"

"Sure. If that's easiest."

"You're unfamiliar with the hydroponic growth system?"

"Entirely."

"Hydroponics is a way of growing plants using mineral-nutrient solutions instead of soil. Even plants that usually grow on dry land—in soil—can be grown with their roots in a mineral-nutrient solution or in an inert medium, such as perlite, gravel, or something called mineral wool—fibers made from minerals or metal oxides. It's the same stuff that gets used to make drywall; it's in gaskets and brake pads.

"In the 1800s plant researchers discovered that the soil itself is not essential to plant growth, that plants absorb essential mineral nutrients when they're dissolved in water. So, when vital mineral nutrients are introduced into a plant's water supply artificially, soil isn't necessary for the plant to thrive. You getting this?" asks Paul, who has delivered the lecture from memory while his eyes wandered around the store, probably taking inventory or wondering why his girlfriend hasn't returned his phone message in two days, but only fixing my gaze when he addresses me.

"Sure. Yes. Sure," I say, wondering how old Paul is and where the hell he gets off.

"Good. There are two kinds of hydroponics: solution culture and medium culture. Solution does not use any solid medium for the roots, just the nutrient solution. There are two types of solution culture: static solution culture and continuous-flow solution culture. The second kind, the medium-culture method, uses a solid medium for the roots like sand, gravel, or, say, rock wool. That's the most common kind of mineral wool. There are two main variations for each medium, subirrigation and top irrigation—watered from the top or the bottom. You clear?"

"Yep. It'll grow vegetables?"

"I recommend you start with lettuce."

"No broccoli?"

"Broccoli requires low temperatures to thrive. That's an added layer of complexity you don't need."

"The kids like broccoli. They have not figured out lettuce, yet."

"Really? The kids like broccoli. That's pretty uncommon," says Paul, totally disinterested.

"Fine. Lettuce, then," I say sullenly, looking around the salesroom to avoid eye contact, and trying to figure out what everybody else has been looking around the salesroom at, when I notice a dozen, maybe more, of those opaque, domed, 360-degree surveillance cameras. This is a big showroom, but that seems like an awful lot of surveillance.

"Okay, I'm going to recommend this book," says Paul, slipping a tabloid-size paperback from the impulse-purchase rack, *Hydroponic Lettuce Production* by Dr. Lynette Morgan. It has a distinctly self-published appearance. "It's the lettuce bible."

"So what do I need to grow a whole lot of lettuce?"

"A whole lot of very expensive equipment."

"Now we're talking," I say.

"I'm gonna suggest that rig by the window for a start,"

says Paul, gesturing over his shoulder at an enormous Amaze-N-Marbles children's toy made from translucent PVC that appears to be circulating nutrient-laden water to a dozen gorgeous orchids. "It's vertical, circulates pretty much by itself, and it'll expand easily, once you get the hang of hydroponic growing."

"How many lettuce plants will it grow?" I ask, doubtful about the rig's ability to satisfy my fantasies of hydroponic domination over hunger.

"A dozen, eighteen, maybe."

"That's not enough."

"Anything more," says Paul, lifting up his baseball cap, and running his hand through the unlikely buzz cut he is sporting, "it's going to be a waste of your money."

"You're right, Paul." I admit defeat. "I better just stick with the lettuce book for now. The rest of this looks a bit too much like science," I say, trying to add levity to an entirely too serious encounter.

"It's all science, friend," replies Paul humorlessly.

That cuts it. "Friend"? Sure, so I did tolerate Paul's self-glorifying ex-Trekkie lecture, but I hate nothing quite so much as a condescending youngster who feels comfortable calling me *friend* when what he really means is *asshole*. What is it that Paul thinks he has on me, talking at me like I'm short a chromosome for an unbearable eternity? My heart rate is slowing down. I can feel my hands going cold; this is never a good sign. In my youth it forewarned of a spasm of violence that earned me the wholly appropriate nickname Dumb Bear.

I need this hydroponics rig, though. Half the day is shot already. If I leave now, it'll take another day to identify and locate an equally well-equipped outfit, and I needed to have some food growing yesterday.

Still, "friend." That is going to be hard to get beyond. Deep breaths, that's what I counsel the kids: "Three deep breaths is all that stands between you and a day-changing mistake." I drop my eyes to the counter, an effort to compose myself. There, laminated to the chipped, beige formica counter is an obituary from February 22, 2005: "Hunter S. Thompson, Out-law Journalist, Is Dead at 67." Scrawled on the obit's margin in black Sharpie marker, R.I.P.

Have the boys here made me for a narc? Me? Maybe. I can't blame them, dressed, as I am, like a pimp dandy from tropical climes. I may not be a narc or a drug-enforcement agent, but ever since I walked into the store I have been doing what my profession trained me to do, ask as many dumb questions as you can think of. If your ego gets bruised along the way, consider another line of work, and meanwhile, comfort yourself that you do this to further your constant quest for a good story with new information, nuance, or a good quote. But I neglected to identify myself as a reporter—because I am not, I am a farmer—so I have inadvertently communicated only a deep desire to burn vast amounts of money on a project I know nothing about. I have spent the last half hour asking after only the most obvious covert growing rigs—ones designed to fit inside closets. I can be one of only two things, the dumbest cannabis grow king ever to step through this front door, or a cop.

Looking around at all this incredibly expensive, narrow-use equipment, narc or not, it is possible that I am the first customer who has ever entered this store with a sincere desire to grow vast quantities of fresh vegetables in his basement. "I'll take the book and think about getting that orchid rig after I have read this," I say, waving the glorified pamphlet in the air and sliding my credit card toward Paul.

"Okay," says Paul, ringing up the sale. "One of the most important things to remember when the plants are young, make sure you have a fan blowing air over them. That makes the plants robust. You don't get overly tall, weak, spindly seedlings that way." My heart sinks as I flash on the killing fields of overly tall, weak, spindly seedlings down in Mannyland. A fan. Of course. I walk out of the store removing the skinny, self-published, 102-page text with the washed-out cover art from its paper bag. Back in the car I glance at the receipt: $42.

Before anything would grow in our backyard, it was necessary to install plumbing. Following instructions provided by a local cement contractor, I dug a dry well through clay until I reached sand. The hole, no wider than a trash can, ended up being nearly eight feet deep. *(Photo by Eric Slater)*

During his entire life, I trained Fergus not to dig holes. *(Photo by Eric Slater)*

The dry well would not work without being fed run-off by a series of French drains. Used by landscapers to eradicate wet spots in sloping lawns, these plastic-and-gravel-lined trenches were dug on a grade leading to the dry well. The dry well was filled with rocks and gravel and capped with a garbage can lid.

After the plumbing was installed, five tons of topsoil was imported from eastern Long Island.

During the preparation process I had casually observed how the sun fell on the plot. After the topsoil was delivered I charted where direct sun fell and for how long. The Back Forty *(far corner)*, just forty square feet, was the only area that received more than five hours a day.

Plants in the Back Forty grew quickly; the other three-quarters of what came to be called the Fields of the Lord lagged behind.

I purchased kid-size shovels for Heath and Bevan Jake, hoping to engage them in the The Farm at its earliest stages. The three of us dug almost two feet before Mom appeared bearing juice boxes, rescuing them from sun too hot to work under.

Like all the structures on The Farm, the rabbit hutch was built on the driveway, without written plans. *(Photo by Gabriel Evans)*

To preserve as much of the limited space on The Farm as possible, and like the chicken coop that would follow, the two-story rabbit hutch was built to take advantage of vertical space. Design alterations included four-inch casters so that it could be moved around The Farm and eventually wheeled into a Dumpster on the curb. *(Photo by Gabriel Evans)*

One of the earliest and hardest lessons learned on The Farm: Doe #2 lies dead on the kitchen floor, a victim of the dreaded infestation known as fly-strike.

The Stray, acquired while buying twenty-five day-old meat birds at the Agway in Englishtown, New Jersey. One morning this very ugly and presumably useless hen laid an egg, instantly changing my sustainability strategy.
(Photo by Daniel Reese Bibb)

Fix what's broken; feed what's hungry.
(Photo by Daniel Reese Bibb)

The Flemish giants refused to breed according to my schedule. In a panic, I turned to chickens for meat and, eventually, eggs. Caleb and Bevan Jake introducing one of two bantams to The Farm from the back of The Tractor, a 1989 Toyota Land Cruiser. *(Photo by Eric Slater)*

This salt-and-pepper team of bantams were the first of many roosters among the twenty-five meat birds to find their voice. It is legal to own hens within New York City. Possession of live roosters is illegal. On The Farm, crowing, no matter your weight, resulted in confinement to the soup pot. *(Photo by Daniel Reese Bibb)*

"On The Farm," Heath Ryan informed her doctor, "we don't name our animals." Simultaneously, she provided her father's proudest moment and her mother's worst fears realized. *(Photo by Eric Slater)*

Overrun by dozens of day-old poultry, Bevan Jake maims one of the ducklings underfoot. Clearly fearing the worst, the little boy looks to his father before whirling around to see what he has stepped on. In that instant, Caleb scoops the dying bird up and behind his back. *(Photo by Eric Slater)*

THE GOOD WORKER

IIIIIIIIIIIIIIIIIIIIIIIIIIIIIIIIIIIIIIIIIIIIIIIIIIIIIIIIIIIIIIIIIIIIIIIIIIIIIIIIIIIIIIIIIIIIIII

I did not know who Wendell Berry was when he took up residence in my imagination. At once professor (though one who claims he's always been "more comfortable out of school"), eastern-Kentucky tobacco farmer, poet, essayist, novelist, and agrarian activist, Wendell Berry is also, and most poignantly, a champion of what someone who knows him well once called the lost disciplines of domesticity—of husbandry and wifery and making do.

Berry is a partisan in the politics of domesticity, and this makes him, in his eyes, so far as I can tell, an enemy of both industrial and postindustrial modernity. More on that later. However, this observation of Berry is written in a letter addressed to him by none other than Wallace Stegner:

> You are a hero among those who have been wounded and offended by industrial living and yearn for a simpler and more natural and more

feeling relation to the natural world. I should add that you wouldn't be as good a man as you are if you were not a member of Tanya [Berry's wife], and she you.

Berry is a vocal critic of what he calls the glamour of newness, ease, and affluence; and a champion of distraction. No one, Berry chides, with too much to do has enough time. "There are some things the arrogant mind does not see; it is blinded by its vision of what it desires. It does not see what is already there." In the context of all that is sacred in postindustrial modernity, Professor Wendell Berry is, clearly, a thoroughgoing pain in the ass.

Here is a prophet of the virtues of moderation, prudence, propriety, and fidelity; the more I learn about Berry, the clearer it becomes that he and I have very little in common. So, when he first started counseling me while I examined the clay that would become my field, I did not recognize the voice. I knew nothing of gullies, nothing of him, never mind the phalanx of disciples and adherents who have rambled after him through time. I did not appreciate how effortlessly he reaches out and back through time to embrace the young Robert Penn Warren, Henry David Thoreau, and, what the hell, Thomas friggin' Jefferson.

All, to my mind, great men, and all as far from fellow travelers as I can imagine. Still, if Berry's first words were not immediately revelatory, ever since I found a moment to look into those gullies Berry was going on about, I have hoped he would return. It turns out nothing pisses a farmer off more than a gully. An extreme form of soil erosion, in its best incarnation a gully is a difficult-to-discern and entirely unproductive seam in a field, one cut by the fierce flow of water and subsequently filled in with useless silt. Gullies only get worse from there, until trees are collapsing into rapidly widening creases, carving away topsoil and creating dry riverbeds, making once productive farmland useless. Named by Scottish farmers after their gully knives, because land blighted by gullies looks as though it has been cut open by a sharp blade. On a farm, gullies usually form as the result of abuse or carelessness at the hands of a farmer (past or present); one who has plowed it without concern for the grade of the field, plants the same crop year in and year out, that sort of thing. Extend the argument, though, as Berry did, and our yard, the yards on the entire block, all of Flatbush, really, was now one big gully.

It didn't seem immediately necessary to share these gully musings with Lisa.

It is early in the morning and the little sun my plot gets has not yet made its way in through the branches of Al and Jane's hemlock tree, nor over the top of our low-slung bunker of a garage and onto my hard clay parcel. Lisa has already left for her office, has been gone from the house for half an hour already, the hand-waxed black Lincoln Town Car, piloted by Alvin Hemmings, gliding up Franklin Delano Roosevelt Drive already approaching the Forty-second Street exit. She is no doubt sitting on the black leather of the backseat, legs crossed, four-inch heel distractedly tapping the magazines in the net at the back of the passenger seat. As she does every morning at Alvin's behest, Lisa will have already looked up from her PDA or a spreadsheet, pausing long enough to enjoy her favorite moment in the commute to watch the sun rising over the East River and behind the Brooklyn Bridge, and then return to busily thumbing her Treo, wordlessly setting the pace of the day for countless people in offices across the country.

I draw from my coffee cup and survey my farm, feeling the chill of the night before still hanging back here. I am deciding what to fix first. So much is already broken or still unfinished.

A farmer does not go to work, says Wendell Berry from his place in the pantheon of celebrated American agrarian men of letters.

I stand stock straight. Did someone say that? Did I think that? Never mind. No, he doesn't, does he? I agree, but with whom I am not quite sure. In my experience thus far, the farmer never does leave his work, except to sleep, and then, apparently, his work follows him to bed and sits on his chest like an angry ghost.

One afternoon, a week or so later, I sit, dejected, staring as I rest on an upturned five-gallon, white plastic joint-compound bucket. There's still so much work to do. I don't want to do any of it. I don't know where to start, how to choose some project I might actually complete before the day ends. Isn't there something, anything, really demonstratively productive to do around here; something I can point to and tell Lisa, "Look at what I did today"? Wonder decays and becomes worry, the heels of my hands, metronomic, rubbing dirt into my cheeks and forehead.

There are times, says Wendell Berry in an offhand way, *when it feels like there are better things for me to be doing.* I later learn that Berry holds strong opinions about the role that enthusiasm plays in American life. Berry contends that Americans celebrate enthusiasm, mistaking the fickle impulse for a virtue. The marketplace encourages our consumerist enthusiasms because our wandering retail eye boosts sales. More dangerously, our practiced whimsy, our ability to cast aside the objects of our desire we impulsively collect, extends to metaphysical yearning as well. The whole culture, a country populated by people, like magpies, on the hunt for the next shiny alternative to whatever it is that occupies their sweaty grip at present.

MEAT RABBIT

||||||||||||||||||||||||||||||||||||||||||||||||||||||||||||||

A spasm of subsequent giant Flemish research makes clear that the perfect breed will be the Flemish giant. Adults top out heavier than twenty pounds. Offspring are edible—what's known as fryer weight, five pounds—in a few months. A doe has between six and ten offspring per litter, but, because she has eight nipples, can only feed that many.

The nearest rabbit breeder trading in the giant Flemish is in suburban New Jersey. He introduces me to his flock—but not his family—and singles out a pale gray doe, tells me that she comes from a fertile line and will probably do well, but he cannot promise anything. The one buck he has for sale is young but also from productive stock. "He will give you rabbits, this one," the suburban breeder says, holding him up by the ears. Clocking my alarm, the breeder explains that this is the best, only really, way to hold such giant rabbits. "It no hurts them, the ears," he assures me.

I choose the pale gray doe and pay for her and the sand-colored buck with cash. He writes me a receipt on an envelope that once held a bill from the electric company. I have neglected to bring anything to put the rabbits in for the trip back. The suburban breeder roots around until he finds a plastic cat carrier and a cardboard box that held a large rotating house fan.

Traffic through the Holland Tunnel is near standstill. I can do nothing but keep up with the flow and wait my turn while ten lanes merge into one at the mouth of the tunnel. My only practical knowledge of rabbits came from the pair my sister, Bevin, had as a kid. Bevin loved rabbits, had two plush toys: Rabby was orange and white, and Bunny was white and blue. The real rabbits, Max, a mottled black-and-white, and Charlie, as pure as snow, didn't turn out to be nearly as cuddly. They lived in a hutch at the bottom of the yard at the house where my mother moved when she and my father split up. Mom was busy making the heap just one hundred yards from the notoriously despoiled Gowanus Canal livable.

The rabbits were intended to cushion the blow of our family's upheaval. As their names would suggest, the pair were purchased with the understanding that they were both males. When Charlie gave birth to her first litter, my mother pretty much wrote them off. They kept breeding. Charlie kept destroying the litters. When Bevin and I couldn't find any evidence of them, my mother was left to explain that Charlie ate them. "Ate them?" we asked, as confused as outraged. It was all very oppressive. Bevin, just eight years old, did what she could, feeding them when she remembered or when she believed doing so would entertain her friends. We didn't know enough to separate the male from the mother and the newborns, so aside from feeding them, we mostly just left them to their seemingly beastly ways. In short order Max and Charlie went entirely feral. Eventually just feeding them required a team effort. During that winter we would bundle up and trudge through the snow to the cage. I held them at bay wearing a baseball mitt to protect my hand, and Bevin filled their bowls. One day, at the end of the Easter vacation, Max and Charlie and their cage were not in the backyard anymore. I don't remember if I asked where they had gone.

Grown-up now, I have every expectation that these rabbits will fare much better than Max and Charlie. I am excited to deliver them to their new home and their, albeit complicated, role in my mission. Not until I return to The Farm do I realize that there is nowhere to house these rabbits, and so I decide to leave them in their boxes in the garage overnight. In the morning it's obvious that they will need something more substantial. Both rabbits have vacated their boxes and have taken up in opposite corners of the dank cement bunker. Rounding them up—stutter-stepping, feinting, lunging, and bending—takes quite a bit more energy and time than I anticipate. This is primarily because I am afraid, less for them than for myself, how they will react if I grab them. Not until I am more frustrated than afraid do I manage to sweep both up by the ears and return them to their entirely inadequate captivity.

It takes twice as long as I anticipate to fabricate their temporary cage. Using chicken wire and found scraps of wood, I build a corral into the corner of the back porch. I divide it in two. The sexes are to be kept separate, says the literature, until it is time to breed. They seem happy enough in their temporary home, and I give them all the vegetables in the crisper before running off to the pet store to buy rabbit food. I am proud of my quick adaptive thinking, and I dub the rectangular, jerry-rigged rabbit cage the FEMA Trailer. The name becomes increasingly appropriate as the summer passes.

Lisa reappears on The Farm but only to check on the rabbits, to feed them carrots and celery from our fridge, and conquer her initial fear of holding them. The more comfortable she gets, the more frequent her visits become. There is not much conversation between the two of us; occasionally Lisa asks me to put one of the rabbits in her lap. She feeds them, cleans their temporary boxes once or twice, and places the timothy grass—which I purchased earlier, mistakenly believing it was for warmth and comfort—as a dietary supplement in their enclosures. While every other project annoys her, these two rabbits provide comfort to Lisa. For the rabbits to successfully fill their function on The Farm, I work hard to regard them with cold calculation.

Eventually Lisa allows the kids to play with the rabbits, as long as she is watching. No names, though. I'm conflicted. Treating the rabbits as pets tangles my plans. The rabbits are tools. Watching the kids laughing at, playing with, and learning about the gentle giants is delightful; watching Lisa's growing comfort on The Farm is exciting. But Buck #1 and Doe #1 are working rabbits—meat machines, nothing more. I remind myself of this a few times a day. I understand that a more experienced hand at animal husbandry is capable of accepting breed-stock duality. I imagine, one day, I will also.

Really, I'm just happy to have the family out back with me. If that means they play house with a pair of rabbits as big as corgis, that's okay by me. The permanent rabbit hutch takes three long days to complete.

THE RAMP

IIIIIIIIIIIIIIIIIIIIIIIIIIIIIIIIIIIIIIIIIIIIIIIIIII

I am pulled away from farmerhood and back into father-
hood by the surprising diagnosis of a congenital defect
in Heath's right knee. Lisa has been worrying out loud for
months about a growing lump underneath Heath's knee.
Until now, I have silently dismissed this concern as Lisa's way
to draw my attention back to the family. Weary of attempting to engage me in conversations about the danger that our
daughter might eventually be unable to walk, ever, Lisa finds
a highly regarded specialist and makes the appointment. All
Lisa requires from me, she says, is that I ferry our daughter
to Manhattan and deliver her to Lisa at the doctor's office
for the appointment at eleven in the morning. I don't even
have to stay if I don't want, but, Lisa says, as though I might
have forgotten that her job is intensely demanding, she has to
return to the office to attend a series of important afternoon
meetings. So, if I do leave, I can't go back to The Farm unless
I want to come all the way back to Manhattan to pick Heath

up—on time—when the appointment is over. It's entirely up to me, Lisa concludes.

I make the delivery and stay with Heath and her mother. The waiting room is populated by parents—some distraught, some stoic—and their children, each one with a crippling ailment of the bone and joint. Most of the kids are confined to wheelchairs. One child is helmeted and belted in. Our daughter is bouncing around the waiting room, chatting to us and asking why we have to be *here*. She then attempts a series of vigorous jumping jacks. Lisa, buried in her PDA, does not seem to notice. I take Heath for a walk around the block. When we return, Lisa has become frantic. The wait is longer than she had anticipated. Now she will have to teleconference in to her lunch meeting and reschedule her two-o'clock. Her two-o'clock, she adds, is with an important client. When the doctor's assistant does call Heath's name, Lisa remains sitting in the waiting-room chair. She is daviting, thumbing at her Treo frenetically. When she looks up, I wordlessly communicate that she should get her butt out of the chair and come with us. "What?" she barks defensively. I toss my head in the direction of the examining room and proffer a hollow smile and furrow my brow. All this to say, let's get this day-killing fool's errand up and over with, please, so that one of these children with serious and challenging, life-altering maladies can get in to see the doctor. "Go ahead without me, I have to finish this e-mail or my deal will explode," she insists. I say nothing, turn to go. "No. Wait. I'm coming," she spits.

In the examining room Lisa is transformed. She is the picture of maternal angst. She can barely manage a smile and stares silently at Heath's right knee. When Heath hops off the examining table in her bare feet and underpants, Lisa shoots me a look, shocked that I would allow such a dangerous maneuver to occur here, in a doctor's office. Heath walks across the room and cranes her neck to inspect a rubber model of an elbow positioned on an aqua-turquoise Formica countertop. "Here, check out the knee, Heath," I say, picking up a rubber knee replica and waggling it at her. "It's a knee. That's why we're here, right?"

Heath smiles. "Dadda," she scolds playfully, and laughs as she reaches for the statue. The surgeon swings into the examining room just as Heath palms the rubber model. He is clearly a pro, wearing a white lab coat over a natty charcoal pin-striped suit, his red tie in a full Windsor knot. He is warm and engaged, at pains to put Heath at ease and to involve her in the examination. The doctor asks Heath and then the two of us what the nature of the complaint is. Heath says her knee hurts. Lisa describes that pain as both dull and sharp, explains just how much it varies, and when and where Heath is and what she's doing (pretty much anything) when she feels it.

The surgeon smiles, trying to absorb Lisa's rapid-fire diagnosis. When she stops momentarily for a breath, the surgeon cuts in, "Let's just have a look, shall we, Heath?"

"Sure," says Heath, putting down the rubber knee that she has been working over intently next to her on the examining table. "It's this one," says Heath, touching her right knee, "not this one," touching the other. The surgeon and I smile. Lisa tries her best. The surgeon extends the leg, applies pressure to the joint in a dozen places, repositioning it a half dozen times.

The surgeon arranges an X-ray, examines the results, and all of a sudden he's telling us that the sooner we can schedule Heath's surgery the better. He says it is impossible to know for certain, but best to prepare for a lengthy recovery. Heath may well be in a wheelchair for six weeks, he says; after that, we will all just have to see. Lisa and I dare not look at each other.

"Shit," I say, when he asks if we have any questions. Lisa is valiantly trying not to weep. The surgeon smiles, removes a digital recorder from his lab coat, and explodes into a clinical digestion of Heath's examination and diagnosis for his records: ". . . have recommended surgery and advised parents"—deep breath while he consults Heath's chart—"Lisa and Manny Howard, that surgery should not be delayed unnecessarily." He turns off the device and smiles broadly, and we all leave the examining room together. The surgeon suggests, gesturing around the corner, that we speak to his assistant about scheduling surgery.

First Lisa calls her own assistant, Peter, and cancels all of her remaining afternoon meetings. On the way home we stop at Paul's Place, a burger counter on Second Avenue at Saint Mark's Place, and buy three cheeseburgers, three bags of french fries, and three chocolate shakes.

Heath's surgery is by no means life-threatening, but her flawed meniscus, the pad of cartilage in the knee that buffers the femur and tibia, has always made climbing stairs, running, jumping, and, occasionally, just walking awkward for her. Now she will spend the summer in a wheelchair, sitting still in the swelter just as Bevan Jake is mastering his scooter.

Before lunch the next day I purchase all the lumber and fasteners necessary for the wheelchair ramp that will link our front porch to the sidewalk. By evening the lumber has been notched and secured to the front steps and stretches eighteen feet along a gentle slope well onto the sidewalk. All that remains is to install the plywood deck and build the railing. All work on The Farm ceases for the day.

My hope is that the instantaneous construction of a wheelchair ramp will provide comfort to Lisa when she returns from work. But when Lisa does emerge from Mr. Hemmings's Town Car at the end of the workday commute, the sight of the enormous ramp hanging off the front of the house like some giant wooden tongue does not have the effect I intended. At first, because the deck and the railing have not yet been built, Lisa does not understand what she is looking at.

When I introduce it as Heath's wheelchair ramp, her eyes leave mine, shifting to the wooden appendage on the front of our house. She smiles weakly, her gaze resting where the foot of the raw lumber extends beyond our property line and well onto the public sidewalk. Her mind working; what element does she object to most? "We haven't even scheduled the surgery yet, Manny."

"Thought it best to be set up," I explain, trying for cheerful ingenuity with a hint of ironic self-knowledge. "The doctor did advise us to avoid unnecessary delay."

"What do we tell the neighbors?" Lisa has moved on.

"That Heath is having knee surgery?"

"I don't want them knowing that!"

"Knowing what?"

"Knee surgery."

"They're gonna figure it out when they see the wheelchair."

"In July!"

"Like Heath's not gonna tell the world before July?"

"It's her news to tell." Lisa's eyes are dead, like a shark's.
"It's not like our little girl has an STD, it's knee surgery!"
"It is a *congenital* defect."
"Better than a motorcycle accident."
"Just forget it." Lisa walks along the ramp's eighteen feet, up the stairs, regarding it like some foul growth. "Why do you have to always be so public about our life?" She closes the half-painted front door firmly, locking it behind her.

"What are you building now?" asks our neighbor Peter enthusiastically, coming up behind me with his dog, Gumbo, on a leash.

"A wheelchair ramp," I reply, more than half-dreading that Lisa can hear the conversation from inside.

"Oh, yeah?" says Peter, concerned, looking at me for the answer to the unspoken question *Who?*

"Heath has to have knee surgery. She has a discoid meniscus. It's hereditary. Not all that serious, but, the surgeon says, six weeks in the chair. Maybe. Probably."

"Uh-huh."

"Then crutches. All summer, really."

"Sucks. Poor Heath. When's the surgery?"

"It's not scheduled. A month, maybe."

"Already built the ramp, though?"

"I just thought . . ."

"Sure."

"Work on The Farm is only going to get crazier," I explain. "A month from now who knows what will be happening back there."

"Sure," says Peter. "Hey, your rabbits 'do it' yet?"

"No. Driving me crazy. The doe won't have anything to do with that great big, stupid, sand-colored buck."

"They call rabbits same as deer? *Does* and *bucks*, huh?"

"Yep. Same as deer." I sit down on a beam halfway up the ramp, rubbing Gumbo's big head.

"Still no babies, though. Do they call baby rabbits *fawns*?"

"Nope. *Kits.*"

"Why *kits*?"

"Fuck knows."

"Hah. Right."

"Hey, what're you building now?" calls Walter from across the street, crossing toward Peter and me and the wheelchair ramp with his dog, Yassie. I wince. Lisa must certainly have heard Walter's call.

"A wheelchair ramp," announces Peter.

"Oh, yeah?" says Walter enthusiastically. "I thought maybe you were turning the whole house into an ark or something! You know, all the animals up two by two!" he singsongs, walking up the beam parallel to the one I am sitting on like a tightrope walker, arms spread for effect. "Who needs a wheelchair?" he bellows.

"At this rate I'm going to," I reply in a stage whisper.

"What?" Walter barks, hopping backward off the beam, and I admire how little flex there is in my ramp.

"Nothing. Just kidding. Heath is having knee surgery."

"When?" asks Walter, looking around as if he expects an ambulance to be driving down the block.

"It's not even scheduled yet," says Peter. Walter laughs.

"Why is that funny?" I say more defensively than I intend.

"You are building an ark. The surgery thing is a cover story," says Walter, rubbing his chin theatrically. Now Peter pops out a half laugh. This ramp thing is getting tired, quick. Examining my joinery, I wonder if there's an efficient way to disassemble it and store it on top of the garage until Heath needs it.

"Is it legal to run the ramp onto the sidewalk?" Lisa asks, trying but failing to disguise her fury from Peter and Walter. She has returned from inside, where she stripped out of her glamorous business kit into jeans and a T-shirt. Lisa steps out onto the porch.

She stands above us, sipping a rum cocktail. She has not made a drink for me.

"Hi, Lisa," Peter and Walter say in cheerful unison.

"Hi, guys," she sings back.

"No, it's probably not legal," I say.

"What are you going to do about that?" Lisa asks with no song in her voice.

"Nothing, probably."

"What if somebody trips over it and sues us?" she asks, as Walter and Peter nod hurried good-byes and continue walking their dogs down the street.

"It's going to have a rail," I explain. "It'll be pretty hard to trip over. Is there more rum?"

"Inside," she says, without gesture. "So all anybody has to do to make a million bucks from us is trip over this giant, silly ramp. Why does it have to be so big? So long?"

"If it's any shorter, it'll be too steep, like a ski jump."

"Why did you build it today?" she repeats, as if she needs to be reminded.

"I thought it would cheer you up. And, anyhow, in July, by the time Heath has surgery, The Farm is going to be crazy."

"The farm? Our daughter is having surgery and all you can think about is the farm? Your daughter is going to be in a wheelchair and you are going to be working on the farm?"

"The ramp?" I sweep an arm over the lumber. "The ramp is all about Heath and your peace of mind." After a considerable pause, sure I have made my point, I add, "I am just planning ahead."

"The farm?" Lisa is looking left and right, anywhere for a witness to what she is sure can only be madness. "Are you even planning on attending the surgery, or will you be too busy on the farm?"

"Oh, please."

The kids come running up the street ahead of Debbie, the babysitter who has taken care of the kids since they were born. They're excited to see us and delighted by the ramp. "What's this for, Dadda?" asks Bevan Jake, swinging underneath it, promptly losing his grip and falling flat on his back with a wind-expelling thud.

"See?" implores Lisa, alerting me to the immediate danger my ramp poses to good and innocent people everywhere.

"What?" I insist. "You okay, Jakey?" I ask, reaching for his outstretched hand.

"What is it?" asks Bevan Jake, unfazed by the fall.

"It's a wheelchair ramp," I say.

"It's *my* wheelchair ramp," insists Heath.

"No, it's mine!" cries Bevan Jake.

"See?" Lisa repeats, identifying the discord it promotes.

"What?" I repeat.

"Is the surgery scheduled already?" asks Debbie, ready to be impressed if it is.

"No," I reply, "just wanted to be prepared, is all."

"He's nuts, Debbie. Right?" asks Lisa.

Debbie laughs. "He's busy these days, dat's true," she says, regarding the ramp's skeleton. "C'mon, kidsies. Inside for your bath. Jake! You come off dat! You'll fall again, y'hear?"

Lisa follows Debbie and the children into the house, again locking the door behind her.

THE MAN WHO
WOULD BE KING

||||||||||||||||||||||||||||||||||||||||||||||||||||||||||||||||||||||||||

I never intended The Farm as a family project. If I gave it any thought at all, I suppose, when all this started, I hoped that Lisa and Heath and Bevan Jake might enjoy occasional visits to the back of their home, in part because we never really used the backyard before the project started, and because I'm not good at sharing my work with my family. I did all I could to shield Lisa from the realities on the ground in Afghanistan while I prepared for my trip in 2005. Lisa had resolutely refused to interfere with my planned change in career from magazine writing to documentary work. That worked for me.

Lisa came to New York after college because, until she discovered what starting salaries were in editorial jobs, she wanted to write. She chooses to understand my inability to do anything else not as the failure of imagination and instinct that it is, but as a passion. She insists that "my unusual pursuits" and my "sense of adventure" are causal to our relationship. Before The Farm, Lisa frequently reminded me that I was responsible for providing the adventure in our life together. When I announced that I was done with magazine writing and fully committed to the craft of documentary filmmaking, starting with the one about the war in Afghanistan, what could she do but support my decision? After all, was there any point in resisting it? This was the most excited she'd seen me about work in months, possibly years.

She never tired of hearing about the project in Afghanistan or the travails of the entire haphazard crew of first-time filmmakers I threw in with, but her support never required any information. A peculiarity of her set of coping skills is that she never does sweat the details, never is overly curious or concerned about the details of the project as it evolves. She was not overly curious about the sorry state of affairs on the ground in Afghanistan and appeared to disassociate all the research I was doing in the office from the possibility that I would, contrary to our original understanding, one day get on a plane and fly to Kabul.

When that day came, I was determined to shield her from any of the details and, at the same time, was doing a pretty stand-up job of ignoring their implications for my own safety. As the production crew prepared for their second trip, I was asked to consider coming along and agreed to go reflexively, and I derived great pleasure in researching the online purchase of body armor and other protective war-zone gear. I was particularly fixated on purchasing the right handheld GPS device.

I did not have any anticipatory anxiety about my first trip to a war zone, even after I asked Josh, who, in addition to being my friend, is a New York City firefighter, to brief the crew on trauma first aid, and the balance of his presentation was that we could do little but stuff shrapnel wounds with maxi pads and bullet wounds with tampons and try not to do additional damage if we absolutely had to move the injured. The day before my departure, however, that blasé front Lisa and I had kept up collapsed in a heap. Mine did anyway. An hour into what had been billed as a regular Sunday winter walk along the Promenade in Brooklyn Heights, the implications of the trip—now thirty-six nonrefundable-airline-ticket hours later—introduced themselves as a chorus of woe. I became convinced that I was leaving my children fatherless. Bevan Jake screeched in my tightening grip. "Sorry, Jake," I said. "Daddy would never hurt you on purpose. You know that, right?"

Bevan Jake looked at me, smiled, and gestured to the statue, a globe wrought from bronze rings, that he wanted to continue climbing. He was not yet two years old.

Lisa was quiet for most of the walk, busying herself, taking pictures of me and the kids horsing around on the bronze statue. I didn't discuss my ballooning fear of imminent death. Apparently, I recovered my lovable zest for adventure. The morning after the documentary crew arrived in Kabul, I sent her this e-mail:

Dear Lisa,

First night in Kabul: It's 11:30 here and I am sitting in a brightly lit living room in the main house, tucked safe behind the 11-foot concrete walls of the American arms dealer's compound where the crew is staying. The room has white stucco walls, lace curtains and the kind of furniture available for lease at chain stores in inner cities all over America.

I've been typing away at production notes (jetlag) for hours and was just interrupted by two drunken female GIs who apparently, so they say, just whored themselves for $200 each to my host (a private contractor—quarter master function—for the Afghan Army) and his Afghan driver/buddy. They didn't want to talk about that, though. They wanted to talk about how sad a place Afghanistan is. "You know what I once saw?" asked the taller of the two. "I once saw a car bomb. That's sad, right? This place is sad."

I agreed with her. Sad. "Sad," I said.

Second Day in Kabul: In addition to a tour of all the Chinese whorehouses in town, Jay, our host, took me on a tour of all the westerners-only shopping markets. Walled compounds holding supermarkets where one's fellow shoppers are men sporting full-body armor machine guns and insignia from every western country under the sun—well, hardly. It's funny to see a gun-toting fellah in fatigues scanning the side of a bran flakes box for nutritional info or trying to decide between chocolate chip ice cream and orange sherbet. We were in line behind three Finnish soldiers who had loaded their cart with all the Beefeater gin on the shelf—another big part of the dueling cultures in this dry Muslim country.

Of course, I've become the guest breakfast chef. Likely will become the dinner chef too but last night we had dinner with a corporate Merc at the Kabul Inn. Bob Shepherd was SAS 1 Regiment and part of the team that, in Gulf One, discovered the, until then, undreamed of SCUD missiles pointed at Israel. The 16-man team spent 6 weeks marking all the targets and fighting the baddies with no air support to speak of and even took what Shepherd called "blue-on-blue" fire. The Americans dropped a bomb on them (well near them) and all escaped, only some with shrapnel wounds. He's 52 and retiring in the beginning of the year. Very sound, sensible fellow, he works for what I've heard is a very reputable British private military contractor, or PMC (Control Risks Group), and his—and his 6-man team's—mission is close personal security for the Japanese Ambassador here.

We return from dinner and Jay has two more lady GIs in his room. He has set to drinking the entire bottle of Johnnie Walker Black that George and I delivered as a gift for his hospitality (and he really has been a wonderful host). We are not allowed to walk around the city so he comes to pick us up. He's loaded. Can hardly speak and in an effort to stop the enormous up-armored Chevy Expedition he is driving in front of the compound gate he drives into a mature tree and uproots it. Though he doesn't seem to notice. All he has to say is, "Good thing that was a short drive."

After being introduced to his new lady friends, I comment that he must be using one of those fine body fragrances marketed to teenage boys that are, so say the marketers, chemically designed to make you irresistible to women. He replies, "Nope all you need here in AFG is some booze and some privacy and you're in business. You can have all the lady GIs you want."

This is a very large world we live in, there's room for all sorts.

This was to be my only contact with Lisa for over a week. The next would be a desperate call to her when, semiconscious, suffering the humiliating effects of a brutal dose of giardia—a pitiless parasite that lived within me well after my return to Brooklyn—I called her for comfort.

So much for protecting Lisa from the reality of my excursion.

I am doing just as good a job protecting her from the mayhem in the back of our home.

Lisa has long since left for work when I pick up the phone and dial Ray Damiani's rabbit farm. If she had been home, I might well have discussed my decision to expand the meat-rabbit operation. But, if my yard is to sustain me for thirty days, I must be strategic; it is going to have to be planted with hardy produce such as collard greens, not arugula, and somehow this farm is going to have to yield meat. I rule out chickens immediately; a month's worth of chicken will be way too much trouble. I'm not opposed to the slaughter, but picking that many chickens—no self-respecting agrarian (not even a rank amateur such as myself) *plucks* anything—is out of the question. The propaganda generated by the meat-rabbit folks is compelling: chicken reproduction is "light sensitive" (whatever that means), while rabbit reproduction is what meat-rabbit people and maybe even biologists call "opportunity sensitive." I determine that rabbits are the only alternative. I figure I will need three does and one buck. Each doe will yield one litter of eight kits in time for The Harvest.

Ray Damiani is a recognized expert in the field of rabbit husbandry, specializing in the monster strain known as the Flemish giant. He has either acquired the moniker or baptized himself Sugar Ray The Rabbit Man; no matter the honorific's origin, it is clear he delights in the title. In a retasked dairy barn on a stretch of road lined by newly developed grand homes in Litchfield, Connecticut, Damiani's warren contains nearly two hundred rabbits. He raises rabbits for show, not for meat, but is not above selling off a few homely or retired show rabbits as breeders for my meat rabbits. After I've acquired a cursory understanding of the ins and outs of raising meat rabbits, it's clear to me that, though rabbits are, of course, masters of reproduction, even an avalanche of baby rabbits won't do me any good at The Harvest if they are not big enough to eat. What I need for The Harvest is a respectable number of fryers. This late in the season, it is not mathematically possible for me to generate any fryers within six months unless I front-load the process with a pair of outsized adults.

This strategy is not without controversy. While everyone in the self-described meat-rabbit community agrees that the Flemish giant is extraordinarily large and gets that way staggeringly quickly, some question the breed's value as a meat source. Rabbits are not officially recognized by the USDA as agricultural livestock intended for human consumption, and the backyard butchering of any rabbit within city limits is illegal, but even the meat-rabbit community (aggressive advocates for a change in these policies) does not recognize the Flemish giant as a suitable source of meat. Of the forty-five recognized rabbit breeds in the United States, just fourteen are both the proper meat body-type and large enough to be suitable for the renegade rabbit-meat industry. Of these, the breed New Zealand white rabbit is the hands-down favorite, followed by the Californian. Members of the American Rabbit Breeders Association go to great pains to make it clear that, though popular, Flemish giant rabbits are not included in their commercial classification because they have heavy bones and a low meat-to-bone ratio. Not a single one of the fourteen recognized meat breeds will grow to fryers on my schedule.

Flemish giants have what is known as a semi-arched spine, resulting in a long, unattractive, and bony carcass. Unlike the membership of the American Rabbit Breeders Association, I could not care less if the carcass is attractive or not. To my mind, the most telling indicator of the value of the Flemish giant is that even the most dire warnings against using Flemish giants are accompanied by the caveat that, though it is preferable to select for size within an accepted meat breed to achieve faster growth rates, it has long been the practice to raise a "shortcut" strain by crossing the prized New Zealand white with the lowly Flemish giant.

After explaining my scheduling conundrum to Sugar Ray on the phone, he assures me his rabbits will provide a solution. I invite myself up to his farm to have a look the very next afternoon. Over the phone Sugar Ray is clearly intrigued by my project and enthusiastic in his offer to help. When I arrive at his barn, I discover that the enthusiasm Sugar Ray had expressed for my project extends to just about everything in his life. He is broad-shouldered and handsome, much younger than I imagined a breeder of prize-winning Flemish giants to be—not that I have ever imagined how old a breeder of prize-winning Flemish giants would be. He is vigorous and robust, neither of which are qualities I associate with a rabbit breeder, not, that is, until I step into the cool concrete barn and stand surrounded by hundreds of twenty-pound caged rabbits.

Sugar Ray extols the virtues of his breed and the waft of rabbity purpose is overwhelming. Low wire cages stand on four-foot-tall metal scaffolds—rows of wire beach homes on stilts. In the cages, either aloof or staring, curious, skipping gingerly over wire floors or sitting stony on tiny paw-preserving plywood beds, are Sugar Ray's prize-winning rabbits; some white, black, gray, or sandy, some spotted, a few mottled. All the adults are larger than spring lambs.

Some of the does keep company with their litters, untroubled by the kits tumbling around and over them. Just a month or so old and even the youngest offspring outweigh the biggest guinea pigs. Sugar Ray, it appears, has solved my problem.

We are standing by a cage holding a black doe that Sugar Ray ballparks at eighteen pounds. He explains that the doe has won all the prizes she can win—in each competition a rabbit can only win a blue ribbon once, and all show rabbits have their ears tattooed for easy identification. He has already bred her once, but not a single champion was among the litter, so he has given up on her. Essentially, Sugar Ray observes, to his operation this doe constitutes a waste of perfectly good food. He is certain that she will more than suit my meat-breeding purposes. Overwhelmed by optimism about the future of my project and the place of Sugar Ray's rabbits in it, I interrupt his sales pitch to explain just how desperately I need to produce enough baby rabbits to feed myself for a month. I tell him I know that I have come up to

115

collect just one buck and one doe, but I am curious, does he have a second female he might part with? Sugar Ray scans the room, his fecund inventory, mostly for effect it seems. "I can do you one more," he says, lighting out for the far reaches of the barn, the afternoon sun through dusty windows cutting swaths across the cages in the barn. "What's more, they'll be a matching set, one black, one white: 'Ebony and ivory together in perfect . . . ,'" he belts, in an impressive church-choir tenor.

Now, an hour later, stuck miles behind some unknowable automotive cataclysm on the Grand Central Parkway with a pair of blue-ribbon does for company, I am joyfully recalling all the propaganda I have read or heard about meat rabbits. Every year, each of the does behind me will produce nearly one thousand times her weight in fryers.

Unlike meat birds (chickens raised as food), rabbits can be raised in confinement. In the sky above the traffic, two news choppers recording the tragic pile-up ahead are joined by a police helicopter hovering in the top right corner of my windshield. Because my rabbits live in cages, the raccoons that live behind the Kentucky Fried Chicken on Coney Island Avenue won't get at them, and neither will the neighborhood cats—not that a mere house cat would stand a chance against my giants.

A second ambulance rattles past me on the gritty median; a Mercedes SUV follows close in the dust cloud like a pilot fish. The propagandists assert that even I can dress and butcher five rabbits in the time it takes to process just one chicken. Hell, I can even trade the pelts of the slaughtered animals if I wish. In my rearview mirror a ribbon of vehicles abandons traffic codes and the Grand Central Parkway, now essentially a parking lot, for the grassy spaces on its verge. They rattle their way over hillocks and around dusty depressions toward an exit ramp fifty yards distant that leads onto the streets of The Bronx. I follow dutifully, making a yawning detour behind Yankee Stadium and southwest through The Bronx on the Grand Concourse.

Upon my return to The Farm I realize that I have neglected to build partitions in the FEMA Trailer and so deposit one of my prize does (the white one) in a cardboard box and the black one in Fergus's travel box.

This is the second time that I have returned to The Farm with rabbits and no place to house them. My repeated lack of foresight, of planning, appalls Lisa. She says so. What I consider the ingenious use of found objects as cages looks to her like ill-considered, reflexive decision-making without a proper support edifice. She thinks giant rabbits housed in appliance boxes is animal cruelty.

I set about building stalls for them, further subdividing the FEMA Trailer. Finally, The Farm has its breeding stock. The relief is palpable as I stand, a Red Stripe beer in my hand, watching the rabbits acclimate to the FEMA Trailer. It is time to build these meat rabbits a proper hutch because they have work to do.

Each pen within the hutch measures eighteen cubic feet. In the meat-rabbit community, little consensus exists about anything. One of the more inflamed debates is whether to house the largest-breed rabbits in cages with wire floors. One school says it is vital in order to maintain cages free of the parasites drawn to feces and the diseases these parasites cause. The competing school asserts that rabbits as heavy as the Flemish giant walking on wire causes such horrific damage, most often characterized by open sores and wounds, that any sanitation benefits provided by wire floors are eclipsed.

Advocates of wooden floors are quick to note that this style of hutch architecture requires vigilant cleaning of the cages—as often as twice a day. In addition to my having a serious disinclination to breed hobbled, possibly blood-soaked, giant rabbits, I find the plywood floor is a valuable design with another specific benefit. The Farm is getting smaller by the day, especially as the garbage piled at the southwest corner of the house grows arithmetically. With wooden floors I can stack the cages. The result is that a home for nearly 120 pounds of rabbit has a footprint of just thirty-six square feet.

As a further innovation, I stack the cages on a sturdy wheeled frame, allowing me to move the rabbit husbandry headquarters wherever conditions are optimal for breeding and, when the time comes, kit-raising. The shelves built into the wheeled frame mean I can store all the rabbit supplies right there. I am proud of the hutch: two stories high, capable of holding six twenty-pound rabbits, with ventilation fans and automatic watering dishes. The modern conveniences incorporated into my hutch shame the amenities of any models I have researched. The cages are larger than most design specs call for, and they are well ventilated. I install a tandem fan at each end of the hutch so that air is both projected into and drawn from the cages. The floor plan is designed so that each buck will have a doe as a neighbor. According to information gleaned from meat-rabbit chat rooms, this will increase pheromone transfer, keeping the brood stock in a constant state of sexual frenzy.

THE CITY IS A CRUST

||||||||||||||||||||||||||||||||||||||||||||||||||||||||||||||||||||||||||||||||||||||

Five tons of blue-black earth arrive in a G&D Landscape dump truck at ten thirty in the morning. The only sound on the street is the trilling of the warning Klaxon as the truck reverses off the street, beyond the sidewalk, and onto the driveway, and the payload glides upward pivoting on its hinge. The dirt begins to tumble onto the foot of the driveway. Moist, somehow obviously fecund, and as dark as a slice of devil's food cake. Joe Gallo stands beside me, wordlessly ordering his crew to begin taking the soil to the backyard. They move quickly with their heavy wheelbarrows, faltering only after the first three tons of loose soil have made the footing unsure. When Joe begins to level the soil, skimming the soil with a rake, I run to fetch mine from the garage. Too eagerly I ask where I can start. Joe waves me off—"Don't worry."

"I'm not worried. I want to help, this is a big moment in my project."

"It's better, quicker, I do it alone." Joe emigrated from a town outside Naples, Italy. His son, Angello, who gave up the physical part of the job to answer the phone five years ago, worries that Joe will work himself to death.

I don't see it.

I take a photograph of the dump truck backed into our driveway just having unloaded the mountain of earth and e-mail it to Lisa, who's on a business trip in Chicago. I never get a response. Teams of three men with wheelbarrows move the soil from the driveway to the back of the house, depositing patches of soil nine inches deep. Standing useless, leaning on my rake, I watch while Joe grades the topsoil on the lifeless clay surface of the yard with the same certitude that a painter moves oil on canvas, maybe that a cook spreads red sauce on a pizza. I just stand and stare, mute with joy while our yard becomes The Farm.

As excited as I am, I also know I'm losing the last excuse I have for not being able to create a self-sustaining environment in my backyard. The dirt is here, it's better than I could have hoped for, and as much as I've read about planting, as many questions as I have asked, I have next to no idea what to do now. *People are joined to the land by work,* says Wendell Berry, announcing his presence. Is that him standing in the shadows of the back porch? *Land, work, people, and community are all comprehended in the idea of culture. These connections cannot be understood or described by information—so many resources to be transformed by so many workers into so many products for so many consumers—because they are not quantitative. We can understand them only after we acknowledge that they should be harmonious—that a culture must be either shapely and saving or shapeless and destructive. To presume to describe land, work, peo-*

ple, and community by information, by quantities, seems invariably to throw them into competition with one another.

Joe and Carlos, the foreman, stand next to me by the garage. I don't think they can hear Berry; still, we all take a moment to admire the black earth. "Well," says Joe, "you've got your dirt now." He smiles briefly, grips his rake at midshaft, toting it in one hand like a hunting rifle, barrel down, and strolls up the driveway.

Carlos smiles broadly; his kind, wet eyes wish me well. After Lisa has returned from Chicago and the kids are tucked in for the evening, I drag a twin mattress from the basement. Lisa, standing in the threshold of the back door, one arm against the jam, looks out at the soil, impressed by the transformation. The black earth has entirely covered up the nerve-crushing dry well and the weeks of my soil and water engineering. I am proud of the results, but I know that the ramshackle system of plastic pipes and gravel impressed her as entirely anarchic, possibly half-assed. She clearly much prefers the uniform earth. Its loamy promise still hangs in the air. She watches while I roll a sleeping bag out over the bare mattress. "What are you doing?" she asks, already knowing the answer.

"It's going to rain really hard tonight," I explain earnestly, smoothing the green sleeping bag out over the uncovered mattress. "I've got to watch, make sure the gully is gone for good."

"The what?" she asks, smiling momentarily.

"Nothing. It's gonna rain really hard tonight."

"So you're going to sleep out here with your dirt, not in our room?" she says, flirting just a little bit.

"There's room in this bag," I suggest, turning to face her, patting the mattress.

"Not for me, there's not." She turns to advance the laundry.

The rain starts at midnight, a storm as strong as forecast. It hammers the rooftops and the water runs through the drainpipes where, at their terminus, my system is waiting to carry it away, down into my seven-foot-deep dry well. After twenty-five minutes of listening to the rain I make a barefoot inspection of the field in my underpants. These are the first steps I have taken on my new soil since it was delivered. It is soft, gives way to each step, cool and wet under the balls of my feet, squishing up over my toes. At the linkages where my system joins the drainpipes there is some overflow, but nothing that concerns me. I may have done this right, after all.

Back at the mattress, I towel the rich mud off my feet and get back into the bag and listen to the storm as it fails to drown my field. Imagining Brooklyn without cement has always been a favorite activity of mine. Once even the anarchic paved ribbon of man and machine that is Flatbush Avenue, seven blocks from here, was little more than a narrow wooden boardwalk. Church Avenue was nothing but a rutted, often impassable two-track. A vital thoroughfare then and now, the two routes intersect half a mile from where I rest, listening to the rain on the new dirt. It is the crossroad where the storied tradition of farming in Kings County came to an end. Western Long Island (now Brooklyn) was the vegetable basket for much of the East Coast, having its trading center in the town of Flatbush and, to a lesser extent, the other four Dutch townships that sat for more than one hundred years on the southern border of Brooklyn.

In 1872, Brooklyn's Committee of One Hundred, all landowning farmers, all Big Men descended from Big Men, prepared a bill approving the annexation by the City of Brooklyn of the five townships that made up the seventy-two square miles of Kings County. Unlike the villages at the core of the other four townships, Flatbush had developed a nearly urban core by the 1870s. The Big Men, or Lords of Flatbush, all of them Dutch, all from the families of original settlers, were convinced that joining with Brooklyn would be a profitable enterprise. In short order, the notion acquired an aura of inevitability.

But annexation was unthinkable to the Boer farmers in Flatlands to the east. Located in the southeastern corner of Kings County, at the time of the first annexation battles in the 1870s there was only one person for every four acres. Flatlands is low-lying terrain just east of Prospect Park Ridge, bordering Flatbush in the west and stretching to Hempstead in the east. At the time of annexation Flatlands (now the area including the neighborhoods Canarsie, Bergen Beach, Mill Basin, and Marine Park) was dominated by fields and woodlands. It had few roads. Its southern reaches, where the territory juts into Rockaway Inlet and Jamaica Bay, had an extended heath on which sheep grazed. Here, the marshland—interrupted regularly by creeks and small bays—was almost entirely uninhabited. Canarsie, the lone, tidy residential pocket, was centered in the lowlands, on the crossroads that is today Kings Highway and Flatbush Avenue. Settled in 1624, the town was first called New Amersfoort by its Dutch founders, after their homeland's even lower-lying southern region.

Not only did the Dutch Flatlanders find comfort in the familiar terrain, they used their technical expertise to build a system of dikes that improved and increased the arable lands used for crops, including tobacco. Cattle grazed on the abundant spartina cordgrasses native to the saltwater meadows. Trade flourished with the native population—the Jamaica nation—living on the Rockaway Peninsula's bay side.

Flatlanders harbored a robust distrust of the modernizing ways of Brooklynites—most all of whom were, by then,
no longer Dutch. The Flatlanders certainly had no use for
modernity's accompanying convenience—luxuries such as
gas streetlights, running water, and paved roads.

Still, on February 11, 1873, the first in a series of annexation bills was filed in the state Assembly. This one, a test of
sorts, called only for the annexation of the town of New Lots.
An important farming center with nearly as many residents
as the four other townships combined, New Lots had been
created when the sons and daughters of farmers in Flatbush
went looking for their own land to harvest. In addition to the
old farming village itself, New Lots consisted of the larger
towns of Brownsville, Cypress Hills, and the industrial center East New York. Its people were almost entirely of Dutch
and German descent. The very next week a second bill was
introduced, intended to annex the county's three most rural
towns, Flatlands, Gravesend, and New Utrecht. The county
commissioners were unanimously in favor of the bill, and the
residents were universally opposed. A war was imminent.

The appointed representatives of each township were all
wealthy farmers. They elected as their president the wealthiest among them, the representative from Flatbush, the most
prosperous of the townships, John A. Lott. A farmer only
inasmuch as he owned the most farmland in Kings County,
Lott was not only a descendant of one of the most prominent
Dutch families, one that had farmed here for two hundred
years, he was also the wealthiest lawyer in the county. He was
the embodiment of modernization and urbanization in Kings
County. The Lott residence stood directly across the Flatbush
Road from Erasmus Hall Academy and next door to the Prot-

estant Reformed Dutch Church of Flatbush. By the 1870s the church, the school, and Lott's impressive homestead were the three institutions upon which the town of Flatbush was built.

During a public career that began in 1838, John A. Lott served as a judge on the Kings County Court of Common Pleas, a member of the state Assembly and later the Senate. Eventually Lott sat on the state Supreme Court and later on the Court of Common Appeals. He ended his career in public service as chief commissioner of the Commission of Appeals from 1870 to 1875. Oliver Wendell Holmes Jr. is said to have considered Lott the "ablest lawyer" in Brooklyn. Lott's long, successful public career was paralleled by his success in the private sector. Lott maintained real estate holdings far beyond Kings County. He was president of one railroad and no fewer than five companies or boards, including the Long Island Safe Deposit Company and Flatbush Gas Company. Lott was also the director of two insurance companies and a trustee of the Flatbush Fire Company on Church Avenue.

In 1870 Lott owned 253 acres of farmland within the five townships he was single-mindedly attempting to urbanize. John Lott believed so completely in annexation and urbanization that he promoted the abolition of the rural town names once they became part of Brooklyn. At first glance his vision of what he called "one city, one government and one destiny" seems at odds with his agrarian financial interests, but it is likely that his income from commercial ventures and legal pursuits eclipsed that of his farms. Because, unlike many of his neighbors, he was already diversified, he stood to profit substantially as he subdivided his rural holdings. Lott's allies in the cause of modernization were Peter Lott (a cousin), representative of Flatlands, and William Bennett of Gravesend, the only British settlement in Kings County. Like Lott, they had already abandoned their farms for other, more portable and profitable pursuits.

Opposing John Lott was Teunis Garret Bergen. If not pilloried then certainly parodied in the press as an agrarian troglodyte and an obstinate old-world Dutch primitive who lived farther south on the family's homestead out on the Bay Ridge, "Uncle Tune," as he was commonly referred to in newspapers, was as dedicated and tenacious a rejectionist as Lott was a modernist. A wealthy farmer who preferred speaking Dutch even if his audience could not, Bergen was also a surveyor and a genealogist, a member of the New Utrecht Commission of Excise, the New Utrecht Highway Commission, and the New Utrecht Board of Health, and a shareholder in the Brooklyn & Flatbush Turnpike. He had been New Utrecht's town supervisor for fifty-three years running. Bergen was also a delegate to the New York State constitutional convention and served one term in Washington, D.C., as a congressman.

Like Lott, Bergen owned farmland throughout the county and beyond its borders. He had substantial holdings across the harbor in New Jersey. His homestead, like those of his closest relatives, was on the banks of New York Harbor just below the narrows. It is possible, and has been suggested, that because Bergen had not diversified his wealth to the same extent as Lott and his allies in anticipation of the wave of modernizing fever, Bergen's opposition was a stalling tactic designed to give him the time he required to broaden his holdings. But if he had not prepared for modernization, he had more than prepared to oppose it. When the bills to annex the five towns were introduced in the state Assembly, Bergen made certain that those bills were accompanied by a petition rejecting the proposal signed by 95 percent of the residents of his district, New Utrecht. The battle had been joined.

In all likelihood, Teunis Bergen's sole motivation was not to protect the region's agrarian past. But, the role of the rural stalwart—one he made it easy for people to believe—did provide the cover he needed while he prepared to profit more completely from the inevitable change. So he was probably secretly delighted when he was satirized as a backward, drunken hayseed in the anonymous epic poem "The Wrath of Bergen," published in the pro-annexation newspaper the *Brooklyn Eagle*.

Bergen, as Uncle Tune, the malevolent clown, drunk on applejack, barrels into Flatbush from the Bay Ridge waving his clay pipe, railing against the progressive efforts of well-meaning local politicians to draw Flatbush and surrounding townships toward modernity.

Marching over hill and moor, Uncle Tune protested as fiercely as Peter Stuyvesant before him, excoriating the gentle majority in an effort to protect the frozen swamp and swales, breaking coveys of timid, starving quail as he marched along the frozen roads and through the swamps choked with bulrushes and over the frozen fields of rotting turnips of his ancestral Flatlands. So dogged was his defense of farmland and wilderness that even good friends, and, importantly, fellow highborn Dutchmen such as Martin Schoonmaker, failed to recognize their once cheerful fellow gentleman farmer.

The appointed hour has come
When Brooklyn, Gravesend and Bay Ridge
Are melted into one.

My Empire of Dirt

Even Flatbush, where Judge Lott resides,
Is equally undone.

No more we hear the bullfrogs sing,
Nor bob for eels at night;
Our swamps will very soon be drained,
And gas lamps give us light.
Adieu to clams and pollywogs
And heaven defend the right.
With that he raised his old time horn,
And blew so long and loud,
That even the silent silver moon,
Dodged in behind a cloud.

Then up came John C. Jacobs,
And with him Dominick Roche,
And pledged that no city lot
Should upon the swales encroach,
Nor any street surveyor
The clams or eels approach.

Then Uncle Tune simmered down,
Resumed his former smile,
And Martin thanked these new friends
In periods of a mile.
So all things stand in status quo,
The bullfrogs still can sing,
And night owls, o'er the stagnant beach,
Still flap their lazy wing,
And Tunis from the Neighboring marsh,
His eels at midnight bring.

However, the condescension that Bergen bore in the cruel lampooning of "Uncle Tune" worked in his favor. He appears to have outmaneuvered the sophisticated, modernizing wannabe urbanites numerous times. Bergen argued strenuously and presciently that the increase in the property tax would quickly bankrupt any small farmer who dared to hold out against speculators for a more reasonable price. Bergen's march was not without its stumbles; his parochial objections about taxation—"Why should I pay for a dock or a school house which is four miles away from my property?"—seem ludicrous today. But in the end, continually repeated protests like this and fearmongering about the social ills of urban expansionism—the anarchy, degradation, and disease that would result from an invasion of urbanizing foreigners—carried the day.

On Election Day, November 4, 1873, predictably 85 percent of Brooklynites voted in favor of annexation. But the initiative was killed when 83 percent of the voters in the five townships rejected inclusion with the boomtown to the north. Uncle Tune strode victorious, abroad in the countryside, sporting his marsh boots and pulling cheerfully on his pipe, momentarily heroic. He made his way back home to the Bay Ridge. The envy of every present-day critic of Our Age, Bergen's triumph was unrepeatable; he had made his stand against modernity and its mirage of limitless choice at its dawn as it closed all around him, just moments before its inevitability was a foregone conclusion. Perversely, a larger proportion of voters in John Lott's Flatbush opposed the plan than in Bergen's New Utrecht stronghold.

The very next year, to John Lott's horror, the citizens of

Flatbush erected a new town hall and continued to resist the urbanizing press of Brooklyn.

Bergen, too, continued to resist annexation, though even he came to see annexation as the inevitable outcome for the county. On the occasion of the opening of the Bay Ridge & Manhattan Railroad, he commented, "We are between two fires. Brooklyn tries to devour us, and New York tries to swallow us."

Hunting parties from Brooklyn often traveled the Flatbush Toll Road on weekends to traipse the marshes, woodlands, and fields of Flatbush for duck, high-holders, woodcock, snipe, and quail. When a drunken member of one such group shot and murdered a farmer who denied the men access to his land, Bergen took up the nativist opposition with renewed vigor. No longer tethered to a theoretical argument about the future property-tax burden, Bergen now argued that with development came debauchery, mayhem, and even murder. These were the values of the city, warned Uncle Tune, and they would bring ruin to paradise.

Into this maelstrom strode Dean Alvord. A newly minted real estate man with modernist dreams of upper-class enclaves for even more freshly minted wealthy Brooklynites, an outlander in a peculiarly tight-knit community that could easily, and often did, trace its lineage to the first settlements, Alvord was precisely the type of carpetbagging speculator Bergen feared would set his sights on rural Kings County. Alvord's Prospect Park South (a gated sixty-acre block of luxurious, grand homes), and developments like it, were heralds of an urban future that Teunis Bergen deplored but was ultimately powerless to halt. By 1912, civic reformers were lamenting the urbanization of America, asserting that cities with more than three hundred thousand residents were unsustainable without interruption by planned, protected, productive green belts and the local farms within to support them. But by then Alvord, president of the Dean Alvord Co., had moved on, heading east, cutting a swath of luxury living as he went, through Laurelton, Queens, and along Long Island. By 1910 he was promoting Belle Terre, his exclusive summer colony on Port Jefferson Harbor. Three years later he was in Clearwater, Florida, building the state's first planned residential community.

By 2003, when we moved to Alvord's Prospect Park South, with its planned greenways and well-managed tree population, it was a verdant, if prettified, oasis in a sea of cement. The Brooklyn I grew up in had been abandoned to fend for itself by both the municipal and state governments. In 1975, President Gerald Ford made it official, refusing to fund a federal government bailout, and in so doing infamously told the entire city, so the New York *Daily News* declared, "Drop dead." The City—Abraham Beame's City Hall specifically, and later, when run by Ed Koch—in turn washed its hands of the four other boroughs, unleashing the latent cronyism of the borough presidents and encouraging unprecedented independence in order to free itself from responsibility in this new sink-or-swim reality of urban America. The decades of corruption that resulted and the blight that greed bore crippled the borough. Now Brooklyn, like Queens, Staten Island, and The Bronx, was no longer the problem of any government that had the capacity or resources to rescue it. Our rivers did not catch on fire—though that's probably only because of their strong currents—but the streets cratered, facades crumbled, entire buildings collapsed.

One of my most vivid memories growing up then was visiting a town house on the corner of State and Hicks streets. Early one evening the north wall that ran along State Street peeled away from the rest of the house and fell in a dusty heap into the middle of the street. The building's interior was exposed like a dollhouse. A visit to the site was easily ten times more fun than a trip to the shambolic South Street Seaport maritime museum. Hell, it was even better than television. As we stood at the gray police barricades, for us, the kids in the neighborhood, the atmosphere was more carnival than catastrophe. We delighted in shouting out the rumor that the man of the house had been in the bathtub when the wall came down. Naked! Delirious at the thought of the physical collapse of our world, we pointed to the details of the family's life now on view for all. My mother told my sister and me that the mom who lived in the house had defied the police and reentered the wreckage to retrieve her dissertation. We were rapt by the story, never mind we had no idea what a dissertation was or if it could be carried by one person or not. My sister, Bevin, grabbed the arm of my duffel coat, gasping and pointing at the gape where the living room was. Ges-

turing to the sideboard, she whispered conspiratorially, "Look. The wineglasses are all still on the shelves."

The decay all around us was never more vividly wrought and caused giddy delight. Twenty-five years later, after Lisa and I purchased a co-op on State Street, just one block from the famous collapse, I learned that under the crust of tarmac, a spring runs off the cliffs that dominate the neighborhood and down the length of State Street, slicing through the sandy soil and leaching through the city's subcutaneous gravel, sand, and clay into the East River, forever undermining the foundations of all the houses along its shifting route. Only a year after our purchase the engineers delivered the news that our building was the latest victim of that subterranean (well, subpavement) brook. When other members pooh-poohed the engineer's report, insisting that walls don't just peel off houses, I told them the story about the Giant Dollhouse. We sold our unit shortly after repairs had begun.

In the 1970s, neither the city nor the state nor the country nor its citizens were responding to what environmental critics were already calling the poisoning of our planet. But my best friend, Matt Prosky, and I, both latchkey kids, didn't mind at all. Dying or not, Brooklyn was our despoiled, ramshackle, often darkly mysterious, occasionally downright venal playland. Brooklyn never failed to produce entertainment. Rumored invasion of the neighborhood by the almost entirely black, marauding orphans who lived in Saint Vincent's Home for Boys was a perennial favorite and was always good for a few hours of hysterical headlong, screaming retreats ending in hiding out, with deliciously skinned knees, in a mountain of someone else's uncollected garbage bags.

During the summer of 1977, while the Son of Sam besieged the imagination of the city's sexually active citizenry, Matt and I entertained ourselves for days on end by flushing readily identifiable objects down the toilet, racing down the eight flights from the Proskys' apartment onto our bicycles and down the hill to a decrepit Fulton Landing. Here we would throw our bikes clattering, wheels wobbling, onto the splintered pier and race to the flimsy metal railing where sewage issued forth, raw, into the East River. We would watch, yodeling with delight, while floating pods of shit, raggedy waving standards of toilet paper, lewdly shimmying condoms, all animated by the current of the gray water over impossibly fouled black rocks, and tampon applicators of every description, bobbed from the outflow pipe below our feet. The stink was intoxicating.

Not once all summer did we spot one of our test objects—the toy soldiers decorated with party ribbons to differentiate ours from just any old toilet warrior. We never saw the dozens of bulletlike Fisher-Price villagers we commandeered from Matt's little brother, Ben. We didn't see the Popsicle sticks painted with brightly colored model-airplane paint. Imagining the sewer as a tree, we would hang our heads over the rail and scrutinize the wonderfully hideous waste spilling from its trunk until concluding that we had simply not covered the distance between Matt's bathroom, a branch and the mouth of our sewage pipe fast enough. We were just going to have to try harder, pedal faster, and choose a quicker route next time.

And there would always be a next time.

TACKLING DAYLIGHT

IIIIIIIIIIIIIIIIIIIIIIIIIIIIIIIIIIIIIIIIIIIIIIIIIIIIIIIIIIIIIIIIIIIIIIIIIIIIIIIIIIIIIII

After my seedlings wither, I am seized by panic. According to my schedule, I had to have plants in the ground by early April. It is now May. The first of the many rules I have set for myself is broken when, after a considerable search, I find a plant nursery that stocks food beyond tomatoes and herbs. There is no shortage of such plants at most plant nurseries, but ask after corn and you only get a funny look. The average nursery has the occasional eggplant and always plenty of lettuce varieties. There is, of course, no end of tomatoes. But trudge down to the neighborhood nursery in search of rhubarb, celery, carrots, or potatoes, and you'll be sorely disappointed. That is, unless you live on a desolate strip of Rockaway Boulevard in Ozone Park, Queens, near C. Verdino & Sons plant nursery. Once upon a time, the multi-acre parking lot across the boulevard here was packed with the cars of racing fans and Aqueduct Racetrack bustled. Today, beyond the chain-link fence that stretches for a half mile, the only vehicles in plain sight are warehoused vans and panel trucks from some unidentifiable city agency.

C. Verdino & Sons is as pregnant with promise as Aqueduct is barren, and once I'm among the plants, my spirits soar. The rows and rows of healthy juvenile food plants call out to me: corn, rhubarb, celery, and carrots. There's a fig tree and callaloo. I pack my cart with broad beans, cantaloupe, beets, four varieties of eggplant, cucumbers, fennel, cabbage, green Scotch bonnet, and jalapeño peppers. I buy eight collard-green plants. I load the car with plants and belt the fig tree into the passenger seat next to me.

The soil delivered, plants on the premises, it is time to tackle daylight. The time has finally come to address The Farm's paucity of sunlight. To conquer my fear I apply the scientific method. The first order of business is to measure it, so I spend the better part of a week chasing the sun around my field. I mark squares using inchwide, orange plastic construction ribbon, hoping to figure how many square feet receive constant sunlight. After twice discarding the painstakingly gathered evidence, I reach the brutally obvious and now unavoidable conclusion that not one square inch in the garden receives constant sunlight. I try for a third time. Same result. I am disappointed, but not discouraged. Good news is mixed in here. The northwest corner, christened the Back Forty because that's how many square feet it comprises, receives by far the most sun. I know that now. I also know that, on good days, I can expect plants placed in the Back Forty to receive two hours in the morning and at least another three in the afternoon. I am still not clear if, according to the brief text and brightly colored charts on the back of the seed packets, this constitutes partial shade or partial sun, but if worse comes to worst, I can always string up those now-dormant grow lights in the basement.

One morning while I'm dropping the kids off at my mother's house, Cathy Fuerst, a dear friend of the family's, inquires about progress on The Farm. I tell her it's going well, but confide that I am amazed and a little overwhelmed by the amount of work required just to get it to a place where I can simply use the space to grow plants and raise animals. Cathy, whose mother grew up on a farm in North Dakota, smiles wryly. I am momentarily embarrassed thinking of my eight hundred square feet and imagining the Fuersts' verdant spread in North Dakota. "I have a proposition for you?" she says. Cathy has an enchanting way of making declarations that sound exactly like questions. This diametric projection is as intriguing as it is confusing; oftentimes the most assertive observations are accompanied by a tentative sweeping away of a phantom lock of hair from her cheek, or a sideways glance—a pantomime of timidity. Her son, Caleb, whom I have known since, as they say, before he was born, eighteen years ago, recently graduated from high school. Cathy explains that she and Craig, her husband, have been desperately trying to get Caleb off his ass. When she told him about my project, he showed the first glimmer of interest since they've been agitating for him to do something, anything at all. Caleb, Cathy says, even asked if I might need help on The Farm. I can feed him but I can't pay him, I interrupt. He's happy to volunteer his services, she assures me.

Apparently Caleb has specific requirements for any project—job or otherwise—during this, the summer before he ships off to college. Whatever it is, it must allow him to set his own schedule, and the work can never conflict with his evening bartending classes up at Columbia University. Unpaid labor on The Farm, no matter how filthy, is better than a paying job with a static schedule that he has to dress up for. This volunteerism satisfies both his preconditions and his parents' requirement that he do something useful.

The next day, just before noon, Caleb hops off his mountain bike and reports for duty. We work like dogs, Caleb and I, to get all the plants in the ground in my backyard. We exert extra effort on the potatoes, since they are my hedge against starvation, as they have been for civilizations across the centuries, a hard-to-fuck-up crop that survives when nothing else will.

The plan is to plant the potatoes in their own long, rectangular box, what is called a drill. Because potatoes are the one necessary plant the Verdino nursery didn't have, I order them online. What arrives in the triple-ply paper sacks are spuds just about as big as golf balls that are already starting to send out shoots, exactly like all the potatoes I've left sitting around the kitchen for two weeks too long—I make a mental note.

Only one thing is stopping us from building our potato drill. The tidy rows of tender plants are a delight, but even after positioning the young plants imprudently close to one another and after only half a day of work, we have run out of space in the garden. Caleb and I stand, each with a small plastic-potted plant in hand, surveying the garden, swivel-heading as if we might miss a vacant patch of earth if we don't stay vigilant. I curse. Caleb nods in agreement. I repeat the curse. "You have any special attachment to those bushes?" asks Caleb.

I thought I was going to be thrilled simply to have the extra pair of hands and the company of a man whose biggest mistakes are still ahead of him. Turns out, it's the fresh eyes that are paying off first.

Lisa and I are finally of one mind about something behind the house: the fate of the low-slung shrubbery that rings the back porch. It has to go. It doesn't matter one bit that we came to this conclusion from diametrically distinct perspectives. Lisa wants them gone because they obscure what, in her imagination, will be, as soon as I have completed this most recent harebrained scheme, a delightful view of the backyard and the newly installed cedar fence beyond. I need them gone because there is no room for the luxury of ornament on The Farm. We are both so pleased to agree on anything that we don't bother to explore each other's motives.

Caleb and I conspire to tear the bushes from their beds with my 1989 Toyota Land Cruiser. We set to loosening the root-ball around each bush with shovels. We attach one end of a bright yellow vinyl towrope to the root base of the first shrub and the other end to the tow hook on the front bumper of the Land Cruiser. We have dubbed the Land Cruiser—like most everything else I imbue with any real value, a coveted collectible in a specific rarefied gearhead subculture—The Tractor. Fully expecting each plant, no higher than my thigh, to pop from the earth at the first suggestion of the Land Cruiser's power in reverse, I throw Caleb the keys, giving him the honor of piloting The Tractor. We both vibrate with anticipation at the prospect of destruction dealt by automotive might.

Caleb drops The Tractor in reverse and steps on the accelerator, too hard for my liking considering how close the vehicle's back end is to the Feders' kitchen window and the back corner of their house. The rope goes taut and the bush shakes, but holds firm. Caleb steps impatiently on the accelerator, and The Tractor's back wheels spin, tracing out a parabola in black rubber on the cement driveway. There is a momentary waft of vaporized rubber. Plan A needs an immediate adjustment. "You're gonna need to put her in four, bud!" I yell over the roaring engine.

Caleb cannot hear me. The engine continues to roar and the towrope, tight as a guitar string, hums. Its roots having absorbed the initial shock from the tractor, the bush no longer even shudders. Caleb looks nervously from the bush, to the back of the Feders' house, to me, more concerned about whether I will continue to let him drive The Tractor than whether he is about to remodel the Feders' kitchen, or tear the front bumper from my collectible, or snap the towrope and disembowel me. All these grim possibilities, it strikes me later that evening while watching the grimy ring forming in the tub I am soaking in, were in the forefront of my mind, but they had probably still not occurred to Caleb.

Caleb's nervous, giddy glance falls on me, and I drag my index finger across my neck. "Cut it," I command inaudibly. Caleb sets the engine to idle in park, hops out of the cab, and just about skips the distance of the taut towrope to where I'm standing among the pugnacious shrubbery.

"Cut the engine when you leave the car, bud," I suggest. Chastened—more so than I had intended—Caleb returns to the cab and kills the ignition. He saunters back to where I am standing, staring at the now impossibly tight knot around the scarred red trunk of the ornamental bush. We struggle to untie the knot in the rope and reset it even closer to the earth. "We're gonna need a bigger boat," he says, grinning, pushing the bramble of hair from in front of his face over the top of his head.

Caleb is wearing baggy, knee-length, nylon, Carolina Tar Heels basketball shorts, a pair of high tops that he has clearly given up on, and a T-shirt. The printed name on his shirt does not cross the generational divide. I don't know if it's a band or a sardonic salute, and trying to parse it makes me feel my age. When he shows up for the second day of work wearing the exact same clothes he had soaked through twice the day before, I offer him a pair of my Carhartt welder's pants and an old denim work shirt. Work clothes should provide more protection than what he's sporting, I insist, handing him a pair of leather work gloves I'd bought for him while on a beer run the night before. "I'm good," he says, rejecting the clothes but appreciatively accepting the gloves. "There's nails and all kinds of crap to get hung up on out here," I warn.

"I'll be careful," he promises, as if I were his grandmother telling him to wear a bicycle helmet to bed.

Over the months, Caleb continues to wear the same gear to work every day. I suppose he washes the stuff. It stops mattering as the various rank odors on The Farm overpower any smell that Caleb's good, honest hard work might produce. I never stop wishing that he'd dress the part—the way I do, especially when we leave The Farm on an errand. But I am no longer a reliable judge on matters beyond the driveway, so I cannot say who looks more out of place when we venture into what comes to be called The World.

"We are going to have to shorten the towrope. Let's double it up," I say. "Also, The Tractor's going to have to be in low four-wheel drive. It's fishtailing all over the driveway." Caleb nods knowingly, in a way that assures me he has absolutely no idea what I have just told him to do. "You want I should still drive?" he asks, unself-consciously mugging teamster dialect and hoping the question sounds ten times more casual than it is. "So you can supervise, I mean."

"You can drive. Yes. But you need to use a lot less gas. Build power slowly, don't let the back end move. It doesn't matter if nothing looks like it's happening. This is just like pulling a tooth, right? Nothing is gonna happen till it's out and on the tray. Big roots. Same theory?"

"Nasty," he says, smiling. "Gotcha."

"Also, we're going to lock the hubs and put it in four-wheel drive."

"Cool."

"Cool?"

"Yup."

"You're a dope," I say.

Caleb smirks. We double up the towrope. I dig out the root-ball to about ten inches. The main stem is completely exposed. The general rule is that trees look the same below the soil line as they do above it—that the root structure mimics the branches. I assume that this is true for ornamental hedges, but suddenly recall that these shrubs have been pruned regularly for something like thirty years. All the same, the Toyota is a lot of tool to be using in such an enclosed space. Having Caleb at the wheel makes the entire project twice as dicey as it might otherwise be, but I'm going to tell him to clean out the entire rabbit hutch and the barn after lunch, so I figure I must let him have some fun. For an instant, standing, staring, first at Caleb's eager grin from behind the wheel and then at the visible top of the root-ball, I'm tempted to dig each of them out one by one, but the sense memory of excavating the spider hole still dominates my upper body, and just the idea makes my ears disappear beneath my shoulders.

142

This time the front bumper is less than four feet from the first bush; still the angle is considerably more horizontal than vertical, which means we're not pulling the roots up out of the hole, but along the ground against the four or more feet of clay that separates the bush from the bumper. Still, low gear with all four hubs locked and 155 horsepower and maximum net torque (whatever that is) of 220 lb/ft at 3,000 rpm; it's a decorative bush for Christ sake.

Caleb fires up The Tractor, guns the engine ferociously in neutral. I shoot him the stone face in response. He grins widely and reflexively brushes the hair from his face with the back of his hand. I can see the reflection of the brake lights when they engage and those of the reverse lights as he shifts into reverse. I wait; watch the rope and the bush, looking for the first signs of movement. Caleb shuts the engine down, leans his head out the driver-side window. "You don't suppose the roots are attached to the house, do you?" he says mischievously. "You know? Grown in around the foundation? Lisa would shit if you pulled the back of the house down."

"She would shit," I agree, knowing how many more horrors would then follow. "Get down from there. Let's have at these plants with a pick for a while."

"I was kidding," protests Caleb, disappointed and confused.

"It was funny. Really, it was, now get the pickaxes, wouldya." We spend the balance of the day digging the row of shrubbery out of the ground by hand. Caleb forlornly looks at The Tractor, wondering if now wouldn't be a good time to try using the truck's 220 lb/ft of net torque again. At the end of the day, though, we have enough room for the all-important potato crop.

My father grew up in the north of England during World War Two and nurses a nostalgia for the privations he endured then. He identifies himself as a war baby, has fond memories of his family's victory garden. On June 22, he informs me that once the seed potatoes have been planted, I must continually build up the potato drill to increase my yield. To create such a heap and not bury the cucumber vines, squash, and collard greens so closely butted up against the row of potatoes, I will need to build a retaining wall. So, delighted to have any direction at all, I construct a ten-inch-high plywood box some eighteen feet long and three feet wide filled with an additional half ton of topsoil. The beans are finally in the ground. The cantaloupe vines are reaching out across the front lawn. I drench the vegetation daily in a solution designed to repel the neighborhood dogs. I am not concerned what effect the active ingredient, methyl nonyl ketone, might have on the produce. My farm is not organic, but the callaloo is thriving.

Before The Farm begins its inexorable slide into depravity and chaos, my father often stops by on his way home from work for a glass of wine and a quick inspection of *his* potatoes. He follows their progress and is excited by what he sees. Now that Jane has left for the summer, excitement, enthusiasm even, is rare around The Farm. He is animated when he predicts how many hundreds of potatoes are busy bulking up under the soil. With each visit his estimate inflates. "There couldn't be fewer than two hundred spuds down there, E," he remarks, eyeballing the near waist-high, deep green plants. Everyone in the family calls me E—short for Emanuel, a name stripped from me by my sixth-grade English teacher, who told me my given name was too long. "No, you are Manny," she pronounced. And she was right.

$\Omega = (N1 + N2)!/(N1! \ N2!)$

||||||||||||||||||||||||||||||||||||||||||||||||||||||||||||||||||||||||||||||||||||||||||||||||||

It is mid-May. I am behind schedule. However, completion of the hutch has brightened my mood. I relegate the personal disappointments from the failures at tilapia farming (or even tilapia acquiring) to the slag heap of history. The promise of rabbit husbandry has buoyed my spirits. The future is bright.

When the day comes to install the rabbits in their new home, I layer a bed of straw in each cage and fill the two metal bowls, one for water, the other for the feed, in each cage. The rabbits take to the hutch with what I understand to be a rabbit's typically understated delight. They appear somewhat startled when I turn on the HVAC system.

Following advice from both breeders and chat room experts, I leave the rabbits to acclimate to the hutch. From my observation post at the living-room window I am delighted to observe the buck and his two female neighbors sticking their noses above the wooden section of the partitions dividing their cages, pressing their noses to the wire grates and, their nostrils working athletically, drawing in great snorts of the rabbit next door. This can only be the precursor to extremely enthusiastic breeding. I allow myself to imagine waves of kits reaching five-pound fryer weight in record time, to predict that I will have to find a way to convince fainthearted friends and neighbors to accept the inevitable excess of rabbit meat.

I notice one unexpected behavior almost immediately. Rather than drinking the cool water I supply, the rabbits prefer to vigorously kick over the heavy metal bowls, splashing the water onto the grass on the bottom of the cage, then sit on the puddle. It is late spring, but spring all the same; it hardly seems so warm that the rabbits would need more relief than the HVAC system supplies, but everything I know about a rabbit's circulatory system I learned while my mother read *Watership Down* to me during one summer vacation in England. It may have been a mild May, but a giant rabbit's coat is no joke. Doe #2, the flawless white, seems especially fond of a good soak. Bottom line? The rabbits want to sit in wet grass. What could possibly be the harm?

The hutch complete, my giant breeders acclimated, all that remains is to begin the multiplication process. The predawn hours are optimal for copulation; apparently the same holds true for rabbits. Early each morning I stumble to the coffeemaker, swipe a cup, and deposit the females in the cage of the sand-colored buck, Buck #1. I vary the method of introduction. I vary the order of introduction. I vary the time they spend in the company of Buck #1. I vary the time at which each doe visits Buck #1. Before long the truth is inescapable. My rabbits don't fuck like rabbits.

For two weeks I stand in my underwear in the predawn,

$$\Omega = (n1 + n2)!/(n1!\ n2!)$$

the hour now twice confirmed in e-mails to Sugar Ray to be the optimal hour for breeding, watching while my does reject the most earnest efforts of the big sand-colored buck, my hopes dimming for that late-summer day when freshly butchered, milk-fed fryers hang cooling in the morning air. Standing, dawn after dawn, in the driveway watching two enormous rabbits dry-humping while holding a cooling cup of coffee is a bad way to start the day. It would be for any-body, but I feel my middle age more acutely each morning that my big sandy buck fails to breed.

I am a product of my generation; even as the father of two, I have never imbued sex with a purpose beyond gratifica-tion (and that is almost always immediate, if not instant). The sand-colored buck's inability to propagate on my orders for my purposes is not simply tedious, not just inconvenient, it is a personal affront. At first the buck's failure is an offense against practicality. But in no time his failure to act on the biological imperative takes on more cosmic dimensions. When the offense is merely temporal, the sand-colored buck is a dullard in my eyes, too dim to keep to my schedule. I view his overeager ministrations as ham-handed, his failed attempts at seduction as sloppy and uncreative at their core. As his early-morning flameouts begin to gnaw at the uni-versal fabric, his inability to deliver on his species' fecund promise seems unnatural, possibly venal. I despair of the sand-colored buck's failures and promptly take them on as my own.

All things in nature move from order to chaos. That's all entropy really is. The speed with which something makes this transition is a function of its multiplicity. It is much easier to roll a seven with a pair of dice (one chance in six) than it is to roll a two (just one chance in thirty-six), thus rolling a seven has a higher multiplicity. The more opportunities a subject has to move toward chaos, the faster it will arrive; multiplicity is a predictor of the entropic character of everything. I know what this says about me. I think that I understand what this says about my Flemish giants. I am mistaken.

Hard work is a tonic. One job in particular, mucking out each stall in the hutch, is less a chore than uninterruptible drudgery. Mucking out keeps you perpetually busy while yielding no durable gain. It is a skill that plateaus very early. The cages are never so clean that the very next morning they don't need immediate attention. Work, life really, on The Farm changes shape and purpose, but rather than change The Farm with work, it is changing me. I no longer strain to fill the space I imagined for The Farm; the force I exert achieves the opposite result. And then, two weeks after the arrival of the last of six rabbits, Doe #2, the white one, dies of a maggot infestation known as fly-strike. She dies because, in my ignorance, I have allowed her to kick over her water dish and sit in the water. I didn't realize that wet rabbit fur in combination with a healthy measure of dung and a little chemical lime (sprinkled in the cages per instructions of one of the first breeders I speak with, to keep the cages sanitary between daily cleanings) creates the perfect condition for flies to lay their eggs (a fly lays eggs an average of fourteen times every summer day). The eggs hatch and the maggots make their way to the warmest, wettest food source and begin to feast. The maggots travel as they feast. It just gets warmer and wetter the farther up the rabbit they range. This is the horror of fly-strike.

I discover the infestation quite by accident. While return-

$$\Omega = (n1 + n2)!/(n1!\ n2!)$$

ing Doe #2 to her cage after yet another failed breeding session, I turn her on her back in my arms, half expecting her to present like a Barbie doll. Having no genitalia at all would have been only half as convincing an explanation of the failure to breed as what I discovered when I brushed her somewhat matted fur aside.

Eggs laid on a rabbit's nethers in the morning will hatch by lunchtime, and the army of maggots that results begins to eat immediately, causing wounds and releasing toxins not only on the surface of the skin but inside the animal's reproductive and digestive tract. The infestation is deadly within days and within hours is too hideous to examine closely. Most all veterinarians understand how fast-moving this infestation is, but I do not. Rather than expose myself as a neglectful rabbit keeper, I opted to treat her myself. I carry her into the kitchen immediately, where I make her a comfy nest from brightly colored beach towels; following website instructions I apply a variety of medicines. The children are delighted to have the rabbit in the house and pretend not to notice my distress when they play with her. I am ashamed of my failure to take Doe #2 to a trained professional. I convince myself that the children's boundless affection will help cure the doe faster than any antiseptic veterinary clinic might. Lisa understands that the perfect white doe is very sick, but also seems to have faith that I am providing a cure. She believes that my newfound concern for this one doe, my constant fussing and ministering, means that the worst of my agrarian role play is finally at an end, that my behavior heralds a return to sanity, and that this increasingly dark pantomime is nearly over.

I know that my ministrations are having little and probably no effect. It is impossible to completely clear this doe of maggots. Believing I have, I leave her alone for just an hour; the infestation is robust again when I flip her over to check on my work. I let Heath name the doe Snow White, and for two days she spends hours feeding the doe carrots. Bevan Jake enjoys enthusiastically hugging the sick rabbit. The idea that he is both increasing what must be her blinding agony and unintentionally squeezing the infestation into his own lap so repulses me that I ban him, clueless as to what he has done to inspire my anger, from the kitchen.

I spend two full days trying to save Doe #2. During the evening of the second day I commit to putting the rabbit out of her misery the next morning, immediately after dropping the kids at school. I return home, grim and determined. But Doe #2 lies dead on the kitchen floor where I have been ministering to her.

I hate my cowardice, my inability to have ended her suffering, the casual way I chose to put off doing the right, if unpleasant, thing the moment I knew there was no saving her. I stuff her heavy carcass in a plastic garbage bag, cover her with a scoop of lime (calcium hydroxide; the alkaline dust speeds decomposition and masks the smell of rotting flesh), and throw her in the trash. Pickup day is tomorrow.

In a terse e-mail to Lisa at work I write, *Snow White is dead*.

I hear nothing from Lisa until 3 p.m., when she sends me an e-mail informing me that she has been asked to drinks by a client and cannot refuse. She asks me to kiss the kids goodnight for her. She will be late, she writes, no need to wait up for her.

I stay up half the night all the same, fixating on how to provide water to the animals in a way that will not allow them to harm themselves. Two hours after Lisa wordlessly

$$\Omega = (n1 + n2)!/(n1! \ n2!)$$

joins me in bed, immediately feigns sleep, and moments after that is sound asleep, I dream up an irrigation system in each cage that operates on a garden timer. A garden hose runs to the back of the hutch to a brass splitter with six spigots. A capillary system of custom-length hoses feeds blue plastic dishes that are screwed to the floor of each cage.

Try kicking that over.

The next morning I build the system that I had in the dark scribbled on the back of a magazine with a laundry marker. I calibrate the garden-hose timer to observed usage patterns. Problem solved. I replace the feed bowls with feed bins that hang through the holes cut in the wire on each cage. The floor of each cage is no longer an inadvertent death trap.

I have trouble reading the rabbits' body language when the automatic irrigation system cranks up, but I am pleased with the automation and think of the generations of yeoman farmers before me who, inspired to solve problems, to avoid continued tragedy, or by Yankee ingenuity, must also have been seized by inspiration in the middle of the night and changed farming methods forever after.

I am alarmed to discover that, after only two days, the automatic water trough is being used as a toilet. Not by one obstinate cuss, but by all five residents of the hutch. Horrified at the health implications if the rabbits continue to hang their nethers over such a fetid stew, I disconnect the hose immediately and swab each cage with a weak bleach solution. Withholding water from the rabbits if they continue to try to kill themselves with it seems reasonable at first. Maybe I can provide water for them outside their cages, monitor their intake, and then, having judged them properly hydrated, return them to a bone-dry cage. This hardly seems in keeping with my philosophical commitment to the laborsaving device that has defined work on The Farm thus far.

In an e-mail to Sugar Ray I neglect to inform him of the demise of Doe #2. Instead I explain that, like Doe #1, the pair he just sold me will not entertain the stud buck either and that my time is running out. I blame the sand-colored buck and ask if Sugar Ray can spare any bucks to sire my herd. He has none to spare but has a friend who is selling off an American Chinchilla buck. Sugar Ray promotes the notion of hybrid vigor, scoffs at my concern that the kits won't grow big enough, fast enough, and offers to broker the deal. In a pinch, I figure, one buck is as good as another and ask if he can spare one more doe—hopefully one much more accommodating than the freeloaders loafing around The Farm. Sugar Ray agrees. Doe #1 is looking a bit worn down. I am too embarrassed to ask him in advance to examine another breeder's merchandise, so the morning the American Chinchilla buck arrives at Sugar Ray's barn, I pack up Doe #1, intending to spring her on him unannounced and see what he thinks.

Sugar Ray is as excitable as ever. I am obviously vexed and insist on getting right to work, but my Rabbit Man doesn't appear to mind. I tell him again that the rabbits aren't doing what rabbits are famous for doing, and the breeder listens. "You can stimulate the doe with your fingers," he offers.

"That's completely out of the question," I reply. If Lisa happened upon me in the barn whilst digitally stimulating a twenty-pound rabbit, I'm pretty certain she would call the locksmith and the police.

"No. It's not bad at all," he explains, putting his index and middle fingers parallel.

"I'm sure it isn't. Still . . . ," I protest, failing to cut short

$$\Omega = (n1 + n2)!/(n1!\ n2!)$$

his demonstration as he reaches into a cage for a steel gray doe. I refuse to watch while he demonstrates, but he demonstrates all the same. At the first opportunity, whimpering now, I repeat that I am running out of time to produce an edible litter of kits.

"So you don't just need a doe," exclaims Sugar Ray, still hugging the steel gray doe. "You need a pregnant doe!"

"Yes. I suppose that's right," I reply gratefully, the straightforward genius of his solution washing over me as the words leave my mouth.

"Well," Sugar Ray exclaims, "let's go rape a rabbit, Manny."

"That one?" I ask, regarding the digitally stimulated steel doe suspiciously.

"She's yours now," says Sugar Ray, strutting off to the brightest corner of the barn. He places the doe in a cage with a light gray buck, one of four in the row, all from the same litter, the breeder explains. The first buck doesn't mount so much as pounce on my stimulated steel doe. Moments later, his work at an end, he flops over sideways off her. Unfazed, she hops over to the water bottle. "Let's make sure this sticks," says Sugar Ray rhetorically, sweeping the doe out of the first cage and into the neighboring confine with one motion so fluid that it seems as though he opened neither door. While the first buck looks on, his brother repeats the process. Looking hard at the first buck, I swear I can detect the instinctive fury produced by sperm competition. I look again. Nope.

A few short moments later, my stimulated steel doe is out from under the jittery buck and back in Sugar Ray's embrace. "That is one pregnant rabbit," he says, stroking her forehead lightly. "You wanna see the Chinchilla?"

"Sure."

In a cage by the door sits a rabbit that at first glance I mistook for one of Sugar Ray's kits. "He's so small?"

"Cute, isn't he?" Sugar Ray smiles, still holding the steel gray doe.

"He's so small?"

"Not for an American Chinchilla, he's not. That's good weight."

"Will it work? I mean, my does don't put up with a buck four times his size," I can hear myself moaning.

"It ought to work," says Sugar Ray carelessly. "Always has before. Truth is, you may even get better meat once you mix 'em up." He's walking to a pile of frail wooden produce boxes. He picks out two and lines them with timothy grass. While he packs the steel gray doe and the Chinchilla buck for transport, I slip out to the truck and return with Doe #1. I ask the breeder if he can cast an eye over her. "Manny, that is one old rabbit you've got there. Where did you get that?"

I tell him that I purchased the fetching pale-gray doe from a Central European guy in New Jersey along with my useless sand-colored buck. "Russian guy?" asks Sugar Ray.

"Sort of."

"I know that guy," he says skeptically, taking the doe from my arms. "His name is Jerzy or something."

"I think that's right." I wonder what the chances really are that my Jersey rabbit breeder is named Jerzy.

"Hell, this isn't even his rabbit," exclaims the breeder, examining my pale gray doe. "This ear tattoo belongs to a friend of mine in Bridgeport. See? 'JZ'!"

"Oh."

"We can give it a try," says Sugar Ray skeptically. "One

$$\Omega = (n1 + n2)!/(n1! \; n2!)$$

of these boys might be into a little MILF action, but she's awfully old. Just look at her."

He turns to walk to the row of studs where we had busied ourselves with the steel gray doe. He turns to me over his shoulder as he briefly promenades the doe in front of his bucks. "What do they say about older women? Much older women?"

I brace for impact, a chimp-fear grin plastered across my face.

"'They don't swell, they don't tell, and they're grateful as hell!'"

Sugar Ray tries to mate Doe #1 with no fewer than six of his most virile bucks.

No go.

"Sorry, Manny, that is one old rabbit. She's like a seventy-year-old person. Rabbits only have but so many eggs to fertilize. When they're done, well, they're done." He draws his finger across his neck.

Spent is not how the breeder with the sun-baked backyard hutch in New Jersey described the doe when he sold her to me. Rather I was buying "an experienced mother who will take great care of her litter."

The claim impressed me at the time, even more so after I see how barbarically some does treat their first litters.

Upon my return from Litchfield, Lisa and I promote Doe #1 to house pet. I do not explore why I consider her departing The Farm a promotion, but with the elevation of station comes a name; we begin to refer to her reverentially as The Old Gray Lady. Lisa, Heath, and Bevan Jake embrace The Old Gray Lady. Watching the kids snuggle a rabbit almost their size is bizarre, but she is always gentle, serene. Lisa and the kids allow her to roam on the porch and sometimes in the kitchen, though she doesn't move around too much. She seems content. They fall in love with her.

The Old Gray Lady dies of something two weeks later.

I put her corpse in the freezer in the barn, and when Lisa notices her absence a few days later, I inform her that her favorite rabbit is dead, explain that, rather than liming her in a garbage bag and putting her at the curb on pickup day as I had done with Doe #2, I have wrapped her carefully and stored her in the garage freezer in case Lisa wants us to bury her out back. Lisa looks at me, wordless for a long moment, says "No," and goes back inside. I don't see Lisa again for a few days. She avoids me around the house and won't let the kids play with the rabbits anymore. When I finally confront her one morning before work, she has tears in her eyes and tells me she can't live in this mess. She doesn't wait for my response before she opens the door and leaves for work.

TAKING FROM TRESPASSER

||||||||||||||||||||||||||||||||||||||||||||||||||||||||||||||||||||||||||||||||||||||||||||||||||||||||||

Sitting on an upturned five-gallon, white plastic bucket watching the riot of squirrels in the canopy behind the house, I am seized with dread. Those squirrels are just waiting to sack the garden. Why haven't I seen this obvious disaster? I'll never see a single vegetable from the garden, never mind eat one, if this tree-borne horde of vermin lays siege. The Internet conjures an exciting and diverse array of anti-squirrel devices, but the solution to this problem can't be put off for overnight delivery. Though by the time I locate a nearby squirrel-trap vendor and set off for Staten Island, I might as well have ordered online and waited for next-day delivery.

I purchase the squirrel trap from a farm supply store on Amboy Road, on the western edge of Staten Island. Pleasingly ramshackle, the feedstore appears a vestige of Staten Island's not too distant agrarian past. The last working farm in the borough, a dairy, was sold for a subdivision in 1980. Today, here outside, looming behind this freestanding, three-story, tumbledown store, the hills of the former Fresh Kills Landfill dominate the horizon. When I was growing up, Fresh Kills was known only as the dump. Each day the dump on the banks of the Fresh Kills estuary received twenty barges, each laden with 650 tons of the city's garbage. The dump was a monument to the varied blight that residents of the city—and especially Staten Island—bore. Opened as a temporary facility in 1947 by the city's infamous construction baron, Robert Moses, when Fresh Kills finally closed in 2001, the dump was the largest city landfill in the country (that honor currently belongs to Puente Hills Landfill in Whittier, California). Even in a city with an ahistorical memory such as this one—a city where the most obscene scandals defy memory because they crash across the headlines, often two at a time, with a regularity that exhausts its citizenry—a testament to the scale of the dump, even here in dysphoric New York City, all these years later, Staten Island's reputation continues to suffer: the home of Fresh Kills Landfill.

Baiting the squirrel trap is no great challenge, assures the proprietor, a big-boned Irishwoman massaging the ash of a Virginia Slims cigarette between her lips while another burns down in the faux-crystal Foxwoods Resort Casino ashtray on the cluttered counter. "There's a trick to the raccoon trap, though," she warns. Having seen the wire box, enormous in comparison to a squirrel trap, I reflexively add it to my shopping list. You never know. In a foolproof method she learned from a longtime customer of hers just down the road, you bait a raccoon trap with a bagel. The bagel has to have a schmear of cream cheese on it (I have since been told that an open can of sardines does the job nicely). The proprietor edges out onto the sales floor between fifty-pound sacks of varied animal feed piled to her waist like sandbags at the mouth of a pillbox. Stepping over a ringworm-medication display that has fallen on its side, she marches toward the western wall of the store and ascends a ladder to what could be called the first shelf, a narrow loft really, about eight feet off the ground. "I have one here somewhere," she calls from behind more sacks of feed. "See if you can find nylon twine. You can tie the bagel in the trap with that. There should be some under the counter." Sure enough, right next to the rubber grip of a .38-caliber Ruger pistol rests a spool of purple nylon twine and a box cutter. Leaving the gun scrupulously untouched, I hold the twine and the knife up for her approval "These?" I call with studied nonchalance. She stands holding a three-foot wire rectangular box in the fingers of one hand, crouching under the loft's low ceiling, nods, and smiles. I wonder if she knows she asked me to go rooting around in her armory.

The trip to Staten Island takes the balance of the afternoon. When I finally emerge from the traffic, there's no time to start a new project. Work on The Farm has become so all-consuming that the evening dog walk is the only opportunity I allow myself to talk with people other than Caleb and the immediate family. Not that the family—well, Lisa—are speaking to me all that much. Gossiping with neighbors on Thursday, June 28, I discover that it has been an eventful day in the neighborhood beyond the confines of The Farm. The police pursued a young man suspected of drug possession through the backyards between my own street and the one behind our house. One neighbor on the scene reports that, when the police apprehended their perp, the alleged drugs were no longer in his possession. The working theory was that the kid had dumped the contraband in one of the yards. . . . Yards? Fine. Farm? Big problem.

Had the perp or his pursuers made it to—worse, through—my garden? If so, what damage had they caused? Is a low-level possession bust really worth the health and safety of my tomatoes, my still-delicate beets, or most important, my potatoes? By early July I will have given up gossiping with the neighbors altogether.

I set the squirrel trap that night, hoping that, if I do a lot of sneaking around and do not then announce its presence in idle conversation, Lisa will not notice it. Discretion is a skill that comes easily to the people I admire most. I am afflicted by the desire to share all, even some of the thoughts I know are best kept close. The charm that Lisa finds in that forth-rightness has waned. When it has a meaningful utility, Lisa does occasionally slap the Southern charm on a little thick, but it's not at all affected. In her bones she has a genteel sensibility I know little about. It is safe to say that the possibility of squirrels barking away blind with panic in traps set at the perimeter of the vegetable garden would produce an equal and opposite reaction in the two of us. I know this when I set the traps. I set them all the same. Too much is at stake to do anything else. I comfort myself with the thought that it is the rare city-dweller indeed who can pick out a squirrel bark from the cacophony of the canopy (Lord knows how a raccoon will react); still, Lisa must have no idea the traps are there. If I can only keep my mouth shut. *And this old place here, it's even more difficult to do right by than Tanya, really, because it's abused and it's steep, and I've accumulated a history of wrong guesses here,* announces Wendell Berry, referring to his Kentucky tobacco farm and then his wife. *And so I live in this com-*

mitment all the time, knowing very well how attractive mobility is. I'd really like to be loved by somebody who doesn't know me—who would be susceptible to charm. I appreciate how fine that would be, but I know it wouldn't last and that I couldn't disguise myself for more than, oh, maybe forty-eight hours.

I nod in agreement. I'm getting used to this fellow Berry's rhythms. He's not done. I place the first trap hard by the fence—the pests' preferred route—and begin staking it to the ground. *Marriage is the inevitable metaphor for the kind of agriculture and community life that I'm talking about,* he says, his words slowing, their camber taking a familiar dip to telegraph significance just in case I'm not paying proper attention, *and it's an inescapable preoccupation for a man who wants to be well married. If you're going to sustain anything, you've got to have populations that are totally committed.*

"So, should I tell her about the traps, or not?" I ask casually, popping the soil from my hands against my workpants, looking around for the strategically perfect location for trap number two.

It is days before a squirrel finally bolts inside my trap. It barks, furious and afraid, hanging upside down from the low wire ceiling, warning others away. The rectangular box barely has room for the critter to turn around. Good. Let him yell. The more he yells, the less tempting my tender shoots will be to the hordes of squirrels that teem in the trees above my garden. He barks for two days, during which time I do not notice a single other squirrel. They'll understand what I have only begun to fully appreciate: my vegetables come at a cost. I consider feeding him, but decide against it, reasoning that a sated squirrel would soon become tame. The last thing I need is another mouth to feed. During lunch on the third day, I empty a trash can and coil a garden hose at the bottom of it. I turn the spigot and the can slowly begins to fill. By the time I finish my sandwich, the can is full. I turn the hose off and fetch up the squirrel trap from the garden.

Caleb is just poking the final bite of his Cuban sandwich into his mouth when I unceremoniously drop the trap into the water. It sinks like a stone. Caleb chokes on his food. The thin, plastic garbage can begins to shake as the squirrel thrashes at the top of his cage, trying to catch his breath less than an inch beneath the now agitated surface of the water. "That is so fucked-up," observes Caleb, with laudable reserve considering the circumstances, shaking his head, wiping his mouth, brushing his mane from in front of his face and looking anywhere but at the trash can even as it ceases vibrating.

"What was I gonna do, release him?" I ask, peering into the can to observe the drowned squirrel pressed against the highest edge of the trap. I did not expect a trash can full of water to vibrate so vigorously as the squirrel thrashed about. I am consumed with remorse, but intent on disguising it. For some reason, projecting the impression that my barbarity has not only dispassionately been executed, but was also rigorously planned, seems important right now.

"I guess? Yes," replies Caleb.

"Just release an angry, starving squirrel?"

"Yep."

"What's the point of trying to scare off the squirrels if they know I'm going to release them?"

"They're going to know? The other squirrels?" asks Caleb, smirking at me.

"They knew he was in the trap, didn't they?" I point at the

drowned squirrel, then up into the empty canopy. "Anyhow, they say that drowning is the most peaceful way to die."

"Squirrels?"

"People say that drowning is easy, not that drowning squirrels is easy."

"Was it?"

"Yes. It wasn't all that hard," I say, making the mistake of peering into the trash can. The squirrel's front claws and orange teeth are frozen in death, gripping the wire. "Not once I'd made the decision to do it."

"So fucked. You mind if I go? I gotta change for bartending school."

"No. That's cool. You wanna bag the squirrel before you go?" I gingerly lift the cage half out of the water with my index finger.

"Fuck you."

Since the drowning, I have seen plenty of squirrels in the trees above my garden, but I have never seen one among the plants in my garden.

CHICKEN RUN

||||||||||||||||||||||||||||||||||||||||||||||||||||||||||||

The passing of The Old Gray Lady has put a point on it for me and Caleb. With her on ice in the garage freezer, we are forced to confront a truth we had treated as suspicion. Like the tilapia before them, the rabbits are never going to provide protein for The Farm. It is agreed. We need to move on. The nearest Agway selling day-old meat birds is forty-nine miles from The Farm. Armed with a newly minted learner's permit, Caleb wrestles the late-model Land Cruiser out over the Outerbridge Crossing and on to Englishtown, New Jersey, while I catch up with the newspaper and try not to look out the windshield.

Caleb and I both prefer it when he drives the truck. He still isn't all that good at it. He is easily flustered by multilane intersections and my barked, last-minute directions, but what Caleb lacks in driving experience he makes up for in enthusiasm. That this combination is precisely the cause of just about every car accident involving teens doesn't deter me. His day is full of such grim and filthy work, I feel obliged to let him drive at every opportunity. The twenty-year-old Toyota Land Cruiser handles like a poorly maintained fishing trawler. The brakes are spongy, and there's enough drift in the steering so that, unchecked, the truck will cross two lanes of traffic over a few hundred yards at a modest speed, but Caleb has little to compare this experience to and seems unfazed by the truck's less than standard performance.

Figuring that, like every other Brooklyn-raised kid I know, he's completely ignorant of the details of internal combustion, I see no reason to burden him with the information that, somewhat miraculously, the engine is running though it fires on just five of six cylinders, the gas tank and the oil pan both leak, and I am keeping a watchful eye on the gamboling needle of the thermostat for fear that what is left of the engine will overheat—not that any of the gauges are the least bit trustworthy.

The Agway is cluttered with fencing and feeding and watering implements and sacks of dirt and rock (various), but don't let these chaotic surroundings fool you. For Lisa this would be the equivalent of her favorite designer-fashion boutiques Scoop and Intermix—stores that limit their merchandise to offerings from such designers as Smythe, Chloé, Stella McCartney, and Adrienne Landau—rolled together. For the agricultural set—of whom I now count myself a member—this is heaven.

After warming up by perusing the ready-made doghouses and discussing what the goat standing on top of a plastic igloo in a metal pen might cost us, Caleb and I just about skip through the front door holding hands. The one-day-old chickens (meat birds) are not hard to find. They are both loud and smelly.

We are like a pair of heartland tourists set loose in the H&M Fifth Avenue flagship store. Playing absolute beginners, we assemble our meat-bird-growing kit—watering tower, feeder, and flytraps.

Flytraps are of special interest to us both. The flies have overrun our paltry defenses, the coils of sticky paper that hang by the dozen from the garage ceiling and that of the back porch. Out of desperation we have resorted to hanging the coils from a lattice of bamboo suspended above the barn. The tape festoons The Farm. So, when we stumble on professional-strength agricultural flytraps we become engrossed, obsessed really. The larger of the two says it will trap and hold sixty-four thousand flies. "How about a couple of these?" I suggest.

"You think?" says Caleb.

"Sure," I say, doubt creeping in, looking at the label one more time.

"You're talking 128,000 flies, dude. You really think there will be that many flies back there?"

"You're right." After a pause, I put a pair of the smaller traps in our shopping cart. Caleb was wrong. Both of the twenty-four-thousand-fly-capacity traps were full in less than three weeks. I order two more pheromone baits for each trap online. I pay the additional charge for overnight delivery.

The average fly lives only about eight days. That's where the good news stops. The female lays eggs on animal excrement, rotting food, and decaying organic matter that the larvae that hatch consume. If a breeding pair of houseflies began their work in April and all of their young were to survive, the original pair would produce an estimated 191.1 quintillion offspring by August. That sounds about right to me. As far as I can tell, the dominant subspecies of the domestic fly that took up residence on The Farm were the house, bottle (both blue, or *Calliphora*, and green, *Phaenicia*), blow, and the reliable black garbage fly.

Houseflies are said to spread disease including but not limited to conjunctivitis, poliomyelitis, typhoid fever, tuberculosis, anthrax, leprosy, cholera, diarrhea, and dysentery. The larvae of the most common flies feed on dead and living tissue of mammals, causing blood poisoning and occasionally death. While feeding, flies puke up the contents of their stomachs onto their meal. The meal dissolves; they then hoover the sludge back up into their stomachs. Flies shit while they walk, wherever they walk. The effective range of a fly varies by species, but most can range from between two and twenty miles. Why any fly would ever wish to leave The Farm is beyond me.

When it comes to selecting our meat birds, Caleb refuses to take any part. He says that he won't take the karmic hit that would result from selecting chicks he knows will end up becoming meat. "Fine," I say, determined, agitated because I'm suddenly also mildly uncomfortable to be doing the selecting alone. "Just hold the box up higher so I can toss them in quickly."

The store manager, inspired by our dizzy spree, offers to throw in a free mature chicken of unknown parentage. Inflamed, we accept before inspecting the offering. The bird is clearly a stray. She's hideous to look at, almost entirely devoid of plumage, with scabrous legs and feet. She's a walking infection—and we are halfway home before we think better of having taken The Stray out of the cat carrier to let her roam the back of the Land Cruiser, spreading who knows what parasites and diseases.

We end up with twenty-five mixed-breed chicks: Cornish Cross, Rhode Island Reds, and blue Plymouth Rocks (or blue Rocks), mixed with a salt-and-pepper team of bantams (strictly a vanity purchase), and four ducklings. This might seem like an overabundance, but based on the experience with the rabbits, we're expecting a pretty significant mortality rate, and a man's gotta eat. We haven't built a coop yet. This detail will not escape Lisa. Tomorrow we will build the chicken coop. Caleb and I are ambitious about the plans.

Lisa's long-simmering resentment about the roiling chaos that I have unleashed on our already hectic life is increasingly hard to manage. She finds it harder and harder to remember that she once thought The Farm would be good for us, would pull me out of my torpor. Daily, she is embarrassed by the growing pile of garbage and the stink of shit. But, given "some space, or time away from the farm," she suggests, she will probably recover. She assures me that deep down she understands the importance of it in my life and will continue to quietly endure the effects of my growing fixation. It is a sincere attempt at reconciliation, and, of course, the right thing to do. I know Lisa wishes that she believed what she says.

Which is why returning from the Agway with twenty-six chickens and four baby ducks without any advance word is no minor tactical error. Lisa requires no explanation, just stands, still in her business rig, staring steely while Caleb shovels livestock out of a box perched on the tailgate of the Land Cruiser and onto the driveway and the kids dance at our feet among a score of day-old chicks. "The rabbits were a nonstarter," I announce, the cheer in my voice entirely unconvincing. "We had to make the switch." The use of the plural is lost on neither Lisa nor Caleb. Both launch disapproving glares that bore into me. Any empathy for me and my agrarian misadventure that Lisa has hidden away in reserve has vanished.

Only just returned from her office, Lisa has not yet made the already difficult cognitive shift she has described as necessary just to enter the front door of Howard Hall. The sight of the chicks on the driveway leaves her dumbfounded. Ambushed, confused, her brooding hostility now open rage, Lisa, angry beyond speaking, tears in her eyes, retreats immediately to her dressing room upstairs. If, rather than continue to wrangle the day-old birds as they, peeping as they go, spread out all over the garden, I had followed her upstairs, I would have found her packing a bag, preparing to abandon our house and The Farm, ready now to take the kids to live in the safety of the Ritz-Carlton Battery Park, her favorite hotel in Manhattan.

Bevan Jake, in an overexcited fit of pique, accidentally steps on one of the ducklings, maiming it. The little boy turns around to see what he stepped on; clearly fearing the worst, he looks to me first, though. In that instant Caleb scoops the dying bird up in his hand, holding it tenderly behind his back. "Jakey crushed a duck," chides Heath.

"No, he didn't, hon," says Caleb resolutely, mugging his best Obi-Wan Kenobi at Heath, "these aren't the 'droids you're looking for."

"Yes, he did," insists Heath, incredulous.

"Did I, Daddy?" Bevan Jake asks, confused, somewhere in his heart knowing the truth, but relieved there is no evidence. My heart breaks for him.

"Jakey, luv, if you had stepped on a duckling, it'd be there on the ground," I explain, pointing, Bevan Jake following with his eyes, as Caleb, slipping past me to tend to Heath, palms the mangled bird to me behind my back.

"He did!" demands Heath. "I saw it!"

"Enough, Heath," I bark. "You want to go inside? Go find your mother." The bird twitches as I slip it into the cargo pocket of my shorts.

"C'mon, kids, let's count the chickies one more time," sings Caleb, leading them away from the driveway among the peeping birds.

Lisa returns from upstairs just in time to watch while I euthanize the duckling by putting it in a plastic shopping bag and, swinging it like a framing hammer, crush it against the driveway. I toss the near-weightless carcass into the garbage can. Lisa and I make eye contact; I smile weakly. "It's a farm. Things die," I say, attempting to ride it out.

Lisa turns from me, expressionless. "You're going to turn them into ax murderers," she spits, gesturing toward our giggling children. Lisa has communicated her fear that the children will be permanently damaged by their exposure to the goings-on back here. I disagree entirely, insisting that contact with the source of their food will make them better global citizens. Well, I made that argument once. I shrug off her repeated objection now, mostly concerned that any substantive discussion about what is good and what is bad about The Farm will end in cataclysm.

"Jakey? Honey? Time for dinner. Heath?"

"Mama, Jakey killed a baby duckling."

"I did not, Mama."

"Then where's the fourth one?" barks Heath, mimicking

what is known as Dad's Stone Voice. Bevan Jake's face collapses in a heap of doubt.

"That's enough, kids," says Lisa. "Dinner. Now."

Early the next afternoon, Lisa calls, says she can't get out of a drinks arrangement after work and won't be home until late.

From this day forward through the summer, Lisa pretty much disappears from our home. She leaves earlier for work each day and suddenly has evening engagements she simply cannot beg out of. Whenever it comes up, she blames a recent promotion, says she never thought the job would require this much face time after work. She used to apologize for making these last-minute announcements. These days, she hangs up the phone before bothering to say sorry for the last-minute change. Today, though, before she hangs up, I overhear her announce, "Okay, we're good. Let me buy the next round."

A CHICKEN NAMED CRAZY

‖‖‖

After breakfast at a diner on Christmas Eve about twenty years ago, my stepbrother, Justin, my friends Evan and Josh, and I are looking for some adventure to pass this long day before Christmas. I suggest we start by seeing what kind of excitement we can wring from the live-poultry market on Twentieth Street in Sunset Park. It's a halal market run by Chinese and frequented predominantly by Dominicans. The early-morning arrival of four outsize white guys, one carrying a late-model video camera (Evan's early ambitions as a filmmaker mean a camera attends any and all nonsense adventures we dream up), doesn't cause any alarm until Justin marches straight back into the slaughterhouse with the camera running, giving no explanation whatsoever. The folks working the market begin exchanging glances, and Josh reacts by adopting the Voice of Officialdom, a carica-ture of a bullhorn-enhanced announcement, part entreat and part command. "Everybody stay calm. Nothing to see

173

here. Please finish your business. And, please, have a merry Christmas."

I busy myself negotiating with the young woman who runs the cash register. How much for a chicken? I want to know. She tells me the per-pound dollar amount. I tell her fine. She makes a point of explaining that the birds are weighed before they are cleaned—often called wet weight in the trade. Fine with me. "We need a big one, please."

The young woman at the cash register barks at a stooped, skinny, older man drowning in a baseball cap from Dyke's Lumber (a familiar local construction-supply outfit), black rubber knee boots, and a matching apron. He walks over to a cage, opens it, and grabs a white hen out of one of the stacked, low wood transport pens. "Bigger! *Massivo!*" I grin, speaking Spanglish to the Chinese and spreading my arms wide. The butcher shrugs, returns the original hen to the cage, moves to another stack of cages. He surveys the inventory and produces a mammoth hen. Held upside down by the feet, she flaps her brown wings aggressively and calls out in full-throated protest, adding her voice to the chorus of lamenting fowl. The butcher ties her ankles roughly with twine secured to the metal crossbar of the scale. The bird weighs a little less than eight pounds. A monster. He sweeps her off the scale and heads back to the abattoir. "No!" I holler. "Wait!"

The butcher stops in his tracks and looks to the cashier. "Alive," I say, smiling conspiratorially. "We want him alive." The cashier shakes her head vigorously. No.

"Alive. Yes," I say.

"No. Only can sell dead chicken." The butcher, thinking the debate is at an end, proceeds to the killing floor beyond the thick plastic curtain. Josh reaches his arm across the door, blocking the old butcher's progress. "Hang one second more, friend," he says, smiling.

"More money for alive chicken," I insist, taking a twenty out of my wallet. "More money for chicken alive," I repeat, looking around at the Latin American patrons now studiously ignoring me.

"No. Alive is not allowed," she barks.

"It is a present for my mother," I improvise. "A Christmas present. More money." I add a ten to the pile and thrust the money at her. By now the customers who have not already quit the converted cinder-block garage have found a variety of things to be fascinated by in the far reaches of the dimly lit market. Justin emerges from the abattoir, obviously eager to tell a funny story. Josh puts his hand on top of Justin's, which is gripping the still-running video camera, forcing it down and out of the cashier's sight. Justin is followed by a retinue of confused and anxious butchers dressed in upside-down, blood-splattered clear plastic garbage bags with a hole for their heads and two arm holes cut into the bottoms of the bags. The cashier barks once and the butchers—all twice her age—disappear back behind the heavy plastic curtain.

"Forty dollars. Okay!" the cashier barks, not modulating her tone.

"Fine," I say, handing over a pair of twenties as Evan relieves our butcher of the big chicken, grabbing its feet and deftly depositing it at the bottom of the plain brown-paper shopping bag we have carried in for just such an eventuality. As we march out in triumphant single file, the cashier mocks us: "Tell your mom merry Christmas."

Pleased by our brash ingenuity and our brusque retail style, we head straight for a bar across the river. Lurching around the East Village, we try and fail half a dozen times to find a bartender who is willing to overlook the specifics of the city health code and help us answer the burning question, what does a drunk chicken look like on video?

It helps, I suppose, that no other patrons are in Joe's Cowboy Bar, surprising for lunchtime on Christmas Eve. The bartender doesn't bat an eye when we tip the shopping bag on its side and out marches our chicken. We take turns engaging the chicken in conversation; we interview her for the camera, try to convince her to join us drinking a draft beer, even serving the beer in an aluminum take-out dish. But the hen isn't interested in anything but bar snacks, which, much to the horror of a nearby body-inked transplant reading the free alternative weekly, the *New York Press*, the bird pecks directly from the common peanut bowl. As the bar begins to fill, the bartender suggests that maybe it is time that the chicken and her boyfriends move along.

Outside now, on East Fifth Street, the day is grayer, wetter, and colder. Our once merry band's mood mirrors the change in the weather. The hen herself looks a little weary, and enthusiasm for continued chicken mischief is cratering when Justin, cradling the bird in both arms, suggests, "Let's buy her a Christmas tree."

We are off, piling into Evan's mother's late-model beige Volvo sedan with only one remaining hubcap and a manual sunroof permanently half-open, driving up Sixth Avenue bound for the busiest Christmas-tree merchant we can locate. Camera rolling, we approach the tree vendors, explaining the annual family tradition requires that a chicken select our family Christmas tree. It is an Albanian cultural thing, we explain. Justin makes a great show of reading retail preference into the chicken's every twitch and change of cadence, and after half an hour we tie a spidery, four-foot Norway spruce to the roof of the Volvo. "Where to?" chirps Evan, as snow dances across the Volvo's windshield, the sky visible between the buildings an ominous slate.

"Macy's," I pronounce. "Henny Penny's final act." At the curb of the department store's main entrance on Sixth Avenue, Josh, Justin, and I bound out of the car. The sidewalk is alive with heavily laden, panic-propelled last-minute shoppers. We ford the human current, marching purposefully through the double brass doors, careful to protect the cargo within our shopping bag from any panic-inducing contact, and into the throng of driven consumers. Once we have our bearings, we head toward the nearby handbag department. Finding a momentarily unattended counter, Justin deposits the shopping bag atop this polished glass surface and quickly steps away. "Tip it over," I hiss.

"You!" Justin protests.

"Tip it now," I say, turning and walking toward the door. I can see Evan idling his mother's late-model Swedish sedan, refracted through the multiple glass panes of the Sixth Avenue entrance, our getaway car, idling by the curb. What is the sentence for animal abandonment? Will the judge consider that it is Christmas Eve as a mitigating or an exacerbating circumstance? The snow is sticking to cabs, and shoppers, but I can't see one flake that has made it past foot traffic to the sidewalk. Josh grabs my shoulder. "Wait."

I wheel around, expecting to find Justin detained by brown-blazer-wearing security guards. But Justin has cleared the bag and is a safe distance from the bird. Our hen steps gingerly out of the overturned paper bag and looks around, confused.

She then takes off down the counter toward a heavyset sales-woman with a spiky but practically coiffed mop of jet-black hair. "Merry Christmas, Henny Penny," says Justin, laughing, as the first exclamation rises over the thrum of the crowd. A scream follows. We quickstep through the grand entryway and pass a guard as his radio crackles to life, sending him in the direction of the handbag department. Pushing through the herd of shoppers, we pile into the backseat of the waiting Volvo. For Evan's sake, the continuation of our holiday prank requires that we imagine hot pursuit. "Drive!" I command. "Drive, Ev! They spotted us!" Evan skids through the slush, driving across the current through a sea of yellow cabs.

Back at the Cowboy Bar, we relive our antics with giddy, beer-fueled abandon until we've managed to bore ourselves and no one is left nearby who hasn't already overheard our shouted repartee or still gives a damn. After a brief, deflating lull, I pimp roll over to the pay phone, pick up the receiver, call information, ask for Macy's. "Lost and Found, please. . . . Yes. . . . Thank you.

"Hello, Lost and Found? . . . Hi. I was shopping in your store earlier today, Christmas shopping, and I seem to have misplaced my bird. I wonder if I may have left it there?"

"Was it a chicken?" asks the concerned gentleman at Lost and Found. I flash to floor-to-ceiling shelves, an aviary pop-ulated by eagles and egrets, ducks, swallows, gulls, piping plovers, a bevy of doves, and our lonely chicken.

"Why, yes, it was a chicken."

"It's good you called, sir," the attendant says, brightening. "I have to close up soon, and I was about to call the ASPCA."

"Goodness. Well, I'll be right over to pick it up."

"I'll wait for you as long as I can."

"Thank you, sir. I'm coming right over." I hang up the phone and order another round. We spend the balance of the evening imagining the Lost and Found at Macy's roiling with birdlife of every description. "Was it a chicken?" one of us shrieks, whenever the hysteria wanes.

"Was it a chicken?"

Chickens inhabit a unique corner in the culture. Flightless, largely senseless, husbanded entirely for human consumption, still chickens are a potent, if unspecific, symbol of the country's agrarian past, the myth of it at least. It's the official bird of contemporary domestic fetishists. There may no longer be one in every pot, but there's a chicken in every Williams-Sonoma catalog. Martha Stewart tended a flock of chickens at her manse in Connecticut for more than a decade. She has periodically updated readers on the flock's welfare, most recently announcing in her magazine the arrival of a brand-new crop of Cuckoo Marans, a French breed known colloquially as the chocolate egger; Mottled Cochins, originally from China and described by her publication as good, gentle mothers; and to finish the collection, the extremely attractive show breed, "one of the prettiest chickens in the hatchery," Porcelains.

Only dogs have been bred for their flesh as domesticated animals longer than chickens. All these handsome, collectible birds descend from a common ancestor, *Gallus gallus*, the marauding scavenger of the bamboo forests in Indonesia. The rooster's fabled cock-a-doodle-do is not the quaint bugle call to, daily, wake the countryside, but rather what evolutionary biologists call a mate investment. It is a much sought-after anti-predator alarm call—and thus, the louder the call the better.

A hen starts her egg career at about twenty weeks. If she's healthy, and regardless whether a male bird is around to fertilize her eggs, she will lay one just about every day. As far as I can tell, for a hen, laying an egg is a fresh experience every time she starts the project. Stewart calls her chicken coop the Palais du Poulet. By all accounts, and just as we've come to expect, Stewart's coop is a spectacular affair.

Stewart is a busier person than I ever hope to be, and still, it is reported, she greatly enjoys watching her chickens wrangle table scraps, especially spaghetti. Stewart has credited the subtle shades of the eggs that her flock produces for some of the more than 250 colors of paint in Martha Stewart Everyday, the home-decorating line she markets through Kmart.

When my friend Sarah installed a small flock of chickens in the backyard of her Brooklyn Heights town house, she called excitedly, soliciting advice about everything from coop construction to sanitation. I was happy to share what I knew, but during the conversation it became clear how much more I had to learn. "Oh, hang on, one more thing," she exclaimed before we hung up. "What kind of treats do your chickens like to eat?"

If it ended there, in domestic idyll, that would be one thing, but there's a dark corollary of America's cult of the chicken, and it finds adherents in the long tradition of fighting game birds.

Roy Jones Jr. cocks his right elbow, lifts his right glove almost above his head, and there it hangs, an implied threat. A challenger, experienced, respected, but fighting for his first title and untested in the looking-glass world of professional boxing, Jones has his body wide-open, exposed to James "Lights Out" Toney, a man undefeated in forty-six bouts, a man measured pound-for-pound the best prizefighter on earth. The young challenger sets his feet apart, his stance wider than his shoulders. This Las Vegas crowd is scandalized, confused. The play-by-play announcers exclaim heresy; the man's boots are both pointed straight at his opponent. Jones's left glove is cocked at his side and well below his waist. Now he's bending his knees—half squat, half pounce, all this promising that something terrible is about to happen to someone. Who, though? Leading, just so, with his face, Jones stands as if he's preparing for Toney to jump into his arms like a small child.

"His unorthodox movement and his unorthodox punches are completely befuddling Toney to this point," barks HBO ringside commentator Larry Merchant, in a masterwork of understatement.

He continues to chatter nervously, wondering out loud if this young Turk is showboating or what, and then it's all over: one, two left hooks connect with Toney's head, and Jones is only now stepping to the champion, delivering a jab with that left and then, impossibly, one and two more hooks with the same fist. Toney is staggering backward, folding like a beach chair, into a sitting position, his gloves covering, doing what they can against the avalanche of punches that does not follow so much as sweep over the champ as he falls toward the ropes in the corner of the ring. Jones is there. Hammering away at Toney's head as if he were chopping wood, walking right alongside and then beyond and away from Toney, now in a heap in the corner of the ring that, less than a minute ago, bookmakers said he owned.

Toney, who earned each of his championship fights, regains his feet almost instantly, but he isn't chasing young Jones down. Toney stands stone still in that terrible corner, waiting for the referee's ruling. The third round not yet complete and Jones has delivered a withering knockdown. Jones has already rolled away, jogging really, across center ring and to his corner beyond, his wings spread wide and low.

"He doesn't set up. Jones doesn't set things up with his left jab. That's the unorthodox part of his style. He doesn't set things up," squawks Merchant. Now, early in the fourth round, Jones disassembles Toney's defense, delivering lefts, two, three, five at a time, from every point on the compass. In his first title fight Jones is busying himself upending the One True Thing left in boxing: you have to be close to do damage. "He'll move with his feet and all of a sudden leap in with that left hook, and it's very, very effective. But again, by doing that, he leaves himself open for a split second. But so far nobody has ever been able to take advantage of it. Nobody that he's fought is so quick."

And nobody will be for years.

In his two-decades-long career Roy Jones Jr. would win fifty-four of his fifty-nine professional fights, knocking out opponents 74 percent of the time. When Jones was still a boy, he learned what no other fighter understood yet, learned how to keep his distance, learned how to close fast and with finality.

Jones learned all this from a chicken named Crazy. A game bird, his game bird, left for dead in a big-money fight when Jones was seventeen years old. The cold metal spur of Crazy's opponent was still stuck in the bird's head, straight in one side and out the other, while the apparent victor flapped and celebrated, still sewn into Crazy's head. Young Jones mourned his game bird, but as he watched, he saw what none of the grown men saw. Crazy wasn't dead. "He's alive!" yelled the teen, who was just months away from a place on the team at Seoul's 1988 Summer Olympics.

And so, according to custom, the fight, already two hours old, started up again. The spur was removed from Crazy's brain. Jones blew on the bird's neck, down the length of the spine, keeping it warm, keeping the blood flowing, until the bird's heart was again circulating fight throughout the rooster.

Raring to go again before he could properly stand, back in the ring Crazy struck and withdrew, enraging the bigger rooster, goading him, Crazy always riding that line, engaged but keeping his distance. Then the big cock, victorious just moments ago, made one mistake and was dead.

Whooping with joy, Jones grabbed up Crazy and hugged him to his chest. That's how Jones tells it, anyhow. And to watch Jones fight, it's hard to imagine any sane human mentor devising those moves. Unlike so many professional boxers, using the fight to escape the claustrophobic crush of a paved world, Jones grew up in the pine woods of the Southeast and never left them, just kept surrounding himself with more and more acres. Jones still raises gamecocks, and he never tires of their ways. Roy Jones Jr. loves his chickens.

I'll settle for like.

"Look how this rooster walks in his cage," says Jones, pointing out one of four hundred chickens as it struts across the run. "See that? It's his cage. He owns it. It's his world. Every other bird has to respect that."*

---

* Gary Smith, "One Tough Bird," *Sports Illustrated*, June 26, 1995.

It's called a lek. Male chickens congregate in leks. The lek has the specific purpose of attracting females. Though researchers continue to disagree about the specific behavioral mechanisms at work within these groups, they do agree that leks provide better opportunities for more males in a flock to breed—promoting hybrid vigor. The presently dominant "hotspot" theory asserts that rather than go it alone like male frogs, angelfish, fur seals, and of course lions, birds—and especially chickens—flock as a breeding strategy. Hens prefer to mate with attractive males, so less handsome males congregate with their more handsome counterparts, waiting patiently for a broody hen to lose her resolve and lower her standards or just make an honest mistake. Behavioralists call this strategy kleptoparasitism, but the move should be familiar beginning in junior high school and ending just about the time that hen loses her resolve and makes that mistake.

A lek is not the riotous, three-deep-at-the-bar party it could be for chickens because this congregation is governed by an extremely rigid social order known as the peck order, or more commonly, the pecking order. A linear dominance hierarchy, not at all limited to chickens, often controls the distribution of food, water, and sex among members of a species who are forced to share the same sandbox. It governs life in most social animals—fish, birds, and mammals. Unlike in a despotic hierarchy—think Saddam Hussein—each individual in a linear hierarchy holds a rank and knows exactly where he or she is located. It's pretty straightforward stuff for chickens. From moment to moment every chicken in a run knows who gets to peck him and whom he gets to peck. According to researchers, neither gender nor body weight has very much, and possibly has nothing, to do with placement in this hierarchy. Unflinching aggression and experience are the key. In the original research, conducted by the Norwegian behavioralist Thorleif Schjelderup-Ebbe, one hen in the study flock demonstrated the ability to recognize twenty-seven other individuals belonging to four different flocks, which may sound pretty impressive, but only if your junior high school didn't have a clique of Popular Girls.

Pecking order is a phrase too casually bandied about. I use it much more selectively now that I have seen its multiplier effect in action. The term has always had the giddy glow of a Warner Bros. cartoon: lots of violence but no permanent damage. I'm probably not unique in making this mistake, but in modern American middle-class experience one hears the term *pecking order* and one reflexively locates oneself right smack, well, in the middle. Watch the goings-on in a chicken run and in no time your gaze will shift from the mundane middle of the order (if you can find it in the first place) to the plight of the omega chicken. The chicken on the bottom of the order doesn't have time to consider the beneficial organizational effects on natural selection that the peck order offers, never mind a moment to compare the relative merits of the linear versus the despotic whatchamacallit.

The omega chicken is moving too fast, trying to hoover up a scrap of corn or a drop of water or grab a sideways glance at an egg vent before another member of his flock, absolutely any other member of his flock, takes a hunk out of the flesh where his tail feathers once were. The last thing on Omega Chicken's mind is the location and disposition of the alpha bird. In fact, life for Omega Chicken is so fraught with danger that he would in a heartbeat happily trade life in the chicken run for good old-fashioned despotism. When food gets scarce, as it did on occasion in my chicken run, it is pretty much all over for Omega Chicken. Because the licks he's taking minute by minute, day in, day out, are just about maintaining flock status quo. This is tame stuff compared to the abuse doled out the moment there's a hiccup in the system and the birds above him (and, remember, all of them are) get stressed in any way. It's simply a matter of time before they've worked through his tail and he's tripping on his own intestines. Why that doesn't kill Omega Chicken outright is beyond me. But he will continue trying in vain to evade the rest of the chickens in the run for hours, tripping over his guts as if his pants were at his ankles. The demise of Omega Chicken provides only a momentary lull in the violence for the birds in the run, unless his gruesome dispatch solves whatever scarcity (real or imagined) has plagued the lek. If the flock is still agitated, it has a replacement omega bird waiting in the wings. There is no election. Every bird in the run knows not only who is in the line of succession, but exactly whom he is standing next to. And if, as one omega passes, that chicken isn't standing between two other birds, he's the next designated omega.

GET OUT

|||||||||||||||||||||||||||||||||||||||||||||||

"**G**et out!" When Lisa started screaming, she was stand-ing in front of me in the hall, but now, after repeat-ing herself twice, she is in a fetal crouch, her arms covering her face. I wonder how she manages to hold herself upright crouching on four-inch heels.

"Get out!" she both begs and demands.

I step back to lean against the doorframe.

"Get out!"

I take it as a generally good sign that I am not panicking. As a rule I am overly dependent on her approval and if I even suspect that she is serious, I would already have set about dismantling The Farm.

"Get out!" Lisa doesn't often have a complete lock on her emotions. I am annoyed by how volatile she is during mildly difficult moments at home. In times of profound distress I always expected, hoped really, that she would be all business-like. It is my understanding from stories told by professional associates that while at work Lisa is steely whenever events conspire and things come apart. If she could be a little more like that around here, our home would be so much higher functioning, I muse.

"Get out!" This tantrum is unprecedented, however. Her exclamations are as regular as a heartbeat, metronomic, really. "Get out!"

"Get out!" Her voice is growing hoarse.

"Lisa?" I say, so calmly that my tone might read as condescension. "Lisa, can you hear me?"

"Get out!"

"Lisa."

"Just get out!" She finally looks up at me. Her face, not flushed as I had imagined, is pale. I was certain I'd see tears. There are none. This breakdown is not fueled by anguish. This is pretty much entirely rage. My name is not on the deed or the mortgage. Howard Hall is, theoretically, hers to decide who gets to stay, not that I think she really means to turf me out, but even as the metrics of my analysis shift, I know enough not to cede this new ground too easily. Domestic precedent is being set here and now. If I leave our home now, like this, in my filthy work clothes, Lisa dressed for corporate success, ordering me out—

"Get out!"

—I will almost certainly return. After all, I reason, if I leave, even for a day, who will feed the chickens and the rabbits? Who will muck out the cages? Who will water and weed the plants? No. If I leave now, like this, I will certainly return.

But I will leave again. Precedent will drift and become pattern. I will be a visitor in my own home, reliant on permission based solely upon what Lisa believes is sufficiently good behavior. That is no way to run a farm.

"Get out!"

"I will leave, Lisa," I hear myself say, interrupting the established pulse of her eruption. "But if I leave, I will not come back." My marital Alamo, and the tomatoes have not even flowered.

She stares for a moment, then wills herself out of her crouch. She runs her hands over her skirt to smooth it, looking through me standing less than two feet away. "Just get out," she croaks, turns on her heel, and clicks upstairs to her dressing room, where she will change out of her business rig into what we call her civvies, her civilian gear. Most days this is a moment I lament. As we rush headlong into our lives each morning, I often waste precious moments watching her dress for the life she has at the office. The authority and confidence she radiates from inside her uniform is inspiring and, simply put, arousing. Lisa's career, its requirements, are as alien to me as her childhood as a prodigy competitive swimmer. Her mother still keeps the newspaper clippings of her record-breaking victories at six and seven years old. She competed, stacking victory on victory through high school and into college, eventually earning a spot at the Olympic trials. She carries herself like a victor. Even when she's sitting on a bench at the local YMCA cheering our tiny kids through their swimming lessons, she adopts an athlete's pose, elbows lightly touching thighs, her right foot cocked away from her core as though fighting a vestigial cramp in her instep.

So, most days, I consider her disappearance into her dressing room at the end of a day a missed opportunity of some kind. Not today. If after Lisa has changed out of her uniform, she still wants me to get out, she'll tell me, I reassure myself. Right now, though, I have a few precious moments. I turn to the back door. If I am going to leave, I better make sure the chickens have enough food and water for a while. As for the weeding, I suppose she'll let me down the driveway through to the backyard if she is not around.

COLLAPSE

||||||||||||||||||||||||||||||||||||||||||||

Lisa has been planning our trip to the wedding of a young cousin. Ryan is getting married in a small lake town in Georgia, and Lisa has decided we need a long family drive together, far away from The Farm. After significant resistance from me about adding two precious days to our itinerary by driving rather than flying, I make careful arrangements for Josh and his wife, Diana, to watch over The Farm, with a promise from Caleb that he will conduct day-to-day management. As I anticipated, Lisa wins the argument in short order, though she is forced to employ her powerful and controlling and rarely resorted-to Money Trick. She expounds on the high cost of flights, tactically inserting the spiraling credit-card debt generated by The Farm into the assault like a flanking cavalry charge. If I wasn't so determined to insulate myself as The Farmer from The World, so dedicated to controlling my cultural inputs, it would be such a simple thing to submit that expense report.

Next thing I know, we're packing the car, Heath's big, fluffy, white flower-girl dress in its special box on the roof rack.

Two days later, we arrive in Georgia. Having driven the entire way, I'm exhausted and angry with the kids. Lisa bounds out of the car and runs straight into the arms of her sister, then her father, and at the same time her six nieces and nephews have rushed out to play with their long-lost cousins from Brooklyn. As just about all of them have migrated from Mississippi, Lisa feels lucky if she sees her family once a year. I am not at all secretly grateful. My family is easy. Lisa's is complex and fraught with what I believe to be a Southern Gothic temperament. They are all overachievers, extremely smart, with successful careers and supportive marriages. Lisa's big sister, Marian, is a pediatrician. Dave, her husband, is an emergency-room surgeon and a hospital administrator. I think that means he's in charge of keeping the kill ratios low, but we get along too well to talk about work. He married into the family years ago and apparently considers it his responsibility to make my immersion as easy as possible. I make this much more difficult than it should be. Dave and Marian are delightful and with two excellent children and the kind of life you imagine for yourself were you to move to Northern California for the quality of life.

Lisa's brother, Brennan, an M&A lawyer, married his college sweetheart, also named Lisa. They live in Atlanta with their four kids and are bravely battling Lisa's rare form of brain cancer, which for a year now has been stable. Lisa's mother, Elise, is the matriarch of the family, heavily opinionated, particularly about me and my career choices. Lisa loves them all intensely—more so for her absence. She left home to train as a swimmer when she was fourteen and has never been back, not really. I have still not left home. Five miles away now, Lisa and I live the farthest I have ever lived from my mother's house. My mother insists we take terrible advantage of her proximity, and we often do, relying on her for everything from child care to a quick stop for a pee on the way home from shopping.

Lisa and I have gotten by on pretty close to the bare minimum of marital interaction for nearly a month now. On the driveway, making my way between the car—still clicking and twitching—and the front door of the vacation house, I am overwhelmed by loneliness.

Lisa's father, John, greets me with a beer and a pat on the back. He's kind and good-spirited, prudent and busy— unless he's unconscious in front of the television. Lisa's adoration of John is childlike. Every morning, to hear Lisa tell it, he exhorted all three of his children to do good, avoid evil, and obey their teachers. Lisa also likes to tell a story about how, when she was growing up, her dad used to shoot the heads off water moccasins in the lake behind their house. There's more to John than Lisa acknowledges; he lives in the world and that's not precisely where Lisa locates him. Maybe that's fathers and daughters; maybe that's walking out the door to go for an especially fast swim one morning when you are fourteen and never, not really, coming home.

Thing is, I don't know much about the transition between being a child and adulthood. My parents and I grew up together. As a result of our proximity, I have an evolving understanding of them independent of the mythology of parenthood.

The preliminary events and the wedding ceremony go off without a hitch. I move aggressively to reverse that trend. It's fair to say that after that first beer John handed me on arrival, I continue to drink steadily, further deepening my isolation from Lisa. At the reception, already happily toasted and oblivious of anybody else's rate of consumption, I am struck by a petulant distaste for the wine. I share this opinion with ungoverned vitriol and further insult my host, Lisa's aunt, by not-so-secretly purchasing what I determine is a superior wine from the venue's reserve stock. In the Ryan family, uncomfortable situations such as this don't get addressed, certainly not out loud. I drink more.

Later that night, much to my frustration, the party returns to our house. I am downstairs in bed now, still drunk, angry, and unable to sleep. Lisa is trying to settle the kids because we have to leave first thing in the morning for the two-day drive back to New York. I can't stand the loud footsteps over my and the children's heads, the even louder talking and inebriated laughter, so I get out of bed, stomp upstairs, and tell Lisa's family, including her grandparents, to shut the fuck up.

Lisa's sister tries to defuse the situation, as we have adored each other since the moment we met. There's no appeasing Dumb Bear, though, and my six-foot-four-inch frame towers over her petite, five-foot-one-inch body. I point my finger at her angrily and begin to make pronouncements. I pull back, alarmed and embarrassed by my ferocity, then storm away down the stairs. Lisa, having heard my outburst, goes upstairs, and her family is cold with shock at my behavior. She apologizes, makes excuses about stress and alcohol, and everyone goes to bed. The alcohol and adrenaline take their toll, and I pass out almost immediately. The next morning I wake to hear Lisa sobbing, knocking on her sister's bedroom door.

Collapse

She wants to say good-bye but her sister is so upset about the night before that she won't face Lisa. Marian doesn't open the door but, through that door and muffled by tears, she says that I have hurt the family and she is scared of me and never wants to see me again. Lisa is shattered. She has always sought approval of me from her family. And she has often sought approval of her family from me. I have betrayed both of these efforts. Lisa shares Marian's opinion about me, but unlike Marian, Lisa has to spend the next two days sitting next to me in our car. She sits on the floor outside her sister's door for a while, calms herself, then makes her way upstairs and, fighting back more tears, apologizes once again to her family. I apologize to her father, but can't seem to face anyone else. I have loaded up the car, put Heath and Bevan Jake in their seats. They're confused and wait patiently for Lisa to say her last good-byes to her family. Lisa does not speak for the first day. On the second day she addresses me once. I have ruined her relationship with her sister, someone she cares about more than anyone else in the world outside our kids, she says. After everything else that's already happened, she doesn't know how she will forgive me, or if she wants to. I tell her that I understand.

The kids are watching movies in the backseat. Upon our arrival home, we get a call from Lisa's sister-in-law, Lisa, who consoles Lisa and asks after me, saying that she and Brennan love us and it will pass. People make mistakes and she wants to make sure that we are okay, that I am okay. Lisa talks to her for about an hour; she is reassured and reminded of my better nature. She's reminded that her family can be intimidating, and that as an outsider herself, she understands what dynamic is at play. At the end of the conversation, her sister-in-law tells her that her checkup earlier that day didn't go well, the brain cancer is back with a vengeance, and that the doctors cannot operate this time.

Realistic or not, she tells Lisa that she won't die—she has four kids and will make it for them. She believes it. We want to. They agree to talk in a few days after her latest chemotherapy protocol is outlined. Lisa is distraught after getting off the phone, but she comes to me and opens up to me. She will forgive me. We have Heath's knee surgery in a few weeks, she says, we need to be strong together.

THE PRICE OF CHICKEN

||||||||||||||||||||||||||||||||||||||||||||||||||||||||||||||||||||||||||||||||||||||||

The Stray, that mature chicken of unknown parentage that Caleb and I adopted at the Agway in Englishtown, New Jersey, turned out to be a laying hen. She is still hideous, her plumage still a travesty. When it finally grows, it does so in tussocks, and her legs and feet remain scabrous, swollen, revolting.

Toward the end of June, after some cursory book learning, I conclude The Stray may be recovering from her eighteen-month molt, a developmental stage of some laying hens that coincides with the onset of a hen's most productive egg-laying period. According to the author Gail Damerow, a fabled chicken whisperer, if a hen's plumage is lacking, supplementing the bird's diet with dry cat food should fix the bird right up, as the cat chow is high in animal protein and, unlike dog food, contains no grain. As an aside, Damerow writes that cat food also has the effect of kick-starting egg production.

As I stand on the driveway outside the barn, gripping her

masterwork, *A Guide to Raising Chickens: Care, Feeding, Facilities*, loosely in dirty, sweat-soaked hands, The Stray's potential as a laying hen opens a whole universe of possibility to me. And once eggs ("Of course! Eggs!") enter my imagination, they immediately become indispensable to the remotest possibility of the success of The Farm.

Maybe I do puzzle briefly over why eggs had never been a deliberate part of my plan before this. I don't recall it, if I did. It is possible, I suppose, that because the chickens were a stand-in for meat rabbits, I'd never really considered them as a source for eggs. But suddenly I could, on occasion, switch an omelet for roast chicken in the evenings, maybe even have lunch once in a while. Breakfast, good Christ in heaven. I could eat eggs for breakfast rather than chicken.

I retreat to the living room, trailing filth as I walk, place an order for eight juvenile, called "started" in the catalogs, pullets from an online hatchery. I fish through my pockets for some cash, hand it to Caleb, and ask him to buy a big box of Whiskas dry cat food and, looking at the position of the sun in the sky and then my wristwatch, a six-pack of beer.

I have high hopes.

My optimism is further buoyed when, only a few days after being fed nothing but Whiskas dry cat food, The Stray produces a warm brown egg. She seems as surprised by this development as I am, and while physically quite nasty, her feathers do begin to grow back in more vigorous clumps than before. The Stray is enormously productive, laying one egg a day for four days.

However, on the fifth day The Stray eats her own egg before I can get my hands on it, and the taste of her own egg has the same effect on a hen (any hen) that crack has on an addict. Apparently, nothing else will do. I don't tumble to this until four days later when the score is three to one in her favor. What ensues is a battle for every additional egg.

The Stray lives in a wire cage with a sloping floor designed specifically to preserve eggs. The theory: bird lays the egg, the egg rolls out of the cage. The bird—very dumb—never notices it was there in the first place. This cage-design theory appears to fall apart if, by some twist of fate, the hen inside it gets a gobful of her own yolk. Then she learns to defeat the design, whirling around as the prize leaves her egg vent and shattering it with her beak. The hen then snorts up whatever does not run through the wire floor onto the filthy guano tray below.

The Farm gives with one hand and takes with another. It is folly to assume otherwise; a hopeless charity case begins contributing to the project, and days later I am locked in a battle with her for every egg she produces. My first jerry-rigged layer-cage design alteration is to increase the angle of floor of the cage and then, after bitter experience, to pad the wire egg-catcher beyond the cage so that the shell does not crack as it tumbles, at speed, away from the hen inside. I get two eggs before The Stray learns to crane her neck through the same break in the wire that allows the egg to pass beyond the cage's wire walls.

I lose one more to The Stray's perverse obsession until I respond by stringing wire in the front of the cage from floor to ceiling. This rig gets me three eggs before, with a junkie's furious ingenuity, the hen learns to weave through the wires and stretch and contort her neck beyond the confines of the cage just as before. I replace the forest of wire with a sheet of mesh in the front of the cage that gives The Stray just enough room to assume the laying posture, but creates a secondary floor in the cage wide enough so that no matter how much she strains—and she does strain—she cannot reach beyond the front wall of the cage.

Two weeks later a deeply confused UPS deliveryman shows up with a cardboard carry case containing the flock of juvenile layers. At seventeen weeks old, they are on the cusp, one week away from laying one egg a day for as long as eight years. I segregate the layers and the meat birds, housing all nine in a cage meant for four full-grown birds. I figure that I'll move the layers into the coop and the run after I have harvested all the meat birds. Once in polite company, The Stray stops eating her own eggs.

Uncoupled from a world that provides two scrambled eggs on a roll for $3, I now know the true price of an egg for breakfast—one without the roll, or so I think.

I reach for the plastic Kool-Aid pitcher we use as a scoop for the chicken food, measure out an equal portion of cracked corn and pellets, and add a few handfuls of ground oyster shells. It occurs to me that though we purchased one hundred pounds of feed, we will run out of food before we know it. The greatest challenge to urban agriculture is that everything you need is sold in the country. No local pet stores carry chicken feed—this comes as no surprise but maybe the proprietors should consider changing that policy. When, eventually, I find a supplier relatively nearby, the outfit is billed as a lumberyard. It's on Rockaway Boulevard, just over the Queens border. I make the drive a few days later. The proprietor is a tall, frail man with a hound's face dominated by an impressive auburn cowcatcher mustache. He wears a plaid shirt from Sears and a trucker's cap sporting the name of his livestock-feed supplier, Blue Label. It seems that livestock supply is the profit center of what was once a considerable lumber operation. I ask Cowcatcher if he carries layer pellets and crack corn. He does not look up from the delivery receipt he is examining, simply motions through a pair of doors to a vast room at the back of the store. Most of the barn-like room is a lumber library, stocked with what looks to me like a pretty good quality selection of hardwood. Stacked in neat rows across from what lumber is left in the inventory are bags of animal feed of every description: homing pigeons and horses, rabbits and chickens among them.

I deposit a pair of fifty-pound paper sacks of feed on the counter. We make eye contact. I smile more enthusiastically than I had intended.

"You raising chickens?" Cowcatcher asks, inspecting the sacks in front of him.

"I am."

"Nearby?"

"Not so close." I'm cagey because, while it is not illegal to own chickens within city limits, as long as they are not roosters (noise complaints), I doubt it is legal to run an operation with as many chickens as I have presently.

"Oh yeah, where?"

"Flatbush." So much for discretion; I really have got to learn to shut my mouth.

"That's a hike."

"It's not so bad," I say, signing the credit-card voucher.

"Is that legal? The chickens? If you don't mind my asking."

"No. Not entirely. It's a gray area," I lie, exhaling while I hoist both bags onto my shoulders.

"You need help carrying that?"

"I'm good. Thanks."

"Well, good luck."

"You, too."

The second time I visit, a month or so later, Cowcatcher remembers me.

"The feed still in the back?" I ask.

"Yup." He follows me out from behind the counter and shadows me to the warehouse out back. "You're the one from Flatbush, right?" he asks, confident that he is correct.

"That's me."

"How're the birds?"

"Doing good. Eating a lot, though."

"They do do that," agrees Cowcatcher amicably.

"You raise chickens, too?"

"Me? Lord no! Not that there's anything wrong. Just, even if I wanted to, my wife would never allow it."

"Unh-huh." I pull two bags from a flat of twenty. There are at least eight flats of each variety of bird food. I help myself to a sack of rabbit kibble. We talk about his lumber. I remark that it looks like really good stuff. Cowcatcher asks me if I know wood. Not as much as I would like is my reply.

He nods. "Funny thing. When my partner said he wanted to start stocking feed for livestock, I thought he'd lost his mind. 'We're a lumberyard, Stan,' I said. But what the hell, right?"

"What the hell."

"Well, you know what, there are a lot of people like you in this city. Not like you, you," Cowcatcher clarified. "I mean chicken people, a lot of chicken people, and all kinds of people. I get a guy from Barbados in here. Some lady all the way from Iran. They're all buying chicken food. And you aren't the one who comes from farthest away. People come from all over the place."

"Yeah?" I say, my knees buckling under the weight as I heft all three sacks on my shoulder.

"You need help carrying that?"

"I'm good. Thanks."

"Yup," says Cowcatcher, wonder in his voice. "Stan was right, all right. Today, I'd say, half of our sales come from live-stock supplies—bowls and bridles and leashes as well as food."

"That right?"

"Unh-huh, there are a lot of chicken people in that city," he says, nodding west toward the city limits.

"Hunh," I say, signing the credit-card voucher. "It's a lot of work." I carry two of the three sacks out to the truck. I return, hoist the third bag onto my shoulder, and nod thank-you and good-bye.

"You need help carrying that?" calls Cowcatcher as I reach the front door.

"No thanks. I'm good."

"Well, good luck."

In the afternoon Caleb and I grind out most of a high-rise coop in a few hours. So that the coop takes up a minimum of the garden's square footage, we settle on an Escheresque design, a vertical coop alive with a tangle of ramps and roosts. We equip it with wheels so that it can be wheeled to and fro; the guano can thus easily be removed from underneath it. We fashion tracks for the wheels out of eight-foot-long aluminum building studs so the coop won't get bogged down in mud or said guano. It has a deeply sloping roof. Remembering that egg production is dependent on available light—we assume that maximizing natural light will positively impact the general well-being of the males—we choose opaque, corrugated plastic. To maximize ventilation we leave about one foot of the walls of the coop open below the roof, sheathing it in chicken wire. When we're done with the first phase of construction, the coop dominates the skyline, towering over the cedar fence.

At about five thirty Caleb scrubs up and gets on his bike to get home in time to tidy up and attend his bartending class. At six thirty I am putting the finishing touches on the coop. I descend into the basement to set up the table saw.

When I was a kid, my mother and Marty, my stepfather, started building a modest real estate empire in Sunset Park. The plan was to purchase nearly derelict buildings, renovate them, and sell them off. The flipping scheme fell apart quickly, after my mother, having grown fond of the houses, refused to sell them, cajoling Marty into renting them. Eventually they had acquired half a dozen buildings, and in addition to one and a half full-time teaching jobs, Marty served as the superintendent for all of the buildings. While they were acquiring this mini-empire, their children, my cousin Gabe, Josh, and any other friends looking for beer money served as the construction crew. Marty is a gifted teacher. Even as teens we had serviceable rough carpentry skills and some piss-poor plumbing techniques. We could pack a Dumpster so tight with framing timber, linoleum tile, and bathroom and kitchen fixtures that the relative density of the contents approached that of pig iron. One immutable rule on Marty's site was that, every afternoon, the tools got unplugged at four thirty sharp. There is always plenty of work to do on the job after four thirty— sweeping mostly—he would say if we protested, almost finished and wanting to conclude some daylong slog. The crew is tired and careless. This way, he argued, everybody leaves the site with all his parts still working and attached. It's a good rule. I have always followed it, until today.

Inspired by the coop design in Nick Park's animated film *Chicken Run*, I am using the table saw to mill one-eighth-inch plywood into strips to make toeholds for the door ramp when I inadvertently cut my pinkie at the second knuckle. It is almost entirely off, the joint no longer holds the finger to the rest of my hand, just dangles from a ribbon of flesh on the palm side. Bone and meat and blood—everything inside the finger a moment ago is spattered on my glasses and face, on the saw table, or in the tool's sawdust bag. I flip my hand away from my body so the limp joint unfolds, then with deliberation belying my inner panic, I flop my entire hand on top of my head and, two steps at a time (can't pass out alone in the basement, after all), ascend from the basement to the kitchen. Right hand still resting on my head, tendrils of blood leaching from my sheared, sweaty hair and running down the left side of my face, I open the freezer and scoop all the ice from the icemaker.

Living a little more than five miles from where one was born often has its advantages. I pry my cell phone out of my work pants using my left hand, holding my right hand above my head, and call Josh.

"Hey," he answers, used to calls from me for advice or assistance or a tool loan.

"I cut my hand."

"Oh, yeah?" He half laughs, grown prepared, over the years, for dramatic announcements from me that segue into vaguely amusing tales of misadventure or humiliation. He waits a moment for my response, but I'm drifting, say nothing. "How bad?"

"Finger's pretty much off."

"Oh, yeah?"

"It's wrapped in this dish towel . . . ice . . . I'm calming down now. Afraid to look, though."

"I'm coming over now," says Josh, who, an indeterminable time later, marches through the front door, down the hall, and into the kitchen and produces a few well-meaning clucks at the sight of me standing weak-kneed at the kitchen sink, covered in blood. He field dresses the mangled wound, then sets about calling all the various matrons who run our universe. From my makeshift plywood desk, still dominating the living room, he makes inquiries about the best hand surgeon in the tribe while I stand around gripping what is left of the pinkie of my right hand, primate-fear grin plastered on my face.

Not only do I not call Lisa to let her in on my little mishap, I am hoping like hell that we can get clear of the house before she returns from work with the kids. Lisa's not good with blood, certainly not lots of it. I injure myself seriously with startling regularity, and on the occasions that Lisa has accompanied me to the emergency room, her vasovagal sensitivity has required that she also be treated or tended by the staff. I have a sneaking suspicion that a nasty wound like this—especially one associated with farmwork—will not go over all that well. Just as we leave the house for the doctor's office, Lisa arrives in the limousine with Alvin, her driver, and the kids. "Lord! We're screwed," I breathe to Josh.

"No. I see an opportunity here," Josh replies.

"Hon, I've banged up my finger and I need to go to the doctor," I say through a rictus grin. "Don't worry, Josh is going with me."

"How? How bad?" she asks.

"Not too bad. With the table saw."

"Uh-oh," says Josh.

"What?" cries Lisa. "Kids, get inside! Now!"

"Can we use your car?" asks Josh, stepping next to the open passenger door of the Town Car and between me and Lisa, who is two-stepping at the curb, one step toward me, then retreating. Fingers on both hands are outstretched at her sides, flexing in disbelief.

"We really have to go," Josh urges.

"Yes, of course," says Lisa, looking at me, forlorn.

From the perch Bevan Jake has scrambled into amid the white dogwood tree on our lawn, he warbles, "Be brave, Dadda!" Then he smiles and waves theatrically. I manage to smile back.

"What have you done, Mr. Howard?" asks Alvin calmly.

"Cut it pretty bad, Mr. Hemmings," I reply, sliding across the backseat.

"Off?" asks Alvin.

"Maybe," Josh and I reply in unison. Twenty-eight minutes later, Josh ushers me through the door and into the office of Danny Fong, MD, PC. Fong's wife and daughters are out of the city; we're here because he is staying at the office late catching up on paperwork and answers Josh's phone call. "A table saw, huh? Why don't you come by the office. I'll see what we can do from here," says Dr. Fong.

Most of the lights in the office are already off, and his two assistants are busying themselves, preparing to leave for the evening. The taller of the two smiles sympathetically at me and asks Dr. Fong if she should lock the door behind her. Fong nods, then gestures for me to follow him down the hall to an outpatient surgery. Josh grabs the summer issue of *Gourmet* magazine from an end table and sits down in the near dark of the waiting room.

Dr. Fong initially reserves an opinion regarding the return to full service for the pinkie, as the saw blade blasted most of the bone below the joint, or proximal phalange, and the cartilage is shredded. Initially he talks of the possibility of a prosthetic joint and some modest hope of preserving the finger and even the slim possibility of some retained motion.

"Hey, do you mind if I ask Josh to join us?" I interrupt. "He's taken great care of me and I'd hate for him to miss the good part."

"Why don't I go ask him? You sit down," Dr. Fong says, smiling. The two return, Josh with *Gourmet*, Dr. Fong with some large hypodermic needles and what I suppose is a vial of anesthetic. "Thanks," says Josh, smiling, sardonic, and plunks himself in a plastic chair that turns out to be a front-row seat.

Dr. Fong ought never to play poker. He does not have the face for it. As he explores the extent of the damage, he alternately grimaces, clucks his tongue dismissively, sighs forlornly, and rolls his eyes in utter hopelessness. By the end of his examination I won't be surprised if he says the whole arm has to come off at the elbow. "If we have to do a skin graft, we'll need to take this show to a real operating room," he offers, both promise and threat.

Josh has been a fireman for twelve years; a hero rookie and a veteran of calls to fatal house fires and car wrecks, countless overdoses, and everything in between. Josh worked The Pile at Ground Zero for months. He never speaks of the horrors he witnessed there, and I have never asked. But this is the first summer since The Attack that the Josh of my childhood memories has been visible through the armor he erected around himself. True to form, Josh has been unflappable since the moment he walked into the kitchen and found me at the sink with my hand wrapped in a bloody towel and jammed in a slush of ice cubes and water. As I knew it would, his calm resolve has kept me moving forward, focused on the only job in front of me: getting my hand to a good surgeon. Now, less than an hour later, here we are and Josh is craning his neck to watch the surgery without blocking Dr. Fong's operating klieg lights.

I feel a hard tug. Josh sits up erect and grips the rolled-up *Gourmet*. His eyes are fixed on the acoustic tile on the ceiling, and the blood drains from his face momentarily. I am also craning my neck to watch the operation, but to get the proper presentation of the wound, Dr. Fong has me positioned in what I suppose to be a quarter nelson, my shoulder twisted at a right angle behind my back so that my straight elbow points at him and my fingers splay with the tension of the twist. I can only see hints and shadows of what is going on. An hour and a half later, over dumplings and beer at Joe's Shanghai, seven blocks away, Josh recounts how Fong had irrigated the last pieces of shattered bone from the wound. "It was crazy," Josh says, shaking his head and slurping up a pork-and-crab soup dumpling. "Fong basically jammed a clamp into the far side of the wound and pushed. The skin stretched about four times the length of your pinkie—like rubber!—and he blasted the last slivers of bone out with the irrigator."

Joe's Shanghai is a venerated mainstay of Chinatown's restaurant scene, and there is always something of a line. The tables seat ten or more, and diners are thrown together as space becomes available. We order a second plate of dumplings and a beef dish that Josh says he likes a lot. We drink a second and third beer while the other diners stare at the hand bandaged to my shoulder, the fresh iodine stains visible on my forearm below the bandaged wrist. We hail a cab and I'm home and lowering myself into bed next to Lisa by ten thirty.

"Does it hurt?" she asks without turning to face me.

"Not as much as I thought it would," I lie.

The next morning the coop still needs final touches, so Caleb, who heard about my injury, shows up before noon—early. Once simply my right-hand man, Caleb becomes both of my arms and hands and half my brain—double-checking pain-addled misdirects on my part, and we get the multistory coop fully operational.

The next day, we follow the advice of my buddy Tex, "A duck must swim," and we build the ducklings an above-ground swimming pool. They will have nothing to do with it, however. We also build the meat birds an eight-foot-long covered food trough from PVC pipe. The legs of the trough are eight-inch lag bolts, each held in place by a pair of nuts and washers. The trough takes up almost the entire length of the run. We build it in the hope that the birds will not crap where they eat with such gusto.

A transparent effort to appease my wife, craven, that's how Caleb characterizes it. All the same, the first day back to work I roll out a five-by-twenty-foot swath of turf against the southern edge of the garden. The kids love it, play house with the ducks on it every chance they get. Usually an appellation granted giant pandas, blue whales, or Asian elephants, here on The Farm the ducks are our *charismatic megafauna*, and so, more equal than others; thanks to Heath, long ago the ducks' death sentence had been commuted. When Heath fully digested the details of my plan, gleaned the true purpose of all the livestock now in residence behind her house, she called me out on the mat. "Daddy, are you going to eat all the animals?" she inquires, stern.

"Yes, honey girl, that's the plan. You can try some, too, if you want."

"No," she said, a reflection of her mother, putting an end to my foolishness.

"I'm building a farm in Brooklyn because nobody else has done this in one hundred years."

"One hundred," she repeats. "Is that a long time?"

"Pretty long."

"Are you going to eat the ducks, too?"

"Yes, hon." Resolute now. I am not sorry and I will not pretend that I am. "Thing is, I need the fat they have in them for cooking. Also, they are very tasty."

"Dad," says Heath, pausing for effect, "I'm serious. You cannot eat the ducks. You can eat as many chickens as you want, but you cannot eat the ducks. Me and Jakey play with the ducks all the time. Ducks are nicer than chickens. You eat them." She points at the riot in the run two yards away.

"I promise," I reply, with every intention of keeping it.

"You have to really promise."

"I really promise."

"I love you, Dadda."

"I love you, too, Heathy."

"I like the little black chicken, too, Daddy," she whines.

"No moaning. No more negotiations. Go on, play with your ducks."

Setting the meat birds up requires two important first

steps. First, Caleb and I built the chicken coop; now, we must set up the caponizing station. Seventy percent of our meat birds are male. Not that we have bothered to determine the sex of the chickens—we simply generated the number in conversation on the journey between the Agway and home— but we plan to act on it all the same. This means we need to castrate the birds before they find their voice. There's no way the neighbors will abide a chorus of cock-a-doodle-do on top of everything else I have put them through. That's all a capon is, a castrated rooster. Like all the other gelded males on a farm, once castrated a male chicken loses all his ambition and gets absurdly big and juicy. Of primary importance for me and the priorities of my agricultural microgeography, castrated roosters lose their voice. Unlike those of most every other livestock on a farm, a chicken's testicles do not dangle, easy prey for a pair of bricks or even a strangulating rubber band; no, rooster testicles are held internally, packed up right against the spine behind the second rib. Castration is, therefore, a surgical procedure requiring a somewhat sterile surface and an assortment of tools. As daunting as the procedure is, all the meat birds must be castrated. Once they start crowing, the neighbors will start to get pissed and Animal Control won't be far behind.

I download the instructions from the 1922 edition of Sears, Roebuck & Co.'s "Easy-On" Caponizing Set. Seven pages long, it includes six rudimentary illustrations and, on page seven, a photograph of a ten-month-old Black Langshan capon that is said to weigh a whopping eleven pounds—proof, I suppose, that the instructions work. A Nasco's Caponizing Kit is already in the mail, on its way to The Farm—such a kit typically contains scalpel, forceps, spreader, probe, needle, gland remover, confinement hooks, and cords. I ordered it yesterday and am told it will be delivered tomorrow.

I dread its arrival.

Caleb figures that the operation—which he has already threatened to be absent for—will greatly reduce the population that survives to the butchering/food stage. His initial wager is that fifteen of the twenty-five will survive long enough to be eaten; now, in light of the information about what caponizing entails and how much of it there is to be done, Caleb says he needs more time to reconsider his bet.

He needn't bother. All the literature supports his grim forecast. Even Gail Damerow, the guru of DIY poultry, is pretty cavalier about the collateral damage associated with caponizing. "If you chance to kill a bird," Damerow counsels, "don't feel bad about it—even the most experienced caponizer occasionally loses one." She warns that if while you make every effort not to kill the bird you're working on, you leave even a portion of a testicle behind in the body cavity, you will have labored in vain. This bird, a "slip," is neither capon nor cockerel; it doesn't grow fat like the gelding bird, and it will remain aggressive and make life hell for the eunuchs. Loyl Stromberg, the author of a fifty-two-page treatise on caponizing and capon management, is just as discouraging.

Caleb will have too much to do come tomorrow morning to worry about the finer points of bird castration, anyhow. Events have conspired, and between my losing the use of my right hand and my imminent departure from The Farm for nobody seems to know how long, Caleb will have to preside over the chaos. At dawn tomorrow Heath is having her knee operated on. It is still impossible to glean whether

her surgeon is skillfully limiting expectations by telling us to anticipate six weeks of immobility, or if that will really be the situation. I'm glad I never disassembled the wheelchair ramp. Lisa would have been delighted if I had taken it down and put it back up. That's make-work. No time for such antics.

The next morning Heath sits on Lisa's knee in the surgery intake room, drowning in a pair of surgery robes that fit her more like a ball gown. Dr. van Bosse, a retinue of surgical internists in tow, greets Heath and presents her with a pair of diminutive stuffed animals, one a pink elephant and the other a white mouse. "Here, these are for you, Heath," the surgeon says, his internists studying the interaction intensely.

"Thanks," replies Heath, polite but all business, trying to make sense of the scene here in pre-op.

"I'll be back in a few minutes. We're gonna do just fine together today, okay?"

"Okay," says Heath, looking up at Lisa, who nods encouragement.

"How's that hand?" asks van Bosse as he turns away from Heath and Lisa. My hand is bound up in a bandage and strapped tightly to my collarbone in a sling so that the wound hovers above my heart.

"It smarts, Doc," I reply. "Not as painful as I thought it would be, though."

"This guy cut his finger off on a table saw," he says to the internists, who perk up at the news, "what was it, yesterday?"

"Three days now."

"Right through the knuckle, isn't that something?" says van Bosse to the young, nodding doctors.

My wife, Lisa, agreed to the retasking of our backyard without much consideration. The Farm was barely up and running before she regretted that decision. After a grueling day in the corridors of publishing power, she wanted her home to be a retreat. The Farm, with its attendant filth, disorder, and tragedy, made that impossible. A master of cognitive reappraisal, her solution: stay away. As the months wore on, Mr. Hemmings, her driver, started picking her up earlier and dropping her off later. By July we were barely speaking.

This five-pound Cornish Cross meat bird registered only 1.5 pounds on the antique produce scale I relied on. This snafu pushed back the start date for my dietary moonwalk almost two weeks.

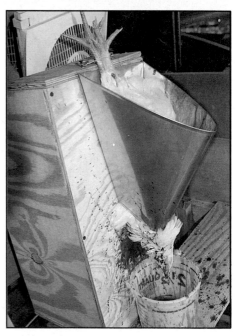

The bird's throat is cut, taking special care not to sever the spinal column and thus stop the heart. It is important to let the bird do most of the work evacuating blood from its body.

After the aesthetically superior antique failed me, a much more reliable twelve-dollar plastic diet scale was added to the tools in the abattoir.

After spending some minutes in a 112°F bath called the scalder, a chicken can be picked (no self-respecting farmer plucks anything) pretty easily. In fact, removing the majority of a bird's plumage is akin to peeling a sock off a warm foot.

When the going was good: growing in The Fields of the Lord when The Farm was at its peak were tomatoes, eggplant (various), collard greens, callaloo, cabbage, corn, beets, pumpkins, peppers, yellow squash, leek, fennel, figs, cantaloupe, and beans.

On August 13, the first tornado to strike Brooklyn in more than one hundred years traveled nine miles from Staten Island, across the strait at the mouth of New York Harbor spanned by the Verrazano-Narrows Bridge, up a glacial moraine, and struck The Farm before dying in a subway trench five hundred yards to the east. It was hard not to take it personally.

The tornado ravaged the world beyond The Farm. There were no human fatalities (or injuries) but scores of trees, including century-old ones like this, were felled, causing all manner of property damage.

After months of working closely and happily with my father on the crop that has sustained civilizations for millennia, come harvest, this is all I found in the painstakingly constructed potato drill (a quarter is used for scale here).

Preparing the First Supper in the blistering heat of Indian summer. Salt, pepper, and coffee beans were the only allowances from the world outside The Farm. *(Photo by Daniel Reese Bibb)*

Chicken feet were a central ingredient for the rich, delicious stock that most of the vegetable preparation relied on. Keeping them in a ziplock bag in the freezer was the least best storage strategy as far as Lisa was concerned. *(Photo by Daniel Reese Bibb)*

The First Supper. *(Photo by Daniel Reese Bibb)*

Initially intended as my sole source of cooking fat, the ducks became our charismatic megafauna and were spared after my daughter, Heath Ryan, negotiated for their lives. "Kill all the chickens you want, Daddy," said the then-four-year-old, "but save the ducks." My wife, Lisa, often lamented that The Farm would turn the children into ax murderers. I believe the experience provided an increasingly important understanding of where food comes from. The verdict is still out.
(Photo by Daniel Reese Bibb)

"Stupid, more like," I say, trying to shift the focus off me and back onto Heath. Lisa scowls. I am upstaging my own daughter.

"You take care," says van Bosse, off to greet the rest of his surgical calendar.

Van Bosse returns a few minutes later. Heath's gurney is in the offing, attended by members of van Bosse's surgical team. Lisa regards them with dread. They smile back benignly. "Hi there, darling," says van Bosse, his preternatural cheerfulness spiking. "Hey, have you named your animals yet, Heath?"

Heath regards the surgeon and then the pink elephant and the white mouse. She furrows her brow, never more serious, and looks right at van Bosse. "We don't name our animals."

Lisa and I while away the morning, drifting like wraiths over the land, from the waiting room to the cafeteria, to the front steps and then back to the waiting room. We happen to be floating near the exit to the surgical suites when the doors automatically open and Heath calls to us from the end of a long hallway. She is grinning wide and so is van Bosse. "It went better than I could have hoped," the surgeon explains. "My guess is she will be up and walking in a soft cast tomorrow, and out of that by the end of the week."

Lisa and I forget ourselves momentarily, hug passionately. The moment passes quickly. Van Bosse clocks it, but it does not register on his face.

I meet Robert Lee O'Neill at a birthday dinner for a member of the documentary-film crew I worked with. Still taken with the brutality of my accident and what I consider to be

its novelty, I have spent weeks recounting the event to anyone who will listen. O'Neill owns a ranch, what passes for a
family farm, in Almeda, Texas, so I assume a kinship and am
overcome by a desire to impress him. O'Neill listens patiently
while I tell the story of my pinkie, using the bent and swollen
digit as a baton. O'Neill is gracious and says he knows how
much that kind of thing can hurt, explaining that some years
ago, while helping out on a neighbor's ranch, he crushed all
four fingers off his right hand while swinging a fence gate
shut. He recalls wrapping his hand—both of his hands look
as if they could still crush a soup can—in a rag, then scrambling to retrieve his fingers from the dust, before rushing off
to the doctor. "The doctor managed to put all three of them
back on without too much fuss at all," he says, clearly still
grateful and a little bit surprised.

"Three? Why didn't the surgeon reattach all four?" I ask.

"The dog beat me to the fourth one back in the stockyard,"
says O'Neill, grinning widely; you win some, you lose some.
"Dog grabbed it up and ran off and ate it behind a cotton
tree."

"You kicked that dog?" I ask rhetorically.

"Nope. Not at all. He was just doing what dogs do."

I nod, pretending to be much wiser than I am. In the
days that follow, the way you do when you join a population you never gave much thought to before, I start to notice
how many broken hands there are in the world. I never brag
about my finger again after that night, not really. Never mind,
then, about price supports and countless agricultural sub-
sidies (both aboveboard and way below) imposed to close
the million-dollar gap between what a chicken costs to make
and the dollar or so a pound that Americans are willing to

pay for it; banish concerns about a looming trade war with China over control of the market for chicken feet. For a few weeks I was certain something momentous had happened to me. I was wrong. I have simply joined the fraternity of old men with gnarly fingers. That is the real price of chicken.

Rabbit Season

IIIIIIIIIIIIIIIIIIIIIIIIIIIIIIIIIIIIIIIIIIIIIIIIIIIIIIIIIIIIIIIIIIII

I still blanch when I recall my behavior among Lisa's family in Georgia, but I have, for the most part, stopped fretting about the fate of my finger. It aches continually, but the shooting pains are gone. While I have been busy disrupting the foundations of my life the garden has turned a corner.

- Tomatoes—are a bramble of robust leaves and branches with fruit aching to ripen.
- Eggplant (various)—pathetically spindly after a life spent seeking more than partial sunlight; the rain has toppled half.
- Collard greens—broad fans of vegetable greedy for space and sunlight.
- Callaloo (Caribbean varietal spinach)—supple delicate leaves and tendrils holding their own against the collards, but not without our help.

219

- Cabbage—never took hold; clearly sun-starved, the plants' hardy stems never developed a convincing ball of leaf.
- Corn—chest high, with some signs of life in the narrow cobs.
- Beets—the greens are convincing, though I have my doubts about the size of the tuber, but there is still some time.
- Pumpkin—plenty of plant; but after an exciting display of blossom, the plant seems to lack all ambition.
- Peppers (various)—the grow boxes in the front yard have been a great success. The plants are strong and the food grows quickly now.
- Squash (various)—there is not a weak sister among the half-dozen plants I put in. Each has produced food and, as long as I keep the food staked up off the wet earth, grows well.
- Leek—certainly wispier than any I am used to buying, but pungent and flavorful all the same.
- Fennel—the bulb is robust, the stalks a little spidery, but the feathery leaves are delightfully fragrant.
- Fig—the limbs are not even remotely robust and it is already producing fruit.
- Herbs (various)—fighting for every ray of sun under the aggressive thicket of tomatoes, but doing okay, considering the neighborhood's aggressive ways.

- Cantaloupe—busy creeping across the lawn,
  I wish it would put as much energy into fruit
  production as land acquisition, but its aggressive growth stops passersby in their tracks.
- Beans (various)—also struggling in the
  shadow of the tomatoes, but the food is
  clearly following close behind the blossoms.
  If they keep this up, these plants will produce
  enough food for at least one meal.

Surveying the garden it seems possible that, when the time comes, if harvested strategically, there will be enough food to sustain me. Suddenly it seems possible that the worst is behind us on The Farm.

Doe #4 kindled ("gave birth," to nonrabbit folk) on Sunday. In the morning I clear eight stillborn, underweight rabbits from the maternity ward, and my mood is dark enough to seriously consider rolling the hutch into the middle of Coney Island Avenue and setting it ablaze. I guess I got busy, because the hutch and the rabbits were still in the barn in the evening when Juan Carlos Lindé, a friend from Argentina—now living in Berlin—whom we are paying to do the plastering and painting on the third floor, a job I had promised to do some months ago, so he can make the money he needs to buy a new surfboard and return to Germany to find a local girlfriend before the notoriously drab and rainy Berlin winter sets in, remarked, "Hey, you have baby rabbits!"

"No," I reply. "The doe had eight stillborn overnight."

"You have baby rabbits, Manny. Lots of them, and most of them are moving," says Juan casually, drawing on the cigarette he had left the dusty confines of the third floor to enjoy.

Sure enough, eleven more rabbits are going cold on the floor of the wire cage while Mom stands by watching. This is her first litter, and my brief experience and casual book learning suggest that she probably won't make any effort to keep them alive. It's not all that hard to empathize after she gave birth to an apparently unheard-of nineteen kits in less than twelve hours. I place the kits in the kindling box in the vain hope that this action might kick-start some maternal instinct. I check the food and water levels and close the garage door for a full day to see if, undisturbed, she does her maternal portion. Twenty-four hours later, six are alive. There is some evidence that she entered the kindling box (adult-rabbit poop), but no suggestion that she is feeding them. Four of the last six starve in a few days. I crush the remaining pair to end their blind suffering and their grotesque, hopeless mewling for nourishment.

It might be one of the only qualities rabbits share with human beings, but some rabbits are just not natural mothers. The truth is, I'm not helping matters at all. I was standing two feet from her when Sugar Ray's randy bucks impregnated her; still I miscalculated the due date of Doe #4. So, when she finally has her first litter, I have not yet built the all-important kindling box, the vessel in which baby rabbits are stored and weaned. All the literature makes it clear that a box must be introduced to a pregnant doe well in advance of the birth so that she will have time to build a nest by filling it with fur. The box has precise specifications, and these are magnified when the doe weighs twenty pounds.

After discovering the newborns, I scramble to build a box. In my haste I use standard kit box measurements for a standard size rabbit. The miscalculation has disastrous results. The box is too small. Doe #4 cannot get in it to feed her brood, and the newborns can scramble, still blind, out of the box and around the cage.

The logistics of keeping track of her first litter prove over-whelming, and not being a natural mother, and not getting any help at all from me, she panics. This is where the com-monalities between rabbits and people end. Rabbits don't turn to drink or call to yell at their own mothers about certain insidious, subtle, repeated cruelties or congenital deficien-cies. Oftentimes when a mother rabbit panics, she simply eats her offspring. I haven't seen it done since my sister raised rabbits when we were kids, but I have read a fair bit about it recently and quietly dread the possibility. Lisa certainly has never considered such infanticidal ticks among livestock. Stealthy, desperate for a break, I recalculate the measure-ments of a new more effective kit box and gather the lumber.

One Saturday in July, I take a planned break from The Farm, the result of my and Lisa's first serious discussion of what she describes as my "behavior." I put Bevan Jake on the back of my bike and we pedal off to Coney Island to watch the Mermaid Parade. Hoping for a mother-daughter bonding moment with the rabbits—it's gotta be good for something—Lisa takes Heath to visit the baby rabbits that Doe #3 has recently birthed. Only moments before their visit, the doe sets about destroying the kits in her first litter, crushing two and tearing the head off a third. Seeing the carnage, Lisa pushes Heath from in front of the cage, but Lisa's retching makes it clear to our little girl that something is terribly wrong.

After the Mermaid Parade massacre, word begins to seep

through my family about the crisis in my marriage. While walking the dog one evening, I receive a call from my father. He is concerned about me—about Lisa and me—and he blames himself. "I feel terrible about this whole rabbit thing," he says. "I should have told you how difficult it is to raise and breed rabbits. I know, you see. I worked on a farm as a child after the war. I should have talked you out of it. I should not have allowed it. I feel responsible."

"Dad? Please. The rabbits were my idea."

"But I knew better and I encouraged you."

"They are pretty impressive rabbits, Dad."

"They are big, aren't they? Twenty pounds. Amazing."

"You never could have talked me out of it. This isn't your bad. It's not on you."

"I should have tried. I know about these things."

We say good-night, but he is still in a lather. I learn after returning home with the dog that he called the house and spoke with Lisa before speaking with me. "Your father called," says Lisa without looking away from *Law & Order: SVU*. "He told me the rabbits were all his fault. Says you could not have known what to expect."

"I know," I reply, stunned that he'd called Lisa. He and I typically use the evening dog walk to catch up on goings-on at The Farm. "I told him he couldn't have talked me out of it," I muse, getting sucked into the rerun procedural on the television.

"I told him the same thing," says Lisa, eyes glued to the set.

"He's really worried. Thinks our marriage is heading for the rocks," I say through a half smile, thinking of my reliably melodramatic father and how regularly he switches his hobby-horses of woe.

"Isn't it?" says Lisa, TiVo-ing through a commercial.

The Voice from the Whirlwind

||||||||||||||||||||||||||||||||||||||||||||||||||||||||||||||||||||||||

Thunderclaps and the flash of lightning wake me at six twenty. As usual, whenever the weather is bad, my first thoughts are of The Farm. It's been unbearably hot and muggy for almost a month now, but a heat wave that descended over the Eastern Seaboard two days ago has made everyone nostalgic for those comparatively mild days. The heat has not been the principal challenge to my crops; rather, it is the unseasonably wet growing season. More punishing rain is bad news.

During the night a summer storm system spawned by this heat wave moved east out of Pennsylvania, gathering strength and dumping rain as it passed over New Jersey. At this hour the sun should be visible above the houses to the east, but it is still dark outside. This storm has a violence that all the others before it have lacked. The rain hammers the windows of our second-floor bedroom at a right angle. Rather than swaying in the wind, the trees on the block that I can see through the murk are all stressed in the same direction, showing the pale undersides of their leaves. Rather than gusting, the wind is a sustained wave. The air feels different, hollow somehow. As I stand at the window, the predawn light starts to struggle in the east. Brightening now, the sky is green; at first a drab olive and after a short while what Crayola crayons calls a Luminescent Asparagus. The rain strikes the bedroom windows as before, and the wind roars and rattles the panes. Lisa, awake well before me as usual, abandons her shower in the upstairs bathroom in a hurry after a thunderclap sounds as if it came from inside our chimney. Her hair bound in a white towel, turban-style, on the way down the stairs she wraps a pale blue silk robe around her wet nakedness. With her eyes she asks if the children are sleeping through the storm. I nod and, as thunder rolls through the house again, shrug.

I pad down to the kitchen. My routine during any rainstorm is to start a foul-weather damage assessment: ignite coffeemaker, query weather.com, and undertake an underpants inspection of the Fields of the Lord (paying special attention to issues of drainage). This morning I make it only as far as Step Two. "A tornado will strike the Flatbush area of Brooklyn at 6:40 a.m." That is the unqualified pronouncement from the Severe Weather Desk of the National Oceanic and Atmospheric Administration. In fact, by 6:22 the twister is alive and has already struck Livingston on the north shore of Staten Island.

I only hear the forty-foot hemlock tree in the Feders' yard next door split in two. Its massive trunk tears twelve feet above the ground and would have free-fallen onto our garage had it not first sheared the gutter off the third floor of our house. Taking two stairs at a time to the picture window on the second-floor landing, I look out over the foliage of the giant fallen conifer now settled across the barn/garage and the back porch. While I'm still inspecting the damage from the first felled tree, with a tremendous crack of splitting wood a secondary limb from a century-old Norway maple in the yard of our neighbors on the northeastern side of the fence blows down, clears our fence, and crushes the Back Forty, the most productive quarter of my vegetable garden. The limb collapses the thicket of tomatoes, snaps the young fig tree in two at the soil line, pulverizes a majority of the collard greens, buries the callaloo, and splinters the roof of the high-rise chicken coop. My wristwatch—set ten ineffectual minutes ahead—reads 6:54 a.m.

Five months ago, when all this started, I would have launched an immediate and manic effort to rescue and repair every corner of my shattered farm. March seems like a long time ago, this morning.

The sick, green sky brightens, the howling wind dies down, and the punishing rain relents. From the second-floor window I watch the scattered chickens regroup, roosting in the dense foliage of the splintered hemlock. I lope back downstairs, poke around a pile of laundry, searching for my filthy work pants. No, this morning, before heading out the back door and tending to The Farm, I walk out the front door and start pulling felled tree limbs out of the road and off the neighbors' cars.

Since 1971 tornadoes have been classified using the Fujita scale, or F-scale. Prior to Professor Theodore "Ted" Fujita's work, quantifying a tornado's strength was impossible because the more powerful ones destroyed everything in their path, especially the delicate anemometers used to measure wind speed. Even less powerful twisters come on so quickly that it is nearly impossible to set up the weather tools that might measure them. What's more, most tornadoes are such brief events that meteorologists don't know they have struck until they are gone, making technology such as Doppler radar useless. Fujita addressed the problems of tornado measurement by examining and categorizing the damage each funnel cloud leaves behind.

The Fujita scale gauges storm-damage severity, then extrapolates the wind speed in the twister from the debris at the scene. A storm that causes light damage to chimneys and broken tree branches is given the rank F-0, with winds judged to be between 40 and 72 mph. Storms causing moderate damage on the ground, ones pushing mobile homes off their foundations or flipping them over, get an F-1 rating, with winds assumed to be between 73 and 112 mph. An F-2 generates considerable damage: mobile homes are demolished and trees uprooted by winds between 113 and 157 mph. Severe damage, such as roofs and walls torn down, trains overturned, and cars thrown around, is caused by winds as strong as 205 mph, earning an F-3 rating. The killer storms (F-4 and F-5) cause what is classified as devastating violent damage. Winds whipping at 315 mph level well-constructed walls, tear homes from foundations carrying them considerable distances, and pick up and toss cars, often hurtling them hundreds of feet at hundreds of miles per hour.

After striking Livingston, our F-2 tornado tears up trees in the Staten Island neighborhoods of South Beach and Fort

Wadsworth directly under the Verrazano-Narrows Bridge and heads east across the Narrows. It strikes Brooklyn as the first such storm to hit the borough since 1899, and it makes landfall at Seventy-fourth Street and Shore Parkway, the precise location of "Uncle Tune" Bergen's farm. Heading northeast packing 135 mph winds, the whirl has no mobile homes to savage, so tears the roof off the car dealership, Bay Ridge Nissan, at Fifth Avenue at Sixty-sixth Street.

At the very moment I am pulling the curtains from in front of our bedroom window, the twister is ripping the face from a row house on Sixty-second Street at Sixth Avenue. As the twister veers east through Leif Ericson Park, it uproots half the trees. At Fifty-eighth Street the winds are 110 mph; they have slowed, but the twister is still powerful enough to tear roofs from eleven houses on one block as it begins to climb the terminal moraine on which Sunset Park is built, shattering windows with debris and shifting cars out of their parking spaces into the street and onto sidewalks.

It skitters along Caton Avenue, reaching Coney Island Avenue with enough strength to topple thirty century-old trees, blocking streets and crushing cars all around our home. The twister rains debris on the tracks of the Q and D trains in the subway trench at East Eighteenth Street, and then, nine miles away from where it was born, and just five hundred yards beyond The Farm, our tornado vanishes.

All the earth's weather occurs within the troposphere, a six-mile band between the earth's surface and the atmospheric lid known as the tropopause. Within this band the air is dense enough to hold moisture. The rapid exchange of this moisture is the source of the planet's most dramatic weather.

Never mind how varied the planet's climate is, never mind

that temperatures range more than two hundred degrees, or that humidity ranges from zero to 100 percent; still, with all this diversity, the atmosphere unceasingly seeks equilibrium. Warm air rises. Cold air sinks. Dry air rises. Moist air sinks. As they do, static air, air closer to equilibrium, flows in to fill the voids the more dynamic air leaves behind.

Cool air sinks and increases in pressure (just as water becomes denser—solid, in fact—when it turns to ice). When falling cool air reaches the earth's surface, it washes out over the landscape, pushing static air ahead of it. Wind is nothing more than air moving from an area of high pressure to one of low pressure. An otherwise unremarkable weather front grows and becomes a thunderstorm if the conditions persist while ever more dynamic air replaces static air.

A cloud is born when moist air is forced upward and cools to a point where it can no longer hold water vapor; that vapor condenses to form minute water droplets. One of the primary ways that clouds are differentiated is by their altitude. High-altitude clouds—*cirrus, cirrocumulus,* and *cirrostratus*—reside between three and seven miles above sea level. *Altostratus* and *altocumulus* are in the midrange, lie between one and a half and three miles above the sea. The low-lying *stratus, stratocumulus, cumulus, nimbostratus,* and *cumulonimbus* are where all the action is. Their bases hang less than one and a half miles above sea level.

Thunderstorms that create twisters can be caused by dramatic weather such as hurricanes, but just as easily by simple low-pressure systems. Typically a thin layer of warmer, drier air gets jammed up between cold, dry air of the upper reaches of the troposphere and warm, humid air sitting on the earth's surface. This sliver of warmer air, sandwiched as it is between the dynamic weather and the cold air above it, serves as a cap on the storm; it both increases the heat and humidity of the air below it and regulates growth of the storm below it. It usually contains a storm long enough for it to collapse in on itself.

The only opportunity a thunderstorm has to become a tornado occurs when that cap cracks, slammed by the arrival of a strong front of upper-level air disturbance. Once the cap is cracked, the warm air in the storm column soars upward through the rupture—sometimes as high as fifty thousand feet at speeds as fast as 150 mph. As this air rises into the upper atmosphere, it expands in the reduced air pressure, cooling as it does so, making the moisture it holds condense and form rain and hail. The storm continues to rise. In stronger storms, as the column rockets upward, the rate at which this transfer of potential (latent) energy becomes kinetic (heat) grows exponentially. At some point the vertical column meets an upper atmospheric wind, which pulls the top of the storm with it, creating the signature anvil cloud of a severe thunderstorm. A severe thunderstorm can become a tornado if the column contains low but persistent winds that rotate the column counterclockwise. The rotating column (a mesocyclone) is drawn down to earth by moisture-laden air. As it does, it is again compressed in the denser air at lower altitudes, and as the column narrows, it rotates faster (just like the whirlpool at a bathtub drain). This entire process can take less than ten minutes.

Still, 999 in 1,000 thunderstorms collapse in chaos. But that one whips itself into that perversely regimented, closely contained weather system: the tornado.

Some tornadoes touch the ground with an impact zone

as wide as two and a half miles; others—some very small to begin with, some savage behemoths already beginning to die—can have a footprint just seven feet wide. Most are no more than one hundred feet wide on the ground. The storm's intense focus is what makes a strike seem so personal.

When a hurricane rolls in, entire communities, huge swaths of coastline, suffer. But when a tornado strikes, it can destroy a home, kill everyone inside, and the neighbor only forty feet away might feel no effect, only hear the twister as it passes by. The individualized havoc reaped by a twister makes the storm so sinister. Hurricanes are introduced to their victims via the media long before charging into them from over the ocean or a gulf. Tornadoes are often gone long before the media or most anybody knows they were there. Twisters don't get names. The twisters that live on in memory are known only for the communities they destroy.

The United States has seen more than one thousand tornadoes a year since 1990, when NOAA began keeping records. Tornadoes strike America more often than any other country in the world. Still, until August 8, 2007, when our tornado crossed the Narrows, a twister had not struck Brooklyn in 108 years. Our tornado lays waste to my lonely little farm just one week before the planned start date of my reliance on it as my only source of food. But the horrible twister is just one more horrible thing that has happened since early last spring when I first put shovel to earth.

It won't be the last.

As bad as it is on The Farm, our tornado has done much more damage on the street in front of Howard Hall. Before I conduct a closer assessment of the damage to The Farm, Lisa, the kids (still clad in pajamas), and I take care of the neighbors. Five trees have come down on our block alone. (Later, police officer Malloy from the Seven-Oh says Westminster Road fared pretty well compared to the four surrounding blocks, especially Rugby Road, where the funnel cloud seems to have traveled down the middle of the street, uprooting or tearing apart every tree. Strangely, the side-view mirrors on the cars parked on the west side of the street are flattened against the cars, while on the east side they are popped out and away from the chassis.) Our block may have been spared the full brutality of the storm; still, five cars are total write-offs, one ornate front porch is crushed, and the top of the street is blocked by a felled one-hundred-year-old elm. Across the way, a birch has been blown down onto Walter and Kate's front porch. Like some Mesolithic spear, a branch from that birch as thick as my forearm juts from the passenger door of Walter's shiny, new black Volkswagen Golf. We both stand by for a moment completely still, then, shaking himself from his actuarial trance, Walter asks earnestly, "My God, Manny? How is your farm?"

"Shit, who cares? Don't worry about that now, Walter. What're you gonna do about your car?"

"Yeah, how're the chickens?" calls Peter from where his brother John's car is parked, the hood stoved in by a smaller tree.

"They're in Al and Jane's hemlock." I shrug.

We set about cutting and moving all the branches we can into one pile on the west side of the street. After three hours, the neighborly work done, I grimace. It's time to return to the ruin of The Farm. An agrarian Alice, I pick my way gingerly through a portal in the tangle of hemlock branches that now bisect The Farm. Yesterday, the Fields of the Lord; today, some of the chickens are picking their way about among the mangled crops. The tomato forest, once a barely manageable tumble, is a heap. The collards are blasted as though by a spectral tantrum. One variety of eggplant escapes unscathed—a four-inch tree limb rests just above the plants. Amidst the wreckage, I now understand: the results of the terrifyingly alien, excruciatingly intense, occasionally terribly hard work of the spring and summer, by its relentlessness alone, affirmed me as no other task has.

- Tomatoes—planted in what turned out to be the most productive corner of my forty-by-twenty-foot lot. A twelve-foot-long tree limb has damaged every plant.
- Eggplant (various)—pathetically spindly after a life spent seeking more than partial sunlight; the rain has toppled half.
- Collard greens—vigorous and greedy for sunlight. Two-thirds of the plants have been uprooted by the branches and foliage of the fallen tree limb.
- Callaloo (Caribbean varietal spinach)—one-half of the plants flattened by the tree limb, but not snapped; might be salvageable if staked before the sun gets too hot.
- Cabbage—gangly and bug-eaten, these heads are as hard to imagine eating as they were before the storm, but undamaged by it.
- Corn—windblown and beaten by rain, every plant is standing at a forty-five-degree angle.
- Beets—the tuber never grew bigger than a

large marble, and now I'll be lucky if the leaves live long enough to eat any of the plant at all.

- Pumpkin—drowned.
- Peppers (various)—like all the other plants in the front yard, entirely unaffected.
- Squash (various)—drowned.
- Leek—windswept, but fine.
- Fennel—discovered undamaged under hemlock trunk.
- Fig—torn in half by tree limb. Two figs already ripe in the dirt (I brush both off on my pants and eat them immediately).
- Herbs (various)—starved for sun by tomato plants. Hopeless.
- Cantaloupe—still visibly crawling across the lawn in the front yard, still no sign of fruit anywhere on the vine.
- Beans (various)—drowned.

As I survey the damage, it seems improbable that there is enough food here to sustain me. But, as has happened over and over through the spring and into this unseasonably wet summer, after every setback my spirits rebound. The motivating mantra was always, Well, now the worst has finally happened.

Now it finally had.

The tornado wiped out the corn, the squash, the pumpkin, half the eggplant, most of the beans, and the fig tree. Of course, some failures weren't the tornado's fault. The cantaloupe never developed the slightest hint of fruit. The cabbage always looked dreadful—sinister, spindly foliage from an episode of the original *Star Trek*. The storm left the tall, dark green potato plants leaning, like the corn, at forty-five degrees, but they are already starting to right themselves in the bright sunshine. I am afraid to take a census of the potato drill, but continue to hope that beneath these robust stalks waits my caloric safety net.

As of today I know what I will be eating: a dinner of chicken, tomatoes (some fresh, some stewed today and stored), and various hearty greens, such as collards and callaloo, and a breakfast, God willing, of a single egg, maybe two.

The potato drill—sixteen by three by one feet of rich black earth—is unaffected by the tornado and, in all likelihood, is brimming with at least two hundred potatoes. This is my anchor crop. As long as potatoes are in my drill, I will be fine. And how hard could it be to grow a potato?

The wind has died down and the temperature and the humidity are now spiking. The chickens scattered in the fallen hemlock still need to be rounded up, fed, and watered.

So, just as I have done for 172 days, I work. The chickens are not at all motivated to quit the hemlock for the present, so the first project is to saw the maple branch into pieces small enough to lift off the crops and carry out of the field. At its widest, the branch is as thick as my thigh and extremely heavy. There will be lots of little pieces of wood. After that I'll need to try to stake the plants to give their trunks a chance to heal.

I lean into the day, and as I do, Wendell Berry speaks. *When one buys the farm and moves there to live, something different begins.* His voice is carried, as usual, on the lightest breeze. An extended pause—just wind in the branches above—then, again, that voice: *One's thoughts begin to be translated into acts. Truth begins to intrude with its matter-of-fact. One's work may be defined in part by one's visions, but it is defined in part too by problems, which the work leads to and reveals. And daily life, work, and problems gradually alter the visions. It invariably turns out, I think, that one's first vision of one's place was to some extent an imposition on it. But if one's sight is clear and if one stays on and works well, one's love gradually responds to the place as it really is, and one's visions gradually imagine possibilities of the highest order thus come within reach: what one wants can become the same as what one has, and one's knowledge can cause respect for what one knows.*

I stand up from the shovel I am working and look to the sky, now a brilliant cloudless blue, while I am listening to Berry. I can see Lisa watching me from the window of her second-story dressing room.

A few hours later, Lisa is standing alone at the top of the driveway, watching the kids play in the tumbledown trees on the empty street, when a police officer arrives. As Lisa backs down the driveway ahead of him, slowing his progress in the vain hope that I will be able to hide all the contraband livestock in the extra seconds she is providing, the officer explains that he wants to make sure we are okay, says he is going house to house through the neighborhood, trying to assess damage to prioritize the work of the city's emergency-response teams.

Lisa has a morbid fear of the police. So, whenever we are out and about and I am behind the wheel, she announces the presence of every patrol car she sees as though the police, guns drawn, intend to pull us over on sight and remove us from our car.

This is an interesting reaction from a white woman raised in an upper-middle-class home in Jackson, Mississippi. Most of the time I respond to these panicked announcements by telling her that patrol is a police officer's job. Only by patrolling can the police perform their duty to protect and serve the community. Protect and serve, I often repeat for emphasis.

So when the police officer enters our driveway, at the end of which is my unambiguously illegal agricultural experiment, I know that, had she been born with even the most modest flight instinct, Lisa would have vaulted the Feders' fence and run until she could not take another step. Lisa holds her ground, but she can only be half-listening to the officer because through the thicket of the Feders' fallen hemlock where I am standing, the din of nervous chickens and aroused young ducks is nearly deafening. The officer must hear this chorus, too. I suspect he has other things on his mind, though. "We're fine. Thank you so much for checking, Officer," she says, her extremely charming, aristocratic Southern drawl lubricating and elongating every syllable.

"You have a tree down," the officer replies, half question, half statement of fact.

"Oh, it's nothing. There is no serious damage to the property. Nobody is hurt," she assures the cop, walking past him toward the top of the driveway. "But thank you so much, Officer. We really are the lucky ones. The real damage is there across the street." She's trying to interest him in Walter's travails or Peter's, or anybody's. "There's all kinds of damage: property, cars, sidewalks. I think that porch over there might be just about ready to go. Can you see? Just there."

My flexible regard for the absolute rule of law—after all, no one citizen can reasonably be expected to obey all the laws all the time—usually makes it difficult for me to empathize with Lisa's inability to distinguish between the severity of one crime and that of another. I am probably less supportive than I should be. But I do appreciate that, for Lisa, when a cop shows up on our driveway headed for The Farm, we might just as well be cultivating high-grade hemp and harboring fugitives on the tiny plot behind our house as growing collards and raising ducks.

When she returns without the cop, she grimaces shyly. Is Lisa mugging for me? Flirting? The smile was one I had not seen for some time. It was hard to know for sure. She is standing still, rubbing her palms on the back pockets of her cutoff jeans. "Do you want to come inside and have a cup of tea, honey?"

"Sure."

It never once occurred to me that Lisa might give my farm and me up to the police. This is an assumption, Lisa tells me, only half-joking, after we have made love for the first time in months, I should not have made so freely.

Still, something changes between us after the tornado. We aren't fixed, the two of us, far from it, but we are suddenly no longer living parallel lives. Not for now, at least.

Not until months later does Lisa recall the moment when she turned around on The Farm and explain why she led the cop back up the driveway. "It wasn't until I watched while you walked into your ruined garden, until I saw you standing in the middle of the wreckage and then you just start working, pulling the place together, saving what you could, just tossing aside all those destroyed plants that you had worked so hard to grow, that I really understood what all this means to you.

"It wasn't something immediate," she cautions. "I stood there at the window watching and thinking, 'We just got hit by a fucking tornado. What is he doing?' Anybody else, anybody sane, would give up, would pick up the phone, call the magazine, and explain that it was over. The tornado killed your farm.

"But that was it. Not you. I'm not saying I understand why, even now. I don't. But I did understand then, I think, maybe for the first time, how much The Farm means to you. And I am very proud of you."

YARD BIRD

||||||||||||||||||||||||||||||||||||||||||||||||

Mind like water, I am clearing the bean rows when a Rhode Island Red, finally a juvenile in full plumage, catches my attention. He stands at the water trough, head cocked, looking at me. The hot afternoon sun baking the pebbles at his feet, he is motionless, momentarily unaware of the other young roosters skirmishing around him. As I regard him, observing the farmer, it occurs to me that he could not possibly weigh a full pound. How is he ever going to grow to the required five pounds by harvesttime? "Eat," I implore him. "Eat." He twitches, blinks, and joins his comrades in the constant free-for-all that is life in the chicken run.

All that fussing burns calories, and those are my calories they are burning in an endless effort to locate themselves one bird higher in the pecking order. I buy more cracked corn, a diet of which, I'm told, puts the weight on a chicken double-quick. I consider ordering more layer cages in order to immobilize the entire flock—a multiplier effect for an all-corn diet.

Yesterday morning, the second day of being awakened at five thirty by the crowing-but-not-growing roosters, I placed the ringleaders, that impulse-purchase pair of bantams, in blackout conditions inside a cardboard box down in the basement. Then I single out for execution the three joiners, roosters exhibiting a sudden enthusiasm for crowing. The offenders are a pair of the blue Plymouth Rocks and a Rhode Island Red. This seemingly drastic measure has a context. Yesterday morning I discovered that applying a high-pressure hose to the offending birds individually does not keep the predawn racket down; in fact, quite the opposite effect is achieved.

So, this morning, as I race downstairs to The Farm to quiet the flock, I am torn between a concern that the crowing will disturb the neighbors' sleep and an abiding desire that somebody, somewhere, will, finally, after all these long months, get fed up with my antics and call Animal Control. My fantasy is that agents of the Humane Society (who for some inexplicable reason all have Geordie accents) surround the house, emergency lights flashing red and blue, sirens blaring. As I exit the back porch, members of an advance team drop me with barbs from the Taser guns they're firing and leave me hog-tied with plastic restraints, facedown on the driveway. The rest of the rescue team move in and remove the various animals to the safety of their bleak facility on Linden Boulevard. Before the team pull away from the curb, the commanding officer issues me a whopping ticket, just stuffs it in the pocket of my damp, soiled work shirt without uttering a word.

No such luck. So, now it is five forty-five, the sun is rising, and on the driveway at my bare feet I've got three cooling young, underweight roosters cut down before their prime or any real usefulness to me at all. What's a half-crazy, middle-aged urban farmer to do?

Make soup.

But first, a nice hot cup of tea. "Honey, put the kettle on!"

All my brutal efforts trying to keep the young roosters from disturbing the neighbors are thwarted when the laying hens come online. It turns out that each egg comes with its own song. Rather than using the egg boxes and roosts inside the henhouse, my birds have taken up residence in the now useless kit box built for the rabbits, using it as a communal laying box. It sits under the one scraggly bush Caleb and I spared because we imagined it might serve as a habitat of some sort. Each morning the hens gather around the straw-lined plywood egg box, about twice the size of a shoebox, with a roof over just one-quarter of it and take turns laying. A great warbling din begins as each bird heralds the laying of her egg. If a hen is particularly vocal, she is joined by the chorus, sharing the interrogative alarm because each of its members has either not yet laid the morning's egg and doesn't realize she's up next or has only now forgotten that she just completed laying her own egg. The ancient grocer's scale hanging from the ceiling in the back of the garage is a beautiful relic, one of the few aesthetically pleasing tools on The Farm. It is as stubborn as it is fetching, though. The days pass and my Cornish Crosses (the most dependable meat birds in my flock, and a favorite of the poultry industry) flourish. Confined to cages and consuming as much corn as I feed them, they certainly look like they weigh five pounds. As I peer through the fogged and fissured glass face at the stolid black needle, the news is never good. According to my venerable antique scale, the broilers are not even close to harvest weight.

One morning in early August, after a frustrating interaction between Cornish and scale, I dig a five-pound dumbbell from the back of the closet in Lisa's dressing room. I hang it from the wire on the scale. The needle leaps on tight springs across the face of the scale, settling reliably, reporting that just like the Cornish Cross that preceded it, that bright blue, rubber-coated, five-pound dumbbell weighs exactly one and a half pounds.

The time has come.

Monday, August 13, the work of the day begins in earnest. I fetch five big, fat Cornish from the prepping pen (water, no food for twenty-four hours prior) and ready them for their reward by hanging them head-down from wires bolted into the ceiling in the garage/barn/abattoir.

I prep the butchering equipment, heat the water in the scalder to 112 degrees. Ice slush fills the receiving (garbage) can. Hanging the birds upside down lulls them. These birds are the only five that have put on enough pounds to harvest. The rest are still well under the five-pound minimum. I purchase still more cracked corn to try to put the needed weight on the others.

Josh Eden, whom everyone calls Shorty, is a renowned chef I have known for more than a decade. Shorty has only just left the stable and comfortable employ of celebrity chef Jean-Georges Vongerichten's haute empire to start his own thirty-two-seat restaurant, Shorty's .32, on Prince Street in SoHo. Shorty arrives early, but demands that, before we start, we drive over to Coney Island Avenue and buy a ten-piece bucket of fried chicken. He thinks it's funny, says it's ironic. I disagree on both counts, but Shorty is raring to go, this is my first of many rounds of slaughter, and good help is hard to find.

When Shorty is finished with his lunch, I deposit the first

Cornish in a stainless-steel cone screwed to a vertical ply-wood plank on the butchering table and wire its feet to the plank. In no time it appears to completely lose consciousness. Using the sharpest, longest knife in the house, I cut its throat, careful not to remove its head completely because severing the spinal column would stop the heart from beating, leaving too much blood in the body. I let the Cornish bleed out into a plastic bucket that has an inch or two of cool water in it to slow coagulation (I reserve the blood to add to an enormous vat of chicken-shit compost I have been collecting as fertilizer in a pair of plastic garbage cans for months—but will likely never use). When the bird has bled out, I remove it from the cone, drop it in the scalder until it appears thoroughly sod-den but not long enough to start it cooking. While the first bird warms, I put the second bird headfirst into the cone. I remove the first meat bird from the scalder, hang it by its feet from the ceiling using bailing string, grasp the bird firmly with both hands, pulling toward the floor to remove all but the most stubborn feathers. In that first pass, almost all of the plumage slips off the carcass like a sock off a warm foot. "Cool!" exclaims Shorty. "Me next."

Shorty puts the knife to the second Cornish. I burn the remaining pin feathers from my bird using a propane torch, then, using a sharp filleting blade, make a single incision at the outer edge of the bird's anus (being careful to hold said anus in place so the contents of the bowel do not leach out and spoil the meat). From here I make an incision in the body cavity just long enough to insert three fingers. Then I do just that, pulling out as much of the contents of the gut bag as I can. To a bird, leaving my abattoir these Cornish Cross (averaging about four and a half pounds) weigh exactly one pound less than they did upon entering. I repeat this process until the cavity is clear of all organs (especially the digestive tract). I dunk the bird in the ice bath until the interior of the bird is extremely cold. As an afterthought I remove the head and the feet (discarding the head, but reserving the feet in the freezer for stock). Finally I bag and store the meat in the fridge for one day before roasting. I'm done with the first Cornish. Shorty has cleaned the second. So I position number three in the steel cone and draw the long blade across its neck.

By nine fifteen in the evening I'm hosing down the cement floor and brushing it with bleach. Five birds are on ice ready for roasting, with ten feet for stock.

Hopefully, not a typical day on The Farm in Flatbush. The work is rewarding, in its way. It doesn't matter if I have any enthusiasm at all for the butchering. Rewarding or not, it's necessary—central to the months of preparation that have preceded this day, and the thirty or more to follow. All the same, I do wish the work were even vaguely enjoyable. It takes hours, and while hunting with Tex in Montana I've killed much bigger animals, I am somehow not prepared for the psychological toll. Harvesting the chickens is tedious, gruesome work. When it is done, after Shorty and I have had one congratulatory beer each, and he has taken his leave, I lie down on the driveway and finish off the six-pack.

Pray for me, a sinner.

THE FIRST SUPPER

|||||||||||||||||||||||||||||||||||||||||||||||||||||||||||||||||||||||||||||||||||||

On August 15, the self-sufficiency project finally begins. As planned, the day starts with a breakfast of one egg, a tomato, and a few cups of black coffee.

The morning after I begin living off the fat of the land, I check the potato drill. I've never fully investigated how many potatoes are under the dirt, in part because I fear we may have started the plants too late, and I never wanted to know the truth enough to go rooting around in the drill unnecessarily if it might damage the crop. My father's enthusiasm and ambition for the crop never flagged. His involvement is a balm, his conviction my only source of confidence. With the potatoes, at least, we were dealing with genuine expertise—genuine and, better yet, paternal. Given how many we'd planted, I am counting on no fewer than one hundred spuds.

I pull the plywood berm away from the drill and attack the soil with a gardening fork. I hit something solid and dig for it with my hands, only to realize it is a clump of compact dirt. I repeat this futile exercise until I've gone through four cubic yards of soil: zero. Sifting through the dirt more closely, like a miner panning for gold, I score ten of the tiniest potatoes the world has ever seen. I call my father. "The potato crop failed, Dad," I say by way of greeting.

"Failed?" he splutters. "How?"

"I dunno," I whine. "But I could only find ten, and they're hardly as big as shirt buttons."

"But I was there," he says, incredulous. "We planted them together. What could you have done wrong?"

Alone again.

"Maybe it was all the rain."

"Your potatoes grew in England, Dad."

My father and mother immigrated to America, arriving in November 1963, the day before John F. Kennedy was assassinated. My father came, recruited by the navy and NASA to work on the Mercury-rocket mission. What does it say about the world that even when using an inexcusably expensive variety of artisanal, organic "seed potatoes," and having a real-life, farm-raised rocket scientist as a consultant, a farmer can't grow the one crop that has sustained even the most primitive cultures since before the beginning of recorded history?

One thing we do know, that we dare not forget, is that better solutions than ours have at times been made by people with less information than we have. We know too, from the study of agriculture, that the same information, tools, and techniques that in one farmer's hands will ruin land, in another's will save and improve it.

This is cold comfort, Wendell.

Maybe with another month in the ground things would have been different, but at least for now, my farm diet will be potato-free. What did I miss this time? What didn't I know?

The First Supper

This is not a recommendation of ignorance, cautions Berry. *To know nothing, after all, is no more possible than to know enough. I am only proposing that knowledge, like everything else, has its place, and that we need urgently now to put it in its place. If we want to know and cannot help knowing, then let us learn as fully and accurately as we decently can. But let us at the same time abandon our superstitious beliefs about knowledge: that it is ever sufficient; that it can of itself solve problems; that it is intrinsically good; that it can be used objectively or disinterestedly.*

The First Supper consists of half a roast chicken, collard greens, and three slices of tomato. It is served with tap water. If my first of thirty dinners grown on The Farm will be potato-free, I hope it will not be family-free. The Farm experience is drawing to a close, with normalcy imaginable. I wish to share that possibility as much as my success, such as it is . . . to share the occasion—if not the actual food, since there isn't all that much—with Lisa and the kids. Lisa is not interested. On the night of the First Supper, she schedules drinks for after work and arranges for Heath and Bevan Jake to stay after school with my mother.

Crushing, sure, but I refuse to eat this meal alone. I invite my friend Dan Bibb to join me. Originally from Alaska, he knows his way around homegrown poultry, and Dan Bibb gets downright nostalgic when a dinner of roast yard bird, collard greens, and tomato salad is served.

I blanch the greens before sautéing them and they stand up well against the green onion; the rock salt clings to the sweet tomatoes without dissolving and muddling the two flavors. My chicken defies comparison to the best, most well-tended, correctly processed chicken I've ever purchased from a local butcher. In texture and strength of flavor the bird's very skin is more robust, resembling pork crackling, just with a parchmentlike delicacy. While roasting, the schmaltz had liquefied, adding flavor to every forkful from the plate. The meat resists a bite not with mere toughness, say, a leathery obstinacy, but with physicality more akin to resolve.

You often hear folks talk of being able to taste a life lived in the meat of a freshly butchered animal; this texture must be what they mean. So for that, I am happy. I don't look forward to the dozens of meals ahead of me. I don't look behind me to the shambles I have made of my home, my marriage, and my finger. My life. Another forkful of my meat bird; I am momentarily unconcerned.

Dan Bibb is less excited about eating the First Supper accompanied only by water than I am.

"Nothing but water for a month?" he asks, incredulous.

"I didn't grow any booze, Dan Bibb," I reply, remembering for a moment that I originally intended to.

"Of course not. Still?"

"You're welcome to open a bottle."

"No. Not if you're not drinking. It wouldn't seem . . ."

"It's fine, Dan. Open a bottle."

"Well, don't mind if I do."

I'm not carrying on when I say that those first forkfuls of that First Supper washed away all the struggle, all the doubt, the disappointment, the heartbreak, and the horror. They would, of course, all of them, be back.

The table is clear and Dan Bibb is long gone when Lisa arrives home with the kids; I rush to them in the doorway, urging them to try some of the remaining chicken. Lisa refuses outright. Bevan Jake looks at his mom and then the chicken and says, "No thanks, Dad."

"Really? Not even a taste?"

"I'm fine," replies Lisa with counterfeit levity. Bevan Jake just watches the two of us.

"It's totally amazing!" I insist. "Not like regular chicken at all."

"I like regular chicken," Bevan Jake says, searching his mother's eyes for a cue, some approval for having taken her side.

August 23. I have lost twenty-nine pounds since March, as much as half of it gone in the last ten days. The fifth meat bird I eat has been in the refrigerator for nine days by the time I get around to cooking it. Coming out of the crisper, it smells pretty rank. I write that off as a part of the whole raised-by-my-own-hand experience. This is real food, not that prettified stuff from greenmarkets. My food rarely looks appealing in the least, but it usually tastes great. I rinse the bird carcass and throw it on the grill. Two hours later I begin suffering from an enfeebling bout of gastrointestinal distress. I had not grown a single saltine on The Farm, but that's all I eat for the next five days.

THE RESTRAINT OF BEASTS

|||||||||||||||||||||||||||||||||||||||||||||||||||||||||||||||||||||||||||||||||||||||||||||||||||||||||||

On day ten of my dietary moonwalk, the rabbits come roaring back into the picture. It has been more than a month since I have thought of them as anything other than a nuisance, a waste of rabbit food, taking up precious space in my barn. I gave up hope of breeding them for food back in July. The remaining does and the two bucks free-range on the strip of lawn I put down in a vain attempt to placate Lisa (but tell everyone is essential for erosion control). Occasionally I might notice a bit of humping and laugh—thanks a lot, guys, where was that action when I needed it?

Then, naturally, on August 25, Doe #4 has a litter, and because the proper kindling box is in place, she doesn't eat them. A few die, but she generally behaves like a responsible mother, and I go about my morning routine: change the water, clean up the poop, and add fresh food. During my rounds two days later, her neighbor Doe #3 lunges at my arm, tearing my work shirt with her claws and, mounting my arm, trying to gain purchase on my elbow with those big rabbity front teeth. A rabbit attack stops being farce when the critter in question weighs upward of twenty-three pounds and she's chewing and scratching her way up your arm to your ear. Fighting her off with one arm is hard work. I muscle her into the back of the cage, but she comes back for more. She scratches and tears at my skin, so I bonk her on the head with the miniature, tin dustpan I use to clean cages. A warning shot, to be sure. But, undaunted, Doe #3 lunges again. One more warning shot. Again she counters. Hell with this. I whack her again, really hard. She is still for a moment, then howls. It is a sound like no other I have ever heard a rabbit make, primarily because, in addition to fear (quite common), there is anger in it, outrage even.

Doe #3 now appears unable to move. I gingerly lift a powerful hind leg, half-expecting her to whirl on me and bite my hand, but when I let the leg go, it thumps on the floor of her cage: paralyzed. Goddamned rabbits, nothing but fruitless misery, and now, fending off a vicious fit of pique, I've crippled one of the last of them. Like others before her, I'll have to put this one out of her misery. Reflexively I go to fetch a trash bag and the lime, but on the way back to the hutch I think better of the plan. This is no occasion for standard operating procedure.

There are practical realities.

My potato crop has failed. I don't have enough food to finish out the month. I'll have to harvest Doe #3, salvage what meat the battle wound has not spoiled, and get her to the stew pot—probably for a good, long time. It's not going to be the best meal I've ever eaten, but I really do have to eat her; there are moral implications to consider as well.

I return to her cage to finish the job. I open the door, and just as Doe #4 did two days ago, Doe #3 is kindling, giving birth to a litter of kits, despite my having paralyzed her. She looks straight at me as the fifth kit of eight slides from between her dead legs.

I close the cage back up and arrange a number of water bottles so that she doesn't have to move to drink, and I leave her to her work. We were both playing rough, I just didn't know why. It was unintentional; still, I can't just hurl her in the trash. Something good has to come of this grotesque error.

An hour later I position the kits where I guess her teats are and I leave them there until sunset. I then remove the kits, hoping that if I put them with Doe #4's litter, she'll adopt them. I rub the maimed doe's offspring on the belly of Doe #4 just as Sugar Ray had advised all those months ago and place them in the kindling box with her babies.

Then I fumble one step closer to completing this horrible process. I pull the chicken-harvesting station away from the wall, secure the plywood covering the scalding tank, and as carefully as such a task can be completed, I lift Doe #3 from where she lies in her cage in a pool of afterbirth. I hang her by her back feet from wire loops hanging from bolts in the ceiling of the garage, and I cut her throat. Unable to even shudder, she bleeds out. After a while, I take her down, still warm, hot really, and put her on the tabletop. Using a heavy, twelve-inch, well-used German kitchen cleaver, I chop her head off in one clean stroke. I hang her back up from the ceiling and prepare her carcass for skinning and cleaning.

"Hey, Manny!" Peter calls from the dimness at the top of the driveway, out for Gumbo's evening walk. "What're yah doing *now*?"

"You don't want to know, Pete," I reply, standing between Peter and the carcass.

"Probably not." Peter laughs and walks on.

When I finish dressing Doe #3, I hang her by the withers in a blue recycling bag behind an out-of-the-way air-conditioning duct in the basement. I hang the meat to tenderize in a location I am certain Lisa will never find.

On Saturday morning, Lisa busies herself cleaning out the basement. "Is that a chicken hanging from the ceiling down there?" she asks, standing at the top of the basement stairs with an armful of Halloween paraphernalia.

"Nope. That's a rabbit. Doe number three." I add after a brief silence, "She . . . died."

"She stinks."

I begin to sob. I tell her the whole story, sort of, and inform her of my plans to eat Doe #3—partly out of desperation to see the project through properly, partly penance, but also as a tribute of some creepy, flaccid sort.

Lisa says this is the first time she feels truly sorry for me since March.

Half an hour later I have thoroughly washed Doe #3 and rendered her into pan-size parts and have started browning her off. The smell is unbearable. No sooner has the meat started to caramelize in the pan than it begins to smell as if some prankster has pulled a footstool up to the stove, mounted it, and pissed directly into the pan. The smell permeates the kitchen and quickly all three floors of the house. I work furiously, cranking the heat to speed up the browning. The logic: the sooner I can get her buried under a sea of chicken-foot stock, the sooner this smell will go away.

Lisa enters the kitchen with her hands covering her nose, one of her more commonly employed gestures. It always precedes her exclamation, made more dramatic by the surgical use of her Mississippi drawl, "Ew! Staaaank!"

I was almost in a fetal crouch when I cut Lisa off. "I know! I know! Don't say a fuckin' word! Just leave! Out of the kitchen! I know! I know!"

Half an hour later, the rabbit is buried under three pints of stock made from the feet of previously butchered chickens, celery, and green onions; I enter the living room to make my apologies. I sit on the floor, where she is sorting and filing household bills.

"I am sorry. That was terrible of me. I was just totally overwhelmed. But I am sorry."

"I know." Lisa looks me straight in the eye for the first time in months. "It must be very hard for you."

I cook Doe #3 for thirty-six hours in a slow cooker, then store the stewed meat in the refrigerator for two days. In the interim I kill five more chickens, eat three, and freeze two (out in The World, I would never consider buying a frozen chicken, but I'm intent on never again eating a nine-day-old chicken). I eat only vegetables for three nights rather than finish preparing Doe #3. On Labor Day, I separate meat from bone and fabricate a pungent tomato sauce aggressively spiked with Scotch-bonnet peppers, salt, and even some contraband garlic. The stink is not as strong, but even through the green onions, garlic, peppers, and herbs, the rabbit gives off a ureic waft. I fix myself a bowl and set to finishing it while standing in the middle of the kitchen. The sauce is powerful enough to mask most of the giant doe's gamy flavor. In truth, the stew is so intensely seasoned that I could just as easily be eating one of the neighbors as Doe #3, and I feel just as guilty. The texture, that of bad canned tuna, or cat food, is a substantial hurdle. I persist. Since the first moment that I accepted the horrible magnitude of this episode, my resolute belief has been that the only thing worse than eating Doe #3 would be not eating Doe #3. I have now eaten Doe #3, and I am not yet certain that I was right. Not a single one of Doe #3's kits was accepted into Doe #4's brood. All are long dead.

I have a grim sense of closure, no question, but this, the final battle of my war against The Farm's entropic collapse, has robbed me of even the most incremental sense of accomplishment during these last six months. Here I am. It is September. I ate the rabbit. As I stand in my kitchen still gripping the empty bowl of rabbit stew, my entire farming experience has distilled into one dreadful, close-to-inedible entrée.

Doe #4 escapes, leaving the three surviving kits sired by the Chinchilla to fend for themselves. They do well and grow quickly, though a plan for a fryer-weight harvest is the furthest thing from my mind. All the same, by October, as the kits reach that all-important five-pound mark, all three vanish overnight. I never suspect Lisa.

Though the contractually mandated self-sustaining period is over, I continue to eat out of The Farm, eventually combining the vegetables still coming out of the garden with food from the outside world.

The sand-colored buck (now called Sandy by the family) goes missing from The Farm in late October. He's run away before, but unlike the other rabbits over the wire, Sandy has always come back. This is the longest he's ever been gone, and I have quietly given up on him, discontinued my dusk and dawn perimeter searches. One evening in early November, as I leave the house to take Fergus out for a walk, Sandy reappears on the lawn. I don't know how you miss a twenty-plus-pound, light brown rabbit sitting in the middle of your front lawn, but I do it.

Fergus does not.

He is off the porch and after Sandy. Trained to hunt birds as a puppy, Fergus is a much more enthusiastic squirrel dog. He enjoys little more than treeing a few squirrels during the course of a walk. The dog runs down Sandy effortlessly, shakes him vigorously once, breaking his neck, killing him instantly.

My heart does not break. I simply pick him up, tuck him under my arm, and sneak around the back of the house with Fergus, who is curious when Sandy will wake up, in tow, through the Feders' yard and into the barn. I heft Sandy into a trash bag and sprinkle a cup of lime over him, not because it's all that warm out anymore, but because when things die around here, that's what I do. I put the bag in the trash for pickup. I never tell Lisa. She asks occasionally what I think happened to him. I reply that I do not know.

As each day passes and I crawl closer to the goal, I can feel the outside world tearing at the fences. For seven months my life has not only changed shape, but function, too. It is no longer taken up in the struggle to expand and fill every possible space I imagine for it (this way to Afghanistan, that way to the Mojave Desert, this way to Ukraine). My life has become a response to The Farm, not just the potential in it, but, much more important, the limits imposed by it. While there is peace in our house again, and The Farm is rarely spoken of, I am seized anew with panic about what the false promise of limitless choice will bring.

I arrange for Carlos to lay more sod on two-thirds of the plot. I can't watch as the grass is laid in prefabricated strips across my earth. In truth the lawn may as well have been asphalt, but my time has passed. Anyhow, I forget my self-ish orthodoxy after just once wrestling with the kids in our newly verdant backyard. I still maintain the flock of layers and now Bevan Jake harvests the eggs every morning. Lisa has taken on the responsibility of the little Chinchilla, the last rabbit standing. The sneaky little sire of two of the three litters has the entire back porch to himself now. After one weekend when he was back East, visiting from Berkeley with his fam-ily, my brother, Justin, egged on by his wife and Lisa, insisted that I help him dismantle and cart away the long-abandoned FEMA Trailer.

The chaos of this past year still reverberates through Howard Hall, though. The discord, almost audible, chasing the children as they charge down the stairs and out into the garden, still lurks. But we are mending. "We are mending." I mutter this confirmation standing in the basement laundry room, folding towels and a raft of the kids' clothes.

We can commit ourselves fully to anything—a discipline, a life's work, a child, a family, a community, a faith, a friend—only with a poverty of knowledge, an ignorance of result, self-subordination, and a final forsaking of other possibilities. If we must make these so final commitments without sufficient information, then what can inform our decisions? This is the first time Berry has ever been inside the house. I smile, finally knowing, I think, where he's going with this one.

In spite of the obvious dangers of the word, we must say first that love can inform them. This, of course, though probably necessary, is not safe. What parent, faced with a child who is in love and going to get married, has not been filled with mistrust and fear— and justly so. We were lovers before we were parents, know what a fraudulent justifier love can be. We know that people stay married for different reasons than those for which they get married and that the later reasons will have to be discovered. Which, of course, is not to say that the later reasons may not confirm the earlier ones; it is to say only that earlier ones must wait for confirmation.

THE WINTER PALACE

||||||||||||||||||||||||||||||||||||||||||||||||||||||||||||||||||||||||||||||||||||||||

The leaves are drying on the trees and the days are shorter now. The few plants still in the field sag, wilt, and harden in a tangled mat on the soil. The only chickens left are the nine layers, so I reorient the chicken-wire line to run east-west across the garden. I pull the coop out of the corner of the yard into the center of a four-foot-wide fenced strip. This will be the hens' winter palace. I staple some foam insulation to the plywood and cover most of the wired openings with clear, corrugated plastic. I stand back wondering whether the hens will survive the winter. The only quality I admire in a chicken is its apparent stoicism. They are rumored to be able to live in temperatures as cold as fifteen degrees, but not much beyond that. I make a note to purchase a heat bulb and to run an extension cord to the coop. It will take me most of the winter to accomplish this one last errand.

In November, Tex calls from Montana. He is excited, says he just found out what happened to my potatoes. "We were listening to the ag report on the radio. Some listener calls in, says her potato crop failed. She said the only spuds she could find weren't as big as a dime."

"Yeah, shirt buttons."

"Right. Tiny. Anyway, the ag report guy says this happens occasionally, especially if you are ordering your seed potatoes online . . . like who does that, Howard?"

"Yes. And?"

"The ag report guy goes on, says fancy people like you who order online do occasionally get bad spuds. The plants look great, but there's no crop."

"So it wasn't my fault?"

"No, it probably was, but you can use this as an excuse if any of those sophisticated city folk you pal around with when you're not out here ask, 'Why no potatoes?'"

"My dad's going to be very excited to be off the hook. He hasn't really recovered yet." I make the call. Dad's thrilled. I have my doubts; root fungus is still my number one suspect.

As far as I can tell the tender, young fig tree is stone dead. The tornado dropped a limb from that Norway maple there. Each of the four secondary branches on that limb was four times the size of the fig. Why it still persists at all is something of a mystery. As I have done so many times before here on The Farm, I get out a garbage bag. This time, rather than putting the tree in it, I wrap it around the nub of the young tree. I wrap the short trunk, more slender than Heath's wrist, and I bind the two together with duct tape. This will insulate the fig through the winter. If it has anything left, we will know next spring.

A few evenings later my dad shows up with his rototiller. It's one of those as-seen-on-TV products, and my old man swears by it. After an excruciatingly detailed lecture on the theory behind, proper maintenance of, and standard operating procedures for the two-stroke internal combustion engine, he asks if there is any wine in the house.

There is.

In the dimming light, after my dad has headed home, I tear up the larger of the remaining expired woody crops. The smaller stuff I intend to plow into the soil. I struggle starting the two-stroke; try to remember what Dad was saying about the priming bubble, warning me against doing something. What, though?

I have to take the bottle of beer out of my back pocket and really lean in and yank the ignition cord, but after I deliver a few frame-rattling tugs, the engine turns over, and what I believe to be my final act on The Farm begins.

As the rototiller churns over the topsoil, its obvious fecundity is exhilarating. This patch is alive. That's clear because I can see, touch, smell its promise. I wonder what that tastes like? Nothing special. Maybe my young fig tree isn't so fucked, after all. The chickens are still jerking worms out of the soil after it rains. This gully has been transformed. It is alive. So focused on my project, so shattered by it, still the real transformation wasn't mine. All the effort I put into preparing the ground for the crops and the livestock, all the thought about and concern for the soil, all was forgotten in the grinding work of watering what was thirsty, feeding what was hungry, and, well, killing what was not dead. *In a conversation, you always expect a reply,* says Berry.

I turn off the rototiller so I can hear Berry more clearly, and am momentarily seized by the fear that the tool won't start again. "Wendell," I say by way of greeting.

And if you honor the other party, you understand that you must not expect always to receive a reply that you foresee or a reply that you would like. A conversation is immitigably two-sided and always to some degree mysterious; it requires faith.

The rototiller does start up again, eventually. Berry is right, of course. All summer I worked without once stopping long enough to even listen for a reply, never mind bother to understand one. I open another beer and clean the blades of the rototiller, careful to collect the soil as it falls from the steel blades as I wipe them down. "Here," I say, tossing this small handful of eastern Long Island's best soil that I'd picked free from the tiller's axle back into The Farm.

My faith collapses in crisis sooner than I'd like to admit. Standing in the new snow, I begin to trim more foam insulation board to fit the outside of the high-rise coop. The nine remaining tenants are The Stray from Agway, and eight layers—four brown pullets, and four white leghorns. It's not fifteen degrees yet, but it's not much warmer.

I have finally purchased an infrared heat lamp—like the ones you see at a banquet-hall carving station hanging over the prime rib. I am cutting the insulation to keep the bulb's heat inside the coop: The Winter Palace. As I begin to screw the panels onto the coop, I am overwhelmed by a wave of doubt. Why do I want to keep these chickens through the winter? Why insulate the obviously dead fig tree in a black trash bag? What good can come of this? The experiment is long over, The Farm, for the most part, plowed under. *Do you recall, I suggested that the good worker will not suppose that good work can be made properly answerable to haste, urgency, or even emergency?* Berry asks rhetorically. I give a nod of recognition. *The other thing that the good worker knows is that after it is done, work requires yet more time to prove its worth. The good worker must stay to experience and study and understand the consequences—must understand them by living with them, and then correct them, if necessary, by longer living and more work. It won't do to correct mistakes made at one place by moving to another place.*

The fig tree blooms in the spring. Not from its shattered trunk; rather, its new limbs grow right from the ground. Two shoots that, through the summer, grow horizontally across the garden, spreading out as wide as they like, just as Bevan Jake does after he sneaks into our bed each evening as we sleep. Predictably, the broad leaves on the delicate boughs shade a good portion of what Lisa and I describe as a non-marriage-challenging vegetable garden that shares the plot with a well-kept backyard.

It was a rough winter for the chickens. It never got so cold that The Winter Palace could not protect them, but it was cold enough to bring the predators around. I lost all four leghorns and two of the red-buff pullets. The three remaining layers, including, against all the odds, The Stray, provide us with an egg each a day. It's been over a year since we have purchased eggs, and we often have a surplus, so we unload them as house presents when we're invited over to dinner.

EPILOGUE

‖‖‖‖‖‖‖‖‖‖‖‖‖‖‖‖‖‖‖‖‖‖‖‖‖‖‖‖‖‖‖‖‖‖‖‖

My enormous failures were so much less devastating than the constant minor mistakes I made, errors born of ignorance, laziness, sloppiness, cussedness, or combinations of any two or more failings. All that stood between complete collapse and modest success was my unwillingness to stop work, an unself-conscious need to, without shame, fix all I had broken, heal what I had injured, clean all I had fouled. Professor Berry writes an eloquent critique of America's work ethic. Work is not an ethic, he insists, work is a necessity. The American fetishization of work as an ideal removes it from practical reality every time it is described as aspirational. I never felt so strongly about work before, never mind a job; never thought of work as necessary.

On The Farm I first met my authentic self. It was not entirely flattering really—driven, uncompromising, solitary, selfish even. Still it was an enormous relief to finally find me, to put aside my fears that I might pass away and never

recognize the real me in the crowd of costumed approxima-
tions. This introduction was the heart of the answer to the
question that is still asked years later: "Why did you keep
going?"

On The Farm, Wendell Berry girded me. Not that I had
ever read a word he'd written until I was back at my desk,
trying to make sense of the year while the dwindling flock
made do on the frozen dirt of their run. The only thing that
really mattered to me was the work. Locavore theory meant
nothing. Neither did the obvious virtues of urban agriculture.
I had no opinion about the strictures and ordinances banning
beekeeping in the five boroughs. Organic? What about it?
I had no attachment to any principle other than that of the
work, and the only dedication I felt was to getting it done.

All I know is that experience is not about analysis and
understanding; experiencing anything requires that you
suffer it, requires that you rejoice in it as it is. As word
spread about The Farm, well-meaning folks began to introduce me around as the Urban Farmer. Simply by doing, I
became, in the eye of the casual observer, an expert. Still,
even my audience's enthusiasm for my experience fails to
make me the expert they require, fails to imbue the expertise they lust after. Once again a phony. If the equally well-
meaning people I was introduced to were familiar with my
story, my "farm adventure," they almost always inquired
whether I was still, even now, "living off the farm." They
wanted me to say yes, hoped that I had (for all of our sakes,
really) persisted, extended the journey, made it mythic.
Some were disappointed when I answered no, not exactly,
but few were surprised, nor entirely sorry, it seemed, when
I prevaricated.

Epilogue

I was asked to lend my name to a community garden. I was approached by producers of various reality-television shows, asked to continue my project for their benefit (and my infamy). I only self-immolate, I assured them. Their counteroffer was to give me a job as a producer, supervising the action of other hapless urban agricultural crash dummies.

Not for me.

The trouble was that once found on The Farm, then returned to the real world, my authenticity wilted, the joy of the discovery fading away a little every day. With every introduction I endured as the Urban Farmer or That Guy Who—Did You Read the Story About . . . ? But I quickly began to fear being discovered once again. I still don't know if I believe urban agricultural sustainability is the right course, not in any productive way, and not at half the price I paid (both life and treasure). My interest in "greening" the urban landscape was still minimal. Community gardens still smacked of the grimmest joinerism. Especially embarrassing were the introductions made to dedicated, hardworking activists such as Ian Marvy, executive director of Added Value, a nonprofit that introduces low/no-income Brooklyn kids to the wonders of gardening—to producing food.

Then, yesterday, attending a backyard barbecue, standing on the back porch of Caleb's mom, Cathy Fuerst, I proudly announced that Flock #2 had arrived. Caleb laughed, the playful, mock scorn you'd hope to elicit from a young man who has just completed two years of college (has it really been two years since he left The Farm for college?). From other friends, those with a less intimate knowledge of life on The Farm but much closer to me in age than Caleb, the horror is equally theatrical, and entirely genuine. The simultaneous question "Why on earth would you start all that again?" is asked by the chorus, crushingly serious.

"God only knows," I replied, rolling my eyes, mugging for the crowd. But, in truth, I know just as well as He.

The uncomplicated (if entirely insufficient for the uninitiated) answer is as rudimentary as because we have not purchased eggs in two years.

And how, in fairness, could anyone be expected to understand who had not answered the doorbell at noon one beautiful day in May, after the rains had finally lifted, and greeted the deliveryman from the United States Postal Service, a red-and-white, two-by-three-by-four-foot cardboard box, marked LIVE BIRDS, at his feet. You asking, "Is this your first box of live chickens?"

The postman replying, without missing a beat, "First today," grinning, and handing me an ocher certified-delivery receipt to sign, Tom Jones's cover of "I'll Never Fall in Love Again" drifting from his truck. "I gotta ask?" the postman, just sayin'.

"Sure. I raise 'em out back." I gesture over my shoulder with my head. "For eggs." As if maybe I need to reassure him. The postman looking just as suspicious as impressed. "I got plenty. You want? Take some home. They're great. Totally different than from the store."

Him saying, changing the subject, and nodding, polite, acknowledgment that he's doing so, "I've delivered pretty much everything. You name it, insects even—live ones! But never live birds . . . chickens. This is a first."

"Just glad to help." Me smiling, handing back the signed receipt.

Him waving—"Good luck!"—over his shoulder as he returns to the truck.

Epilogue

I'll never fall in love again.

"Haven't bought an egg in two years." The claim authenticates my secessionist insurgency, a largely ceremonial war against slavish consumerism. Is it really too much to describe the laying hens as the foot soldiers in this battle against the gully? Because if not them, who?

ACKNOWLEDGMENTS

IIIIIIIIIIIIIIIIIIIIIIIIIIIIIIIIIIIIIIIIIIIIIIIIIIIIIIIIIIIIIIIIIIIIIIIIIIIIIIIIIIIIIIIIIIII

This book grew out of a feature I wrote for *New York* magazine and published in the fall of 2007. Without the faith and patience of the editors there, this very unusual story would never have made it into print. Thanks to Adam Moss, Hugo Lindgren (who, in his inimitable way, was once heard to say, "Manny, the hard part is over. Anybody could write this story *now,* nobody could have done what you just did. So, shut up and write." So, as usual, Büg, thank you and f*ck you), John Homans, Ann Clarke, and Jody Quon. Special thanks to Faye Penn, who assigned the original piece, and kept the lines of communication open to The Farm through the dark days.

I am fortunate to have Scribner as a publisher. Thanks to Susan, Nan, Anna, Dan, Steve, Isabel, Meredith, Brian, and, especially, my editor, Brant Rumble, for his confidence, insight, and wisdom. At the Gernert Company, thanks to David, Sarah, Stephanie, Allison, Courtney, Will, Erika, and,

Acknowledgments

above all, Chris Parris-Lamb for his endless encouragement, straight talk, sound judgment, his regular indulgences, and his mad skills as a reader.

All I know about Roy Jones Jr. I learned reading Gary Smith in *Sports Illustrated*. Thanks, Gary. The same can be said of Gail Damerow when it comes to raising chickens. Marc Linder and Lawrence S. Zacharias added clarity and context to my understanding of the agricultural history of King's County. Ray Damiani showed me how to handle rabbits and I will never be the same.

I am profoundly grateful to Wendell Berry and his canon, without which I may never have understood why The Farm cast the spell that it did.

Thank you, Caleb Townsend.

Thanks to Al and Jane Feder (especially you, Jane), the McCorkel clan, and a raft of similarly deeply patient and generous neighbors. Thanks to Angello, Joe, and Carlos from G&D Landscape. Ta to my big cousin, Gabriel Evans, for a smattering of technical advice and his unrelenting enthusiasm and damn-the-torpedoes encouragement. Nice save, Dr. Danny Fong.

I am blessed to have such smart, supportive, patient friends; I relied on all of their gifts while I wrote, and even more so when I did not. Tina Fallon, Cathy Fuerst, Suzanne Sullivan, Michael Wylde, and Eric Slater received daily updates about The Farm both when I was working there and when I was writing about it. It must have been excruciating. Daphne Klein and Trilby Cohen read an early draft and, somehow, found encouraging words that propelled me forward. Thanks to CPL, Eric, Nancy Messereau, Sarah Burnes, and Sam Sifton, who read the last working draft, for their

Acknowledgments

focus and insight and the brave face. Dan Bibb, Evan Brenner, Catherine Brophy, Jim Cooper, Craig Townsend, Andrew Eccles, Page Edmunds, Samantha Gillison, Joanna Hershon, Bill Hogeland, Emily Jenkins, Peter Lodola, Josh and Diana Lomask, Jonathan Mahler, Danielle Mattoon, John Merz, Eric Simonoff, Robert Sullivan (who led me here, wherever *this* is), Mark Tarbell, Chris Boyer, Brendan Coburn, Ward Welch, Paul Rice, the brothers at Holy Cross Monastery, and Norman Vanamee were all there when I needed them.

Because of the boundless love, sacrifice, and quiet confidence of my parents, Jos, Gabrielle, and Marty, and my sister, Bevin, I did not plummet. Thank you.

To my wife, Lisa Ryan Howard, whose pride in me I can only hope to one day earn, whose faith in me makes it possible to greet the day, whose sacrifice while The Farm was operational was enormous and aspects of which remain beyond measure, who did not sweep our children, Heath and Bevan Jake, up in her powerful arms and leave when she had every right to, I thank you.